STUDENT AFFAIRS FUNCTIONS
IN HIGHER EDUCATION

STUDENT AFFAIRS FUNCTIONS IN HIGHER EDUCATION

Edited by

AUDREY L. RENTZ, PH.D.

and

GERALD L. SADDLEMIRE, ED.D.

Professors
Department of College Student Personnel
Bowling Green State University

Forewords by

Paul Bloland

Chair and Professor
Department of Counseling Psychology
University of Southern California

and

Arthur Sandeen

Vice President for Student Affairs
University of Florida

CHARLES C THOMAS • PUBLISHER
Springfield • Illinois • U.S.A.

Published and Distributed Throughout the World by

CHARLES C THOMAS • PUBLISHER

2600 South First Street

Springfield, Illinois 62794-9265

© *1988 by* CHARLES C THOMAS • PUBLISHER

ISBN 0-398-05480-0

Library of Congress Catalog Card Number: 88-4586

With THOMAS BOOKS *careful attention is given to all details of manufacturing and design. It is the Publisher's desire to present books that are satisfactory as to their physical qualities and artistic possibilities and appropriate for their particular use.* THOMAS BOOKS *will be true to those laws of quality that assure a good name and good will.*

Printed in the United States of America
Q-R-3

Library of Congress Cataloging in Publication Data

Student affairs functions in higher education/edited
by Audrey L. Rentz and Gerald L. Saddlemire;
forewords by Paul Bloland and Arthur Sandeen.
    p. cm.
    Includes bibliographies and index.
    ISBN 0-398-05480-0
    1. Personnel service in higher education — United
States. I. Rentz, Audrey L. II. Saddlemire,
Gerald L.
LB2343.S793   1988
378'.194 — dc19   88-4586
                                     CIP

THE AUTHORS

AUDREY L. RENTZ is Professor in the Department of College Student Personnel at Bowling Green State University. Dr. Rentz's educational background includes the Ph.D. from Michigan State University, the M.S. from The Pennsylvania State University, and an A.B. from the College of Mount St. Vincent. Practitioner experience in student affairs administration in Pennsylvania, Virginia, and Michigan preceded a graduate faculty appointment at Bowling Green State University in 1974. National professional association memberships include A.A.H.E., A.C.P.A. (Commission XII Directorate), N.A.S.P.A., and N.A.W.D.A.C. (Journal Editorial Board). Dr. Rentz is co-editor of *Student Affairs: A Profession's Heritage* (1983; 1986) with Gerald L. Saddlemire and co-author of *Careers in the College Student Personnel Profession* (1987) with Gary H. Knock.

GERALD L. SADDLEMIRE is Professor in the Department of College Student Personnel at Bowling Green State University. Dr. Saddlemire's educational background includes the Ed.D. and M.A. from Teachers' College, Columbia University and the B.A. from the State University of New York at Albany. From 1969 to 1985 Dr. Saddlemire served as the Chair of the Department of College Student Personnel and Interim Dean, the College of Education and Allied Professions during 1985-86. Practitioner experience as Dean of Students in New York and Director of Counseling in Ohio preceded a graduate faculty appointment in 1969. National professional association memberships include A.A.H.E., A.C.P.A. (Commission XII Directorate, Chair), and N.A.S.P.A. Dr. Saddlemire is the co-editor of *Student Affairs: A Profession's Heritage* (1983, 1986) with Audrey L. Rentz.

MICHAEL D. COOMES received his Ed.D. from Indiana University and is a Visiting Assistant Professor in the Department of College Student Personnel at Bowling Green State University.

v

MICHAEL DANNELLS received his Ph.D. from the University of Iowa and is an Assistant Professor in the Department of Counselor Education and Educational Psychology at Kansas State University.

JUDITH J. GOETZ received her Ph.D. from the University of Toledo and is the Assistant Director of the Division of Undergraduate Studies at The Pennsylvania State University.

DON HOSSLER received his Ph.D. from the University of Iowa and is an Assistant Professor in the Department of Higher Education and Student Affairs at Indiana University.

GARY H. KNOCK received his Ed.D. from Indiana University and is the Associate Dean of the Graduate School and Professor in the Department of Educational Leadership at Miami University.

JOANN KROLL received her M.Ed. from Kent State University and is the Director of Placement Services at Bowling Green State University.

JOHN H. SCHUH received his Ph.D. from Arizona State University and is the Assistant Vice President for Student Affairs at Wichita State University.

ELIZABETH YARRIS received her Ph.D. from the University of Iowa and is a Counseling Psychologist and Assistant Professor in the Counseling and Career Development Center at Bowling Green State University.

FOREWORD

MY INITIAL academic introduction to the field of student personnel work was at the University of Minnesota during the fall quarter of 1952 when I enrolled in Education Psychology 250, College Student Personnel Work. Taught by C. Gilbert Wrenn, our text was his new book, *Student Personnel Work in College,* published just the preceding year. It is now 37 years later as I write these lines in my study and, having just reviewed this book compiled by Audrey Rentz and Gerald Saddlemire, I pulled the Wrenn book off the shelf and paged through it. He organized his book into five parts, discussing the needs of students and the organization of the student personnel program in the first section. The next section talked about counseling services and procedures followed by a section by Ruth Strang on group experiences, i.e., activities, orientation, and housing and dining. The next two sections dealt with health services, financial aid and student employment, job placement, admissions and records, and discipline, concluding with a chapter on research and evaluation.

Reading through Wrenn's book whetted my curiosity so I picked up the oldest book on student personnel services I could find in my personal library, *Student Personnel Work: An Outline of Clinical Procedures* (1937) to see what Ed Williamson and John Darley had considered important then. Most of their book dealt with counseling techniques but one chapter out of nine covered the field of student personnel work. In it the authors described the following functions: selection and prediction of student achievement, admissions, orientation, testing, readjustment of curricula, counseling, vocational information, and placement.

That really got me going so I then pulled all of my texts out of the bookcase, dusted them off, and scanned their contents. While a wide variety of programs was covered, most of the texts on student personnel work have included over the years such topics as student activities, counseling, housing, health services, orientation, financial aid, admissions

vii

discipline, religious counseling, and career planning and in roughly that order of frequency. Because textbooks, of necessity, attempt to incorporate contemporary thinking concerning the scope, nature, and organization of the discipline being covered, they can present an instructive snapshot, frozen in time, of the state of the art at the time they were written.

It is clear that the field today is far more complex in its details and in its emphasis upon certain topics such as student development and legal considerations than it was in the early years. It is also clear that it has been many years since a single author has attempted to write a textbook that endeavors to encompass the entire field in the span of a single volume. In the 50 years since the publication of the *Student Personnel Point of View* (1937), the depth and breadth of the existing literature has inevitably grown to the point where seemingly no one individual can write with any great authority on all of the major elements of the field which must be included if a textbook is to have both credibility and utility.

I have taught a survey course for student affairs graduate students since 1965 and have, perforce, used a wide variety of texts, articles, and materials in an effort to keep the content current and relevant to the needs of my students. The centerpiece of the course has almost always included one or two required textbooks. Over the years, for example, I have used Williamson (1961); Mueller (1961); Shaffer and Martinson (1966); Fitzgerald, Johnson, and Norris (1970); Harrington (1974); Williamson and Biggs (1975); Miller and Prince (1977); Packwood (1977); Delworth and Hanson (1980); and, most recently, Miller, Winston, and Mendenhall (1983) supplemented by Saddlemire and Rentz (1986).

As an educator, what do I want to know and, therefore, what do I look for in the kinds of textbooks that I would list as required reading for the beginning or survey course in student affairs? Because I believe that it is important for the students to obtain an over-all, birds-eye view of the field in this initial exposure, I would like to have most of its constituent elements touched on so that the parts can be viewed in the context of the whole. It is not nearly as important that the student learn specific competencies in this course as it is that the student learn how to read the road map.

First I want students to acquire a sense of the history of the field. What social and economic trends and shifts in our society spawned the philosophic and pragmatic roots of student personnel work? Whose ideas and dreams helped to shape the field over the years? These and other questions need to be answered if the student is to understand fully the field as it exists today. It didn't just happen: it evolved, idea by idea, concept by concept. Next, I want students to acquire a firm grounding in the foundations of the field, those philosophical and theoretical underpinnings which provide the scholarly and research-based basis for our view of higher education and our unique role in it. And finally, I believe that every graduate student should have a grasp of the field of student affairs as it is presently constituted. What services are we providing and what functions are we performing within the higher education mission? Here the student should obtain an overview of the various service elements of the contemporary student affairs program, the major functions of administration and student development programming, and professional directions and issues.

To identify one textbook that will adequately handle this task has been impossible to date but, luckily, it is possible to assemble a package which appears to be up to the task. And interestingly, it is the editing team of Saddlemire and Rentz, motivated in part no doubt by their colleagues on the American College Personnel Association's Commission on the Professional Education of Student Personnel Workers in Higher Education, that has contributed a substantial component of the answer to the problem.

Certainly, their *Student Affairs—A Profession's Heritage* (Rev. Ed., 1986), admirably meets my need for an historical overview based as it is upon the seminal documents and influential writing that helps us to understand the beginnings of our field and its evolution over time.

And for an overview of the services and functions being performed by the prototypal student affairs division, we now will be able to turn to this volume by Audrey Rentz and Gerald Saddlemire. Within its covers, the graduate student will find chapters describing everything the person new to student affairs needs to know about the major service functions of the modern student affairs division. Wisely, the editors have not attempted to incorporate every service that has been or might be subsumed under the student affairs rubric (that task awaits the advent of an encyclopedia of student affairs) but they have obtained a thorough presentation of those principal functions that have withstood the test of time and that constitute the core of a comprehensive campus program. Of those most frequently described student services I listed earlier, Rentz and Saddlemire have added only academic advising while omitting religious counseling, a service that no longer appears to be featured in the most often cited textbooks in our field.

I, for one, am most pleased that the editors and their authors have contributed such a fine portrayal of contemporary college student services. That it will find a welcome place on the reading lists of professional preparation programs, I have no doubt. Students in the field and, for that matter, experienced practitioners and administrators can all add to their understanding of our profession, its growth and present status, by a thorough reading of *Student Affairs Functions in Higher Education*.

Paul A. Bloland
University of Southern California

REFERENCES

American Council on Education (1937). *The student personnel point of view*. American Council on Education Studies, Series 1, Vol. 1, No. 3. Washington, D.C.: Author.

Delworth, U., Hanson, G.R., & Associates (1980). *Student services: A handbook for the profession*. San Francisco: Jossey-Bass.

Fitzgerald, L.E., Johnson, W.F., & Norris, W. (Eds.). (1970). *College student personnel: Readings and bibliographies*. Boston: Houghton-Mifflin.

Harrington, T.F. (1974). *Student personnel work in urban colleges*. New York: Intext.

Miller, T.K., & Prince, J.S. (1976). *The future of student affairs*. San Francisco: Jossey-Bass.

Miller, T.K., Winston, R.B., & Mendenhall, W.R. (Eds.). (1983). *Administration and leadership in student affairs*. Muncie, Indiana: Accelerated Development.

Mueller, K.H. (1961). *Student personnel work in higher education*. Boston: Houghton-Mifflin.

Packwood, W.T. (Ed.). (1977). *College student personnel services*. Springfield, Ill.: Charles C Thomas.

Saddlemire, G.L., & Rentz, A.L. (Eds.). (1986). *Student affairs—A professions heritage: Significant articles, authors, issues and documents*. Carbondale, Ill.: Southern Illinois University Press.

Shaffer, R.H., & Martinson, W.D. (1966). *Student personnel services in higher education*. New York: Center for Applied Research in Education.

Williamson, E.G. (1961). *Student personnel services in colleges and universities*. New York: McGraw-Hill.

Williamson, E.G., & Biggs, D.A. (1975). *Student personnel work: A program of developmental relationships*. New York: John Wiley.

Williamson, E.G., & Darley, J.G. (1937). *Student personnel work: An outline of clinical procedures*. New York: McGraw-Hill.

Wrenn, C.G. (1951). *Student personnel work in college*. New York: Ronald Press.

FOREWORD

POLICIES, programs, and priorities in student affairs reflect the major issues in the society of the times, and the particular emphasis of the institution. Student affairs administrators work to provide effective education and services to students within these contexts. With the complexity and diversity of higher education in 1988, the challenges for student affairs practitioners are considerable.

Student affairs administrators face many different expectations regarding their roles on the campus. Presidents and board members may see the chief student affairs officer as a benevolent, but stern Mr. Chips; faculty may think of the dean as the "person who handles the riots"; parents may expect the student affairs professional to be a "warm, caring advisor"; the other institutional vice presidents may view the chief student affairs officer as just one more competitor in the relentless drive for resources; the student affairs staff may expect their leader to "champion their cause, get them what they need, and redirect the priorities of the institution"; students (depending on the group and the issue!) may think of the student affairs administrator as leader, enemy, counselor, service provider, red tape cutter, or even friend.

Chief student affairs administrators are likely to view themselves in 1988 as an integral part of the institution's management team. They must be skillful in dealing with the different expectations that others have for them, knowledgeable about issues and problems in their own field, and able to provide leadership to the campus in their assigned responsibilities, and in a number of areas that often cannot be anticipated. Among their most important challenges is to convince others outside of student affairs (presidents, provosts, academic deans, faculty, parents, community leaders, and students) that the policies and programs they propose are worthy of support. The success of student affairs on any campus is dependent on the ability of the chief student affairs officer to articulate the needs of the various programs in an understandable and persuasive manner.

It is very common for student affairs administrators to be on the campus over 70 hours each week. The pace of their lives is fast, and the expectations from so many diverse groups do not encourage a contemplative, solitary life style. Yet, there is a strong need to learn about current developments in the field in order to improve programs on the campus. This is especially true in 1988, as the student affairs profession has become increasingly specialized, and there are distinct literatures, strategies, and issues in each area to learn. The current volume edited by Rentz and Saddlemire is directed to this need.

Student affairs administrators will find the 12 chapters in this book very helpful in furthering their understanding of the major functions in the field. In addition to the excellent background and descriptive information in each chapter, there are many useful discussions of issues, organizational patterns, models, and staffing. For staff who want to read further, there are up-to-date references at the end of each chapter.

Most student affairs administrators are not likely to read this entire book all at once. It will be helpful primarily in situations such as, (1) the director of financial aid has resigned, the admissions program is faltering, and the president is restless about next fall's entering class . . . read the chapter on "Enrollment Management"; (2) The chief student affairs officer wants the directors of housing, counseling, health service, and career planning to know more about financial aid . . . read the chapter on "Financial Aid"; (3) Three college deans propose that they be given authority to administer their own separate student judicial programs . . . read the chapter on "Discipline"; or (4) The chief student affairs officer needs to hire a new director of the student health service, and wants to establish a campus wellness program . . . read the chapter on "Health Services."

Student affairs administrators have the responsibility of providing the best programs and services they can for the students on their campuses. This volume, *Student Affairs Functions in Higher Education,* can be a very helpful resource for them in their efforts to achieve that important goal.

Arthur Sandeen
University of Florida

CONTENTS

STUDENT AFFAIRS FUNCTIONS
IN HIGHER EDUCATION

CHAPTER 1

THE PHILOSOPHICAL HERITAGE OF STUDENT AFFAIRS

GARY H. KNOCK

THE MISSION of the student affairs profession is to personalize and humanize the educational experiences of college students. Efforts toward this goal are initiated and sustained by an institution's administrative requirements and by educational philosophy. While administrative requirements may appear to be more immediate and more influential, philosophy is not absent from the decision-making which shapes and supports the activities of an institution's student affairs division. Professional practice has been and continues to be influenced directly and indirectly by institutional values and beliefs of individuals about the nature of human beings and the purposes of higher education.

The *Student Personnel Point of View* (American Council on Education, Committee on Student Personnel Work, 1937; American Council on Education, Committee on Student Personnel Work, 1949) shaped professional practice in student affairs during the profession's formative years, and the influence of this document continues to the present. The philosophical heritage of student affairs, however, is not limited to the *Student Personnel Point of View*. This landmark statement in both its original and revised forms is more a declaration of purpose and commitment than a philosophical dictum. The statement incorporates more than one educational philosophy, and the purposes and practices outlined are subject to both philosophical and operational interpretation. While the *Student Personnel Point of View* has provided a foundation for college student affairs, the richness of the profession's philosophical heritage can be considered and appreciated only by an examination of the effects of certain educational philosophies upon both policy-making and practice.

WHAT IS PHILOSOPHY?

It has been said that philosophy promises truth and delivers only argument about its definition. Bertrand Russell observed that "Science is what you know; philosophy is what you don't know." In a literal sense, the word "philosophy" means love of wisdom. In a technical sense, philosophy can be thought of as an activity, a set of attitudes, and a body of content (Marler, 1975; Smith, 1965). Historically, philosophers have been expected to combine the aims and achievements of scientists, moralists, and theologians (O'Conner, 1957). The fact is these expectations are really unattainable in any true and complete sense. Contemporary philosophers have settled on a somewhat limited but more reasonable purpose: the study of questions. The crux of the matter is asking the "right" questions. "Right" refers to questions that are relevant and meaningful and make a difference in various aspects of life and living (Morris, 1961).

Philosophical Categories

The body of philosophical inquiry has been organized into three categories of questions. Metaphysics is the study of questions concerning the nature of reality. Epistemology is the study of the nature of truth and knowledge and how these are attained. Axiology is the study of questions of value.

Metaphysics

A transliteration from the Greek that means "beyond physics," metaphysics represents the synthesizing and speculative efforts of philosophy. Metaphysics provides a framework that permits creation of a world view of a phenomenon and development of hypotheses that can be tested according to basic assumptions. The synthesizing role of philosophy is concerned with assisting human beings to possess a comprehensive and consistent view of life which provides a basis on which to unify thoughts, base aspirations, and interpret experiences (Knight, 1982). The speculative dimension of philosophy is based upon the limitations of human knowledge. Because human knowledge at any time or place is limited and incomplete, it is both desirable and necessary to move beyond empirical knowledge or "What we know." Knight (1982) explains that it is the speculative function of philosophy that allows a rational jump from known to unknown and which permits attempts to define the undefined.

The alternative to speculation is to be stymied by doubt (Knight, 1982). In science, in particular, the synthesizing and speculative qualities of metaphysics are necessary and useful. Theories of science are ultimately related to theories of reality. Other areas of inquiry including professional fields such as college student affairs must also be concerned with answering questions of reality.

Metaphysics is usefully divided into four subsets which depict different types of questions. Cosmology concerns the study of and theories about the origin, nature, and development of the universe as an orderly system. Cosmological questions focus on the nature of time and space and the purposefulness of the universe. Theology, the second subset of metaphysics, concerns conceptions of and about God. A third aspect of metaphysics is anthropology which asks questions about human beings: What is the relationship between mind and body? Are people born good, evil, or morally neutral? Do human beings have free will? Does man have a soul? Ontology, the study of the nature of existence, is the final division of metaphysics. Ontological questions are concerned with what it means for anything to be: Is reality orderly and lawful? Has man created a condition of order? Is reality friendly, hostile, or neutral to humans? Is basic reality the world of human senses or of spiritual energy?

Epistemology

The branch of philosophy which concerns studies of the nature of knowledge, the sources of knowledge, and the validity of knowledge is epistemology. What is truth? and How is truth known? are central issues of epistemology. These issues cause thoughtful consideration of questions about the absolute or relative nature of truth, about the objective or subjective nature of truth, and about whether there can be truth independent of human experience.

At least five sources of knowledge can be identified. Empirical knowledge refers to knowledge gained through the senses. Revealed knowledge presupposes a transcendent supernatural reality which is accepted. Religious faith is a concrete example of revealed knowledge. Authoritative knowledge is that which comes from experts or from tradition. Rational knowledge is gained from reasoning, thought, or logic. Intuition is knowledge which results not from conscious reasoning or sense perception but from direct apprehension and comprehension, a "flash of insight."

Issues concerning the validity of knowledge center on criteria for determining what is true and what is false. Agreement with empirically determined fact is one test of truth. If a judgment corresponds with facts, it is true. If it does not, it is false. Another test of the validity of knowledge is to determine if a judgment is consistent with other judgments which have been accepted as true. A third test of truth is based upon the assumption that truth is neither static nor absolute. Within this context, truth is what works, and the test of truth lies in its utility, practicality, or satisfactory consequences.

Axiology

Axiology is that division of philosophy that attempts to answer questions of value. Morris (1956) has labeled values that are verbalized but not always actualized as "conceived values." Values that are acted upon are referred to as "operational values" (Morris, 1956). Rational living is based upon systems of value. Both individuals and societies develop value systems which are constructed on conceptions of reality and truth. Tensions develop when different conceptions of good or of value are held by the same society or individual.

Axiology has two subdivisions, ethics and aesthetics. Ethics is the study of moral values and conduct. Ethical theory is concerned with indicating right values as foundational to right actions. Ethical issues cause direct and regular consideration of the absolute or relative nature of ethical standards, the existence of universal moral values, and the basis of ethical authority. Aesthetics deals with principles and standards governing both creation and appreciation of beauty and of art. As such, aesthetics is closely related to creativity and imagination. The making of aesthetic judgments involves both cognitive understanding and affective experiencing. Knight (1982) asserts that the aesthetic experience enables people to move beyond the limits imposed by purely rational thought and weakness of human language.

Educational Philosophy

Educational philosophy is the application of philosophy to various aspects of education. Similarly, philosophy of science refers to philosophical considerations of aspects and dimensions of scientific inquiry, and philosophy of art is the philosophical consideration of questions related to the creation and appreciation of art forms. Educational philosophy may be concerned with education in a broad or limited sense. Educational philosophy may also focus concern upon a level of education, educational goals, specific subject matter, approaches to teaching and learning, curriculum development, or the development of institutional policy.

EDUCATIONAL PHILOSOPHY OF HIGHER EDUCATION

Philosophical efforts which attempt to take into account broad conceptions of education are often of limited value to higher education. Many general philosophies of education are concerned primarily, if not exclusively, with elementary and secondary schools. Brubaker (1982) notes that these philosophies do not recognize that higher education has problems of its own not found in lower schools. In an historical sense, only certain schools of philosophy have been concerned with higher learning and higher education.

The Yale Report of 1828 was the first formal statement of philosophy of higher education in the United States (Brubaker & Rudy, 1976). This statement by the Yale faculty asserted that a prescribed curriculum (traditional classical curriculum) was the only appropriate approach to learning for college students because it was based on two principles: the discipline of the mind (faculty psychology) and the "finishing" of the mind (inclusion of knowledge that developed the mind and exclusion of knowledge that could be learned elsewhere) (Brubaker, 1982). The spirit, if not the prescription, of the Yale Report influenced the philosophy and practice of higher education for the rest of the nineteenth century. President Charles Eliot of Harvard, however, fomented serious challenges to the Yale Report with the introduction of an elective system which allowed students to choose alternatives to prescribed classical studies.

During the final decades of the nineteenth century, a number of American colleges and universities began modeling approaches to teaching and learning after the German university. Graduate education with an emphasis upon pure research was the German model. While this model was based originally upon an understanding of philosophy and a commitment to research, it was to be adapted in the twentieth century to fit the needs of professional education. The Select Committee on Graduate Education of the University of California at Berkeley stated in 1966 that "First and foremost [graduate education] is training and only as a by-product is it education" (Passmore, 1980, p. 40).

In the early twentieth century, concern was expressed by individuals who feared the influences of a middle-class business culture would undermine the intellectual heritage of American higher education (Brubaker, 1982). The first philosophical critique of the increasing dominance of the middle-class business culture was Veblen's (1918) *The Higher Learning in America*. In this book Veblen attempted to preserve the value-free objectivity of research against the corrupting influence of the "captains of industry" (Brubaker, 1982). Hutchins (1936) added his criticism of the trend toward pragmatic concerns in higher education in a book by the same title, *The Higher Learning in America*. Brubaker (1982) notes that Hutchins would have anchored his philosophy of higher education in theology except for the separation of church and state. Instead, Hutchins based his views on a metaphysics that held to perennial absolutes about the nature of man, the nature of truth, and the nature of values (Brubaker, 1982).

Hutchins was an advocate of rational humanism in the sense that his philosophy of humanism was not grounded in the study of theology. With his colleague Mortimer Adler, Hutchins sought to establish a philosophy of higher education which drew upon a classic conception of intellectual excellence as the proper aim of education in all societies. This conception, like that of Aristotle and St. Thomas Aquinas, glorified the life of the mind as the good life. The content of the liberal arts was defined as the "wisdom of the ages" which was to be found in studying the "great books." Adler (1951) held that the value of liberal studies does not depend on the use to which they can be put in the world but rather is self-contained and valuable in and of themselves. Hutchins argued that "Education implies teaching. Teaching implies knowledge. Knowledge is truth. The truth is everywhere the same. Hence education should be everywhere the same" (Hutchins, 1936, p. 66).

The rational humanists of the first half of the twentieth century did not regard themselves as holding aristocratic views. They maintained that a liberal education which emphasized the development of the human intellect was for everyone. A liberal education as opposed to vocational training would guarantee a common universe of discourse so necessary for the solidity of democratic institutions (Adler, 1943).

The philosophy of rational humanism has been refuted by Dewey (1937), Hook (1963), and Whitehead (1929). These educational philosophers regarded rationality not as an end of higher learning but as instrumental to finding solutions to problems of current living. Their philosophy has been called pragmatic naturalism, or often instrumentalism or experimentalism. They did not conceive of liberal education as having a constant quality no matter what the time in history or the place in the world. Dewey and his colleagues thought of liberal education as necessarily undergoing changes and alteration to meet the demands of time and place. Their reference point was not a metaphysical view of man, but was rather rooted in democracy, liberalism, and pragmatism, and they regarded human intelligence as a means rather than an end. Dewey expressed concern with the authoritarianism of Hutchins and Adler which implied a higher education resting on a metaphysic of ultimate first principles. Since someone must decide which principles of education ultimately come first, Dewey believed that such a decision posed a dangerous threat to the intellectual freedom of higher education (Brubaker & Rudy, 1976).

Dewey, Hook, and Whitehead also objected to the notion of the human intellect as divorced from human emotion. Furthermore, the pragmatic naturalists objected to the rational humanists' view on the relation of theory to practice. In particular, they objected to isolating conceptualization to colleges and universities and practice to life and technical institutes (Brubaker & Rudy, 1976). They believed that theory and practice are mutually supportive, with theory anticipating consequences and practice determining whether consequences corroborate theoretical expectations.

Arguments concerning a philosophy of rational humanism versus a philosophy of pragmatic naturalism have continued to the present. An effort at resolution of these two philosophical perspectives was attempted by the Harvard University faculty in 1945 with little immediate or long term success (*General Education in a Free Society,* 1945). It is probably impossible to synthesize these two incompatible philosophies. Of greater significance is the fact that at the midpoint in the twentieth century, many people were beginning to seek a both/and rather than an either/or answer to the philosophical problems of higher education (Green, 1943).

The expansion of American higher education after World War II caused attention to be drawn away from philosophical consideration to accommodating greater numbers of students. This period of expansion started with the influx of veterans supported by the Servicemen's Readjustment Act of 1944, more commonly called the G. I. Bill of Rights. The "baby boomers" followed the veterans to college, and a concern with expansion continued as a matter of immediacy. Philosophy came back into focus in the late 1960's and 1970's when issues related to the Vietnam War and civil rights precipitated student unrest and activism. Brubaker (1982) has observed that the Vietnam War and struggles over the civil rights of minority students agitated campuses not only about the direction of public affairs but also about the role of higher education in them. "The importance of a philosophy of higher education was recognized as never before" (Brubaker, 1982, p. 7).

Despite efforts to develop a philosophy of higher education in the United States which is consistent and coherent, (Brubaker, 1982; Carnegie Commission, 1972; Carnegie Commission, 1973; Gross & Grambsch, 1986; Smith, 1955) a single philosophy has not been broadly accepted or endorsed. Instead, philosophical questions such as the purposes of colleges and universities, the nature of students, the relationship between education and training, and the transmission of values in teaching continue to be approached and considered by a relatively small number of established schools of philosophy that have considered the uniqueness of higher education.

EDUCATIONAL PHILOSOPHY AND COLLEGE STUDENT AFFAIRS

Just as higher education in the United States has not accepted or endorsed a single educational philosophy, the area of college student affairs has not grounded its professional identity in but one philosophical position. As noted previously, professional practice in college student affairs has been and continues to be shaped by the *Student Personnel Point of View* (American Council on Education, Committee on Student Personnel Work, 1973; American Council on Education, Comittee on Student Personnel Work, 1949). However, since this landmark statement is really a statement of purpose and commitment and accommodates more than one philosophical perspective, there is purpose in examining and analyzing those schools of philosophy which have shaped professional practice. Four schools of philosophy, in particular, have had influence and impact: rationalism, neo-humanism, pragmatism, and existentialism.

Rationalism

One of the oldest philosophies of western civilization is rationalism. Early statements of rationalism are attributed to Aristotle. The emphasis of this philosophical perspective is upon the nature of man and the nature of knowledge rather than upon the nature of reality itself. A fundamental assertion of rationalism is that the essence of human nature is its rational character. It is the human being's intellect and reasoning power that creates a separation between the human organism and other living creatures. The rationalist assumes that ideas are absolute and asserts that Great Truths and Great Ideas are contained in the writings of classical thinkers. The task of the learner is to discover these Great Truths and Great Ideas and apply them to contemporary life.

Rationalism holds that the essence of education is the cultivation of the intellect alone. The aim of education, therefore, is intellectual development. At the undergraduate level, this aim is achieved through a liberal arts curriculum based upon classical writings. Only those individuals who are capable of understanding Great Truths and shouldering the responsibility of the wisdom resulting from a study of classical thought are regarded as legitimate students.

Rationalism had considerable influence upon the purposes and practices in American higher education during the final decades of the nineteenth century. At this time, the leadership of scholarship had passed from England to Germany, and a number of American colleges and universities were modeling approaches to teaching and learning after the German university. The goals of developing the intellect of students and the assumption that the truth can and must be verified empirically were becoming more widely accepted in America. In those institutions which embraced rationalism, the individuality and personal development of students were not matters of concern, nor was the welfare of students outside of the classroom and laboratory. To the rationalist, intellectual development is the primary purpose of higher education.

Rationalism provided and continues to provide limited but definable philosophical support for college student affairs practice. This philosophical perspective has shaped practices which are primarily concerned with creating and controlling a campus environment in order that students will develop intellectually. In a campus environment where decisions and practices are based on rationalism, educational policies and practices are designed to transmit Great Truths and to train the intellect. Knowledge is regarded as exact and rational. Rationalism dictates that the essence of education is intellectual development, and the task of the academic community is to make certain that carefully selected students progress toward goals in accordance with institutional values.

The rationalist believes that the policies and practices of a student affairs division are intended to support and enhance such an environment. Such practices as selective admission policies and transcripting policies which document only academic performance and conduct transgressions reflect rationalism. Residence hall programming is geared only to academic matters which are supportive of intellectual development. Student activities may be available but are not regarded as contributing to the education of students. Counseling and career development services are viewed as not directly contributory to intellectual development and, therefore, nonessential. Rationalism supports an authoritarian approach to student discipline. Student conduct regulations are viewed as universal and based on absolute concepts of right and wrong. Students who cannot or will not accept responsibility for their conduct jeopardize membership in the academic community. The legal concept of *in loco parentis* fits natrally and logically with rationalism. Those who honestly believe that student affairs professionals should enforce an established and accepted code of proper behavior in the interest of promoting students' intellectual development often support their view with reference to basic tenets of rationalism.

Since rationalism regards education as development of the intellect only, the mission of college student affairs is a limited one. Those efforts which support academic endeavors are viewed as appropriate and necessary. A philosophy of rationalism does not embrace efforts by college student affairs professionals to foster the development of students outside of the cognitive domain.

Neo-Humanism

During the early twentieth century, the significance of the emerging psychology of individual differences caused divergent thinking about the nature of college students and the processes of teaching and learning. Field theories of learning and personality and the science of psychometrics gave rise to a view that the individual is and functions as a total entity with each of the parts contributing to total growth and development. Neo-humanism represents a perspective on the human being as learner and departs from the rational humanism of Hutchins and Adler. A philosophy of neo-humanism requires that the individual learner be assessed and that curriculum flexibility exist to satisfy individual interests and abilities. This philosophical perspective recognizes the primacy of cultivating the intellect and reason but assumes a dualism of mind and body, thought and action, reason and emotion. Higher education is viewed as embracing more than intellectual development and including intentional efforts to develop many dimensions of human personality. It is accepted that education at all levels should address the needs of the total person — intellectual, physical, social, and emotional.

The notion that providing services to and for students is a responsibility of a collegiate institution is supported philosophically by neo-humanism. A concern for more than just the intellectual development of college students and attempts to meet a variety of human needs within the environment of the campus lead to a broadening of the concept of *in loco parentis* by the mid-twentieth century. This legal concept was reconceptualized by some practitioners to mean that an institution should be attentive to many dimensions of the growth and development of students and like a caring parent should seek to nurture, support, and direct this development. Neo-humanism supports a view of education which includes more than cognitive learning. This perspective, however, supports a concept of college student affairs work as extracurricular in nature. To the neo-humanist, the primary goal of a student affairs division is to support and enhance the academic experiences of students. Efforts to promote the development of students in the affective and psychomotor domains of human learning are regarded as appropriate but of secondary importance. Student affairs policies and practices should support the academic mission. Counseling, for example, should focus on academic goal-setting, improvement of study skills, and decision-making about academic majors and career plans. Student activities are regarded as valuable opportunities for leadership development but not essential to a student's educational experience. Residence life programs should complement the content of academic courses and also provide social and recreational outlets. Student involvement in organizations and service projects should be encouraged but managed by student affairs staff so that students have sufficient time for study and academic pursuits.

A philosophy of neo-humanism is concerned with more than just the intellectual development of college students and is supportive of college student affairs work as a part of the extracurriculum. The needs of the total student — intellectual, physical, social, and emotional — are recognized as responsibilities of the college or university. The intellectual need is primary and is to be addressed by the faculty. The other areas of human needs are to be addressed by the student affairs division.

Influence of Rationalism and Neo-Humanism

Both rationalism and neo-humanism influenced the thinking and motivation of persons who accepted student affairs positions in the early and mid-twentieth century. Cowley (1957) has commented that three kinds of people engaged in college student affairs by the mid-1950's: the humanitarians, the administrators, and the scientists. The humanitarians came first and tended to be sentimentalists in that "they often advocate building Utopias without knowing much about architecture and construction engineering" (Cowley, 1957, p. 21). The first wave of student affairs professionals in the twentieth century came largely from the ranks of humanitarians. The second wave who entered the field between 1930 and 1960 were appointed "primarily because of their administrative ability rather than because of any compelling interest in students" (Cowley, 1957, p. 21). The psychologists, the scientists in Cowley's depiction, arrived upon the scene just after World War I and brought a rigor and commitment to counseling and research that contributed significantly to giving increased status to student affairs as a profession. In reality, these three groups had relatively little in common. It has been observed that the student personnel movement of the post World War I period was not a movement at all but instead was "a collection of independent wheels turning at different rates and often in different directions" (Cowley, 1957, p. 20).

The realities noted by Cowley reveal that college student affairs, like the rest of higher education, had not established philosophical anchor points by the middle of the twentieth century. Questions and issues related to purpose and mission were not addressed or answered from an accepted educational philosophy. Both rationalism and neo-humanism influenced practice in college student affairs during the early and mid-twentieth century, the formative years of the profession. The influence of both of these schools of philosophy has continued into the second half of the century; however, professional practice in recent years has been more affected by pragmatism and existentialism.

Pragmatism

Pragmatism, sometimes referred to as instrumentalism, has roots in the writings of Bacon and Comte and gained popularity as a philosophy of education in the United States through the writings of the nineteenth century psychologist and philosopher William James and the twentieth century educator, John Dewey. To the pragmatist, knowing involves an interrelationship between the object to be known and the knower. There is not a separation of fact from value, body from mind, or the world to be known from the knower. Theories of knowledge and of values emphasize the continuity of knower and unknown and of object and observer. Pragmatism begins with specific and particular experience rather than with universal truths. It is assumed that all things are known within a context that involves their utility. While the rationalist seeks to answer the question, "Is it true?" the pragmatist asks, "Does it work?" Truth is viewed as dynamic rather than static and subject to constant change in a world which is subject to change.

Values are important in all areas of knowledge and living. Pragmatists perceive values as particular to the individual observer and the result of human choices involving an interrelationship of the person and the environment. Education is geared toward harmony of the rational and emotional states of human beings. Students are encouraged to learn by doing and to apply knowledge to find solutions to problems. It is believed that the curriculum of higher education should provide for application of theory to practice.

Pragmatism emphasizes the full and creative development of the whole student. Programs and services which intentionally provide opportunities for students to experience the utilitarian value of various forms of knowledge evidence institutional policies based on pragmatism. Student organizations which offer opportunities for applying knowledge to real situations such as defining and pursuing common goals, preparing for and meeting financial obligations, participating in democratic decision-making, and contributing to conflict resolution reflect a pragmatic approach to learning. Student affairs efforts such as career development, counseling, student activities, living-learning environments, student government, and leadership training reflect directly a philosophy of pragmatism in that students are openly encouraged and supported to gain understanding by using and applying knowledge. Providing opportunities for students to participate in institutional governance and to govern and manage the activities of a residence hall or fraternity or sorority house evidences student affairs leadership which accepts the assumptions of pragmatism.

Unlike neo-humanism, an assumption of dualism of mind and body, thought and action, reason and emotion is not consistent with pragmatism. However, arguments for a separation of the curriculum and extracurriculum have, at times, been supported by pragmatists who honestly believe in the value of out-of-class learning experiences but as separate and distinct from learning which occurs within the classroom. Some academic administrators, teaching faculty, and student affairs professionals alike have and do argue that a division between academic affairs and student affairs contributes to acceptance and respect for the goal of educating the whole student. Acceptance of pragmatism has caused academic administrators, faculty, and student affairs professionals to value learning experiences which occur within and outside of the classroom. This educational philosophy however, has not caused consideration of the value and potential of joining the curriculum and the extracurriculum.

Existentialism

A philosophy of existentialism comes from the writings of such nineteenth century European thinkers as Kierkegaard and Nietzsche. Existentialism places existence prior to essence. "Essence" refers to the substance of things that is permanent and unchangeable. In contrast, "existence" is neither created by human beings, nor can it be analyzed by rational thinking. The existentialist asserts that a person exists first and subsequently thinks, speculates, and contemplates this existence. Existentialism rejects a dichotomy between subject and object. A human being is not a subject who perceives an object. Rather, a person is considered to be with and a part of every object encountered.

The individual's existence is the central force in the analysis of things because each individual creates a uniquely personal world and gives meaning to phenomena in that world. The twentieth century French philosopher Jean Paul Sarte asserts that "Man is nothing else but what he makes of himself" (Sarte, 1957, p. 15). Existentialism views the human being as moving toward personal essence, as bridging the gap between the finite and the infinite. People are and must be responsible for what they are and for what they become. If essence (what a person consists of) preceded existence, (the fact that the person is) then human beings would be predetermined. However, since people are regarded as not having a predetermined essence, each person is considered to be both free and responsible. Decisions are possible and necessary, and each choice made moves an individual closer to the person which he or she is becoming.

Within the context of higher education, existentialism places responsibility for learning and development upon the student. The existentialist believes that each student creates his or her own curriculum within the context of a course, an academic program, or a social learning situation. What one has learned in the past does not determine what one will or should learn in the future. The teacher is the facilitator of learning, and the subject matter provides the focus for self consideration by the student.

The 1970's marked a period of restructuring of roles and relationships for college student affairs professionals. Facilitation of the growth and development of students replaced concern with controlling student behavior. Direct involvement in instruction became a new responsibility and diminished the notion that student affairs is a part of the extracurriculum only. Addressing institutional policies, procedures, and organizational structures that affect the environment and culture of the campus in positive or negative ways was recognized as a necessary action for deliverying quality student services. These changes were a result of advancements in knowledge of human growth and development during the adult years, the demise of *in loco parentis*, a felt need on the part of the student affairs profession to recast its purpose and mission (Brown, 1972), and the influence of existentialism. The concept of student development (Crookston, 1972; Miller et al., 1974; Miller & Prince, 1976; Parker, 1974) provided a framework for restructuring professional roles and relationships. Student development is the application of human development concepts, knowledge, and skills within the context of the collegiate environment and culture. Crookston (1976) observed that the emergence of the concept of student development in the late 1960's came out of the recognition that out-of-class education of college students would never be fully effective until it became incorporated into the philosophical and educational fabric of the institution. Existentialism with focus on the self, the belief that existence precedes one's essence, and a conviction that each individual must take responsibility for his or her own life provides philosophical support for the concept of student development.

Student affairs practice has been significantly influenced by the concept of student development and the philosophy of existentialism. In particular, this concept and this philosophy influenced a refocusing of professional practice to both the in-class and out-of-class life of college students. Crookston has noted that "As the examining of one's life becomes academically legitimate, the pedagogical focus must necessarily turn from the subject to the student" (Crookston, 1976, p. 28). Acceptance of a philosophy of existentialism by individuals and collegiate institutions results in a shifting of the primary emphasis from teaching subject matter to students to helping students make personal decisions about the knowledge to which they are exposed. This shifts in pedagogical focus represents a major departure from established notions about teaching and learning which have been developed for centuries. One implication of this shift is that college student affairs professionals become directly and intentionally involved in the facilitation of student learning. A separation between the curriculum and the extracurriculum is not maintained. Teaching becomes a collaborative function involving faculty and college student affairs professionals and takes place in a number of campus settings. Learning is recognized as a unique and individual responsibility of each student.

Programs and policies developed by college student affairs professionals which emphasize the importance of students being participating members of the academic community reflect the influence of existentialism as do open admissions, personal wellness programs, educational programming for non-traditional students, alcohol awareness efforts, learning assistance, and support services for special student subcultures. The goals and policies of such traditional areas as residence living, counseling, campus judicial programs, student government, and leadership training have also been influenced by existential concepts and principles. These activities are designed and offered by college student affairs professionals to foster individual decision-making on the part of students and not as forums for prescribing decisions or answers. Perhaps the influence of existentialism is most obvious in institutional policy changes which place responsibility for personal conduct with each student and remove that responsibility from both parents and the institution. The college student of the late twentieth century is generally regarded by members of the academic community and by off-campus observers as well as an adult who is responsible for both personal conduct and personal development.

SUMMARY

Philosophy has influenced the nature, goals, policies, and procedures of higher education in the United States. While the *Student Personnel Point of View* has provided the foundation for professional practice in student affairs, this landmark statement is actually more a statement of commitment and a declaration of purpose than a philosophy. The philosophical heritage of the student affairs profession is appreciated more completely by an examination of philosophical positions which have influenced policy and practice. Four schools of philosophy — rationalism, neo-humanism, pragmatism, and existentialism — have had significant influence and impact upon the profession. As an applied professional field, student affairs has been and probably always will be primarily concerned with immediate needs and current problems. Philosophical matters or what Tripp (1968) has called "philosophical anxieties" are considered less frequently. Nevertheless, philosophy, both institutional and personal, contributes to policy-making and program development. It is necessary to reflect regularly on both the "Why" and the "How" of the student affairs mission. This is the role of philosophy.

REFERENCES

Adler, M.J. (1943). God and the professors. In M. Van Doren, *Liberal education.* New York: Holt.

Adler, M.J. (1951). Labor, leisure, and liberal education, *Journal of General Education, 6,* 175-184.

American Council on Education, Committee on Student Personnel Work. (1937). *The student personnel point of view.* Washington, D.C.: American Council on Education, 1, 1, 3.

American Council on Education, Committee on Student Personnel Work. (1949). *The student personnel point of view (Rev. Ed.).* Washington, D.C.: American Council on Education, 6, 1, 13.

Brown, R.D. (1972). *Student development in tomorrow's higher education — a return to the academy.* Washington, D.C.: American College Personnel Association.

Brubaker, J.S. (1982). *On the philosophy of higher education.* San Francisco: Jossey-Bass.

Brubaker, J.S. & Rudy, W. (1976). *Higher education in transition.* New York: Harper & Row. (Originally published 1958).

Carnegie Commission on Higher Education. (1972). *Reform on campus.* New York: McGraw-Hill.

Carnegie Commission on Higher Education. (1973). *Purposes and performance of higher education in the United States.* New York: McGraw-Hill.

Cowley, W.H. (1957). Student personnel services in retrospect and prospect. *School and Society.* Jan., 19-22.

Crookston, B.B. (1972). A developmental view of academic advising as teaching. *Journal of College Student Personnel, 13,* 12-17.

Crookston, B.B. (1976). Student personnel — all hail and farewell. *Personnel and Guidance Journal, 55,* 26-29.

Dewey, J. (1937). President Hutchins' proposals to remake higher education, *Social Frontier, 3,* 103-104.

General Education in a Free Society. (1945). Cambridge, MA: Harvard University Press.

Greene, T.M. (1943). *Liberal education re-examined.* New York: Harper.

Gross, E. & Grambsch, P.V. (1968). *University goals and academic power.* Washington, D.C.: American Council on Education.

Hook, S. (1946). *Education for modern man.* New York: Dial.

Hutchins, R.M. (1936). *The higher learning in America.* New Haven, CT: Yale University Press.

Knight, G.R. (1982). *Issues and alternatives in educational philosophy.* Berrien Springs, MI: Andrews University Press.

Knock, G.H., Rentz, A.L., & Penn, J.R. (1987, March). *Our philosophical heritage: Significant influences on professional practice and preparation.* Paper presented at the national convention of the American College Personnel Association, Chicago.

Marler, C.D. (1975). *Philosophy and schooling.* Boston: Allyn & Bacon.

Miller, T.K., et al. (1974). *A student development model for student affairs in tomorrow's higher education.* Washington, D.C.: American College Personnel Association.

Miller, T.K., & Prince, J.S. (1976). *The future of student affairs.* San Francisco: Jossey-Bass.

Morris, C. (1956). *Varieties of human value.* Chicago: University of Chicago Press.

Morris, V.C. (1961). *Philosophy and the American school.* Boston: Houghton Mifflin.

O'Conner, D.J. (1957). *An introduction to the philosophy of education.* London: Routledge & Kegan Paul.

Parker, C.A. (1974). Student development: What does it mean? *Journal of College Student Personnel, 15,* 248-256.

Passmore, J. (1980). The philosophy of graduate education. In W.K. Frankena, (Ed)., *The philosophy and future of graduate education.* Ann Arbor, MI: The University of Michigan Press.

Sarte, J.P. (1957). Existentialism and Human Emotions. New York: Philosophical Library.

Smith, H. (1955). *The purposes of higher education.* New York: Harper & Row.

Smith, P.G. (1965). *Philosophy of education: Introductory studies.* New York: Harper & Row.

Taylor, H. (1952). Philosophical foundations of general education. In National Society for the Study of Education, *General Education.* 51st Yearbook, Part II. Chicago: University of Chicago Press.

Tripp, P.A. (1968). Student personnel workers: Student development experts of the future. *NAWDAC Journal,* Spring, 142-144.

Veblen, T. (1918). *The higher learning in America.* New York: D.W. Huebsch.

Whitehead, A.N. (1929). *The aims of education and other essays.* New York: Macmillan.

CHAPTER 2

ACADEMIC ADVISING

JUDITH J. GOETZ

INTRODUCTION

THE ACTIVITY of academic advising provides students with guidance in identifying and developing suitable programs of study using the curricular structure of the institution. The breadth of this activity is dependent on many institutional factors, such as curricular complexity, enrollment configurations, procedural organization, and staffing options.

Academic guidance began as a faculty responsibility to help students make appropriate course selections from the increasingly complex college curriculum that evolved at the end of the nineteenth century (Rudolph, 1962). Prior to this time, academic programs were highly structured, curricular choices were limited, and few persons enrolled in college.

As society's need for educated people grew to meet the demands of technological advances and increased occupational opportunities, colleges and universities broadened their curricula and widened their bases of enrollment. Academic guidance became a visible need, joining other newly created student guidance programs as a necessary part of institutional operations.

Today, with the diverse enrollments in institutions and the demands placed upon higher education to be ". . . not merely a preserver and transmitter of culture but an integral part of . . . economic progress and [the] national well being" (Study Group on the Conditions of Excellence in American Higher Education, 1984), the activity of academic advising has taken on increased importance as a potential contributor to student persistence and success.

DEFINITION

Academic advising is a fairly recent institutionalized term. Early academic guidance focused on faculty interaction with students to discuss curriculum, institutional procedures, course selection, and choosing a field of study (Brubacher & Rudy, 1968; Crookston, 1972; Hardee, 1962, 1970; Kramer & Gardner, 1977, 1983; McKeachie, 1978; Moore, 1967; Mueller, 1961; Rudolph, 1962). These components are still fundamental in the academic advising process, as is the faculty role. Today's programs broaden the wide range of personnel involved in academic advising to include professional advisors, student advisors, and various persons within student service units (Ender, Winston, & Miller, 1982; Grites, 1979; Levine, 1978).

Academic advising has evolved toward increased curricular diversification and expanded definitions of the faculty role. Academic advising as an activity varies widely in the degree to which organizational and programmatic efforts are provided.

PURPOSE

The purpose of academic advising is closely associated with both the institutional mission and the evolution of the task of aiding students to develop educational plans. College faculties formed the original core of the advising process, so early organized programs of advising concentrated on this faculty role. Mueller (1961) differentiated advising from counseling, stating that advising was more restricted than counseling, and that ". . . the term 'faculty advising' is usually reserved specifically for aiding a student in planning his academic program" (p. 210). Hardee (1962) described faculty advising as a three-part activity of identifying institutional purpose, student purpose, and assisting the student to identify options. Schneider (1977) identified choosing courses for a specific program of study as the narrowest purpose of academic advising. Levine (1978) described the purpose of advising to include those areas related to the curriculum, such as course selection, major field requirements, and student performance.

More far-reaching purposes of academic advising have broadened the base both in who does the advising and what constitutes the process. Grites (1979) noted that academic advising is ". . . a decision-making process during which students realize their maximum educational potential" (p. 1). Grites saw the process as ". . . ongoing [and] multifaceted" to include a wide range of persons within the academic community providing comprehensive services to students (p. 1). Winston, Grites, Miller, and Ender (1984) identified four components that characterize academic advising: a teaching-learning activity, a way to stimulate personal and intellectual growth, a support function, and a record keeping function. Crockett (1978b) associated six tasks with academic advising: (1) values clarification and goal identification; (2) understanding the institution of higher education; (3) information-giving; (4) program planning that reflects the student's abilities and interests; (5) program assessment; and (6) referral to institutional resources (p. 30). These tasks expand the student's educational experience and the purposes for academic advising.

Borgard (1981) uses ideas derived from John Dewey to discuss a philosophy of advising that rests on ". . . the principle that learning begins in experience" (p. 3). He indicated that the advisor should help students to arrange experiences and to assist them in seeing the learning process as "a constant revision through systematic inquiry" (p. 4). Such an approach encourages students to become actively engaged in the learning process, with advisors serving as " . . . the bridge between the student in his present environment and his environments to be" (p. 4). Borgard noted that the purpose of advising should be to encourage the use of skills derived through content courses as the foundation for ". . . growth both in and out of college" (p. 4).

Although the scope of academic advising today is much broader than issues solely associated with curricular choice, a fundamental task of the student is to decide from among alternatives the most appropriate direction to take in planning a program of study. The purpose of academic advising is therefore intimately tied to the curriculum, both in the general education components that frequently form an introduction to the curricular structure and in the concentration, or major field component, that forms the specialization. From the earliest days of faculty advisors helping students to understand the curriculum (McKeachie, 1961), to the most sophisticated and comprehensive advising structures currently conceived (Grites, 1984), the basic task of identifying appropriate choices of courses remains fundamental to the advising process. Thus, as pointed out by Grites (1979), ". . . the most significant guide in academic advising is still the curriculum" (p. 30).

The basic curricular foundation of an institution directly affects such tasks as deciding on a field of study, selecting and monitoring the proper alternatives for required and elective courses, and determining the need for remediation or acceleration in skill components of the major field. The advising delivery system takes into account the complexity of academic departments and the breadth of academic support services available within the institution. Administering an advising program also must consider the degree to which computer technology for program exploration and record keeping is viable in the advising process (Aitken & Conrad, 1977; Kramer & Megerian, 1985; Kramer, Peterson, & Spencer, 1984).

Crookston (1972) stated that "[h]istorically, the primary focus of both the academic advisor and the vocational counselor has been concerned with helping the student choose a major or an occupation as a central decision around which to begin organizing his life" (p. 12). In recent years student interest in the vocational outcomes of the college experience has increased, although colleges have always focused on advanced education for vocational reasons (such as the traditional law, medicine, and the clergy). The proliferation of professionally oriented fields of study have meant wider ranges of choices open to students today; because of this, it is apparent that the vocational emphasis students place on the purpose of a college education is greater.

Perhaps the main thrust seen by many students is the desire for the practical application of course work and other learning experiences to a career. Since academic advising is an activity related to the curriculum, the purpose of advising becomes tied to the vocational applications that are possible as a result of choice for a program of study. Consideration should be given in an advising program to helping students translate their immediate needs for marketable skills into what Grites (1981) called ". . . functional skills that are related to all majors and jobs" (p. 45). The traditional components of learning that are transmitted as part of becoming "an educated person" should not be lost in the immediacy of collecting skills for a future vocational interest.

HISTORY

An early effort to provide academic guidance to students was provided at Kenyon College in the late 1820s (Levine, 1978). Perhaps the first recognized systems of advising existed at Johns Hopkins University and at Harvard University in the late 1800s (Brubacher & Rudy, 1968; Rudolph, 1962). The Harvard student advising program focused on faculty helping students "to select those programs which were best suited to their needs and interests" (Brubacher & Rudy, 1968, p. 432).

The Harvard advising plan developed as an outgrowth of the broad curricular experiment of the elective system instituted by President Charles Eliot in the latter part of the nineteenth century (Brubacher & Rudy, 1968). By 1895, Harvard freshmen were only required to take two English courses and a modern foreign language, with the remaining courses chosen from an array of electives. According to Rudolph (1962), "[t]he creation of a system of faculty advisors at Johns Hopkins and Harvard . . . was apparently the first formal recognition that size and the elective system required some closer attention to undergraduate guidance than was possible with an increasingly professionally-oriented faculty" (p. 460).

The Harvard elective system, as well as similar curricular innovations at other colleges, was in part a reflection of the expansion of knowledge that was occurring in the latter part of the nineteenth century. This was especially true in the sciences and the newly developing professions, such as social work, education, and economics. According to Wiebe (1967), universities played an important role for the professions with the " . . . power to legitimize, for no new profession felt complete — or scientific — without its distinct academic curriculum" (p. 121).

The expansion of knowledge as embodied in the curriculum required specialists (Light, 1974) who became organized into departments that represented academic disciplines. These affiliations became ". . . the focus of the *identity* of an academic professional" (Parsons & Platt, 1973, p. 113). Differentiation into academic departments increased the complexity of programs of study and encouraged the subject-matter specialization of the faculty (Brubacher & Rudy, 1968; Weaver, 1981).

As the American college and university system adapted to include more course offerings, wider ranges of choices for programs of study, greater diversity of students, and increased faculty specialization (Levine, 1978), the concern for educating the "whole student" resulted in the student personnel movement, which attempted to restore the concern of the "old-time college . . . for the non-intellectual side of the student's career" (Brubacher & Rudy, 1968, p. 331). Developments in psychological measurement and new approaches to viewing human behavior and learning laid the groundwork to help the student to be successful. Educational counseling became one area of interest within the broader framework of the expanding area of student personnel (Brubacher & Rudy, 1968).

Recent developments in higher education contribute to the visibility of the advising function. Concern with student/institutional "fit," a fairly recent area of interest in researching institutional impact on students, acknowledges the need to examine such issues as the effects of student-faculty interaction on persistence and satisfaction (Astin, 1977; Feldman & Newcomb, 1969; Jacob, 1957; Pascarella, 1980; Pascarella & Terenzini, 1977; Terenzini, Pascarella, & Lorgan, 1982; Tinto, 1982; Vreeland & Bidwell, 1966). The issue of student retention has become a key focus for those concerned with academic advising (Carstensen & Silberhorn, 1979; Creamer, 1980; Crockett, 1978b, 1986; Ender, Winston, & Miller, 1982; Glennen, 1976; Habley, 1981). Achieving excellence through involvement, especially through a strong academic advising system, has been a key topic in national studies, such as that produced by the Study Group on the Conditions of Excellence in American Higher Education (1984) and the Carnegie Foundation's investigation of the undergraduate experience (Boyer, 1987).

Two professional associations have been formed for administrators whose primary concerns include academic advising. In 1971 the Association of Academic Affairs Administrators (ACAFAD) adopted a constitution which included in its purposes, "to strengthen the quality of higher education by focusing on the individual student and the academic environment." Membership is open to academic affairs administrators whose primary concern includes academic advisement. Regional meetings and a newsletter are used to encourage professional dialogue.

In 1979, the National Academic Advising Association (NACADA) was established as a new organization specifically created to address issues and concerns of practitioners in academic advising. The Association produces a journal devoted to the topic of academic advising and hosts national and regional conferences. The Association has participated in the preparation of academic advising standards that contain the mission, administration, resources, facilities and ethics (Council for the Advancement of Standards for Student Services/Development Programs).

The American College Testing Program (ACT) has addressed issues related to academic advising by providing training sessions and developing resource materials (Crockett, 1978a, 1979, 1984), as well as conducting national studies of academic advising (Carstensen & Silberhorn, 1979; Crockett & Levitz, 1984). These efforts have proved useful to practitioners faced with establishing new academic advising programs and enriching existing ones.

In 1981, the term "academic advising" became a descriptor for the

Educational Resource Information Center (ERIC) information retrieval system. This recognition of academic guidance as an identifiable programmatic effort brings together under one rubric the varied efforts of formal and informal academic planning assistance to students.

PROGRAMS/SERVICES

Although no single program or set of services for academic advising is appropriate for all institutions (Grites, 1979), certain factors do form a core considered to be fundamental to the advising activity. The curriculum is crucial to the advising process because it forms the fundamental structure through which the student accomplishes the basic task of choosing a program of study. Student enrollment is a key aspect to program planning in the advising process because the entering needs and characteristics of students can help to frame the approaches used. Procedural functions that are mandated as part of the bureaucratic structure of the institution must be considered as part of the advising process.

Institutions whose foundation is based on the more traditional liberal arts will find that different approaches to advising are needed at those institutions that have very structured "career-oriented" programs. The multiversity that provides a wide range of programmatic options will find that different services are required than would be true for those institutions that have a more restricted purpose in their curricular aims.

All institutions need to consider student demands regarding the relevance of education to future possibilities that exist in the world of work. Regardless of the type or size of an institution, academic and career planning should be integrated (Beatty, Davis, & White, 1983; Habley, 1984). Such integration can allow for students to see how skills in information retrieval, decision-making, and assessment can be used in identifying and developing an academic program of study as well as constructing the foundation for a career plan.

Crockett (1982) identified the following four areas that students consider important in advising programs: "(1) accessibility; (2) specific and accurate information; (3) advice and counsel; and (4) a personal relationship with the advisor" (p. 41). In an analysis of advising tasks as perceived by students, Trombley (1984) found that defining educational goals, clarifying the choice of major field, and identifying career areas were important to students.

In the American College Testing Program (ACT) study of academic advising (Carstensen & Silberhorn, 1979), the informational needs of students were seen to be of primary importance in most advising programs. A follow-up study conducted by ACT in 1982 found an increase in informational resources used in advising programs (Crockett & Levitz, 1984). Accurate information that is accessible to students is fundamental to any advising program (Creamer, 1980).

The traditional functions associated with academic advising include record keeping associated with course registration, schedule adjustments, and monitoring progress toward a degree. These tasks, as defined by Trombley (1984), are technical in nature and important to a comprehensive advising program. The degree to which an institution can create efficient procedures that do not overwhelm student-advisor interactions will help to establish a successful program.

ORGANIZATIONAL PATTERNS

Various organizational patterns exist to provide academic advising to students. As pointed out by Ender, Winston, and Miller (1984) and Grites (1979), no one form of organization exists for all institutions because the individual institutional mission must be considered for the process to be effective.

Early advising programs were developed when the college president selected a core of faculty to aid in the process of providing counsel to students about their academic programs of study (Rudolph, 1962; Brubacher & Rudy, 1968). The two studies of academic advising programs undertaken by the American College Testing Program (ACT) showed that faculty advising has remained the major pattern for advising over the years (Castensen & Silberhorn, 1979; Crockett & Levitz, 1984). This decentralized approach of assigning students to faculty advisors acknowledges the curricular influence for advising (Grites, 1979).

Recently, increased attention has been given to organizing advising around a center, an idea pioneered by community colleges (Grites, 1979; O'Banion, 1971, 1972). The advising center, a centralized approach, combines a number of personnel (faculty, professional advisors, peer advisors) to provide information to students and to assist students with their academic decision-making (Crockett & Levitz, 1984). The advising center may exist for the entire institution, for specific academic units, or for delivering services to special subgroups of students (Crockett & Levitz, 1984; Gerlach, 1983; Grites, 1984; Johnson & Sprandel,

1974; Polson & Jurich, 1979; Spencer, Peterson, & Kramer, 1982). Crockett and Levitz (1984) found that advising the undecided/undeclared major was a primary function of the advising center approach. The advising center has also become a realistic mechanism to handle the large numbers of students in today's colleges and universities (Grites, 1979).

Another approach to academic advising has been through formal courses, providing to students an extended academic orientation. Orientation courses have been used for many years as mechanisms for integrating students into the institutional environment. Higginson, Moore, and White (1981) found that students report significant need for academic information as they begin the college experience. Recently, increased emphasis has been placed on the potential for using formal courses as an aid to understanding basic issues and strategies related to advising (Beatty, Davis, & White, 1983; Gardner, 1982; Gordon & Grites, 1984).

STAFFING

The major staffing patterns for college and university advising include faculty, professional staff advisors, and student advisors (Barman & Bansen, 1981; Crockett, 1986; Crockett & Levitz, 1984; Elliott, 1985; Grites, 1979; Habley, 1979; Hardee, 1970; Kramer & Gardner, 1977, 1983; Upcraft, 1971). Various individuals may work independently, or as teams, depending on the degree of centralization of policies and procedures (Crockett & Levitz, 1984; Grites, 1979; O'Banion, 1972).

Heavy reliance on faculty depends on the extent of their availability. Usually faculty will play the key advising role for students who have entered a major academic field, where the advising tasks will be carried out through the academic department of division housing the appropriate field of study. Faculty are also used as resource persons in both general and specialized advising centers. They may also serve their academic departments as resources to students seeking information about various fields of study.

Use of professional staff advisors as support to faculty advising has taken on increasing importance with the involvement of student affairs staff and the emphasis on "collaborative efforts for student development" (Ender, Winston, & Miller, 1982, pp. 12-13). Professional staff advisors whose full time responsibility is academic advising are usually part of advising centers or specialized academic or support units. These advisors frequently work with the students who have not yet declared majors, helping to identify options and to develop basic curricular plans that can provide a structure to future decisions.

Student, or "peer," advisors can be found at the academic department level as well as in general or specialized advising centers. These students may be graduate or undergraduate students who are integrated into the advising support system. Competency building programs are extremely important when using students (Grites, 1984).

MODELS

Grites pointed out in 1979 that "few theoretical models of the complex process [of advising] exist; rather, descriptions of various advising delivery systems prevail in the literature" (p. 1). The literature does cite two early models that have been widely identified as important to the basic activity of advising (O'Banion, 1972; Crookston, 1972). In both cases, as described by Grites (1979), the emphasis is on process, or sequencing of events that identify advising as a teaching-learning experience. According to Crockett (1986), advising models such as the one developed by O'Banion should acknowledge that there exists ". . . a logical and sequential set of steps to the advising process" (p. 246-247).

Recently, increased emphasis has been placed on the use of developmental theory as an organizing model for advising (Winston, Ende, & Miller, 1982; Thomas & Chickering, 1984). The notion of "developmental academic advising," as described by Ender, Winston, and Miller (1982) offers ". . . a systematic process based on close student-advisor relationship intended to aid students in achieving educational, career, and personal goals through the utilization of the full range of institutional and community resources" (p. 19). Frequent student-advisor interaction to encourage personal development has been described as a necessary part of an advising program (Greenwood, 1984). Using a framework that addresses the needs of students at various points in their development can provide a way to help students view educational planning as part of a life process.

Organizational models for advising programs as seen from the administrative level note the need for support throughout the institution to develop goals, personnel selection, and adequate funding (Greenwood, 1984). The emphasis on coordination among various academic units and student service support areas are important to address, along with a ". . . systematic program of guidance and advisement that involves students from matriculation through graduation" (Study Group on the Conditions of Excellence in American Higher Education, 1984, p. 31). These considerations can be highly political, affecting the very nature of the organization. Implementing campus-wide models for academic advising reaches down to the fundamental questions of the purpose of higher education, the definition and importance of the faculty role, and the distribution of financial resources to programs and services.

ISSUES

Issues related to academic advising are heavily dependent on institutional configurations, such as curricular options available to meet student needs, ever diversified preparation levels of entering students, demands on information retrieval systems with increasing use of the computer for information management, and retention/attrition concerns. Fundamental factors such as financial resources, institutional size and control, and commitment to the value of the advising process necessitate juggling educational demands from various constituencies with institutional realities from a management perspective. Developing a mission or theoretical structure that can serve as a commitment to academic advising by the persons involved is crucial as an element to bond together the rationale and the implementation of academic advising programs.

Any advising program, to be effective, must be structured using some type of organizational plan guided by a statement of purpose (Crockett & Levitz, 1984). Included in such a plan is the issue of selection and training of the advising staff (Crockett & Levitz, 1984; Goetz & White, 1986; Gordon, 1980). Evaluation of the advising program is also an important consideration (Polson & Cashin, 1981), and forms a key part of a reward system frequently found lacking in advising programs (Carstensen & Silberhorn, 1979). The main issue associated with this concern is the degree to which the institutional decision-makers recognize and support the need for a strong advising program. Once such a commitment is made, the organizational factors associated with the development of a coordinated system must be considered, such as the degree to which the advising program will be centralized under a specific academic unit, or the extent of uniformity in the selection and training of the advising staff, or the mechanisms for budget control.

The degree to which an institution's academic advising program can affect student retention has taken on increased visibility (Crockett, 1978a). Creamer (1980) pointed out that a model is necessary, involving many aspects of the university community, in order to address the notion of "institutional holding power" (p. 11). One major issue associated with the concern of retention is how to help students make realistic assessments for the proper selection of academic fields of study so as to maximize the likelihood of success. Another issue related to retention is how to address student-institutional interaction by defining ways to help students become involved in the advising process, and then by developing methods of evaluating these designs.

Various efforts have been made to address the needs of subgroups of students for special advising. Considerable work has been reported in the literature to determine the best ways to identify and to structure academic advising programs for groups such as underprepared students, minority students, undecided students, reentry students, women students, and student-athletes(Clayton, 1982; Gordon, 1983; Grites, 1982, 1984; NACADA Journal, 1986; Peterson & McDonough, 1985; Ware, Steckler, & Leserman, 1985). Although the fundamental tasks of identifying and developing an academic program of study exists for all students, special needs may exist in remediation for students with weak backgrounds, or in support for individuals returning to school after an absence who need careful review of college credits accumulated during a previous period of enrollment in college. Regulations that apply for academic progress of student-athletes competing in inter-scholastic sports may necessitate specialized training for academic advisors. Continuing research on socialization factors that have an impact on the academic progress of students previously underrepresented in college add dimensions to advising programs that attempt to meet individualized needs of students.

Attention has been drawn to the importance of the freshman year as critical for the advising process (Gardner, 1982; Study Group on the Conditions of Excellence in American Higher Education, 1984). The major issue associated with attending to the specialized needs of students through academic advising programs is the degree to which an institution can support these advising efforts within the organizational and financial resources that are available.

Recent demands on certain curricular areas have forced some institutions to consider the population of students unable to enter the fields of study they desire because of institutional or departmental limitations on enrollment (Gordon & Polson, 1985). The implications of student consumerism on curricular demand forces the issue of advising into the notion of "alternative advising" based on supply and demand (p. 78). The major issue associated with this consideration rests with the comprehensiveness of an advising program, especially from the information support area. Interaction among academic units is needed to make information readily available to those students so that contingency plans can be developed and alternative program requirements met.

The advising experience should reflect the needs of the students set in the framework of institutional capabilities. Using the academic advising structure as a mechanism for developing complex educational and life-planning skills requires a clear understanding of the tasks to be accomplished, the staffing available to accomplish these tasks, and the commitment to the importance of the endeavor. As Crookston pointed out (1972), advising is broader than specific choices that are made, such as that of a vocational decision. The ability of the institution to provide a multifaceted approach to helping students realize their goals means a broadly-based effort to support a range of options that will help students effectively negotiate the experience. The main issue associated with this concern is the philosophy under which the advising program operates. As an example, for staffing to be addressed, the entire advising program must be envisioned as having a central role in the programmatic and the reward system of the institution.

Thomas and Chickering (1984) point out the following observation for those concerned about academic advising on college and university campuses:

> Thus, given the intricate interplay of academic and personal development, separating the two is administratively convenient but obviously absurd and ignores the wholeness of each student. Academic advising based on the developmental theory legitimately recognizes this wholeness and serves to encourage effectively wholesome development of each student's life in and out of the classroom. (p. 90-91)

The major issue associated with the notion of advising from a developmental perspective, as discussed in Thomas and Chickering's observation, rests with a clear understanding of the developmental process. Such an understanding is essential for handling the comprehensive task set forth in the above observation. Organizational factors affecting various campus units must also be addressed for comprehensive programs to be accomplished.

FUTURE CONCERNS

The activity of academic advising has undergone tremendous changes since the early efforts to give counsel to students. The need for academic guidance in the future will not diminish; continual updating of this activity so central to the nature of higher education must address organizational, fiscal, and theoretical issues. Several areas need to be addressed.

1. Perhaps the most far-reaching concern that faces institutions is how to identify services to students in such a way that the services are used by students to accomplish the tasks for which they were created. The activity of academic advising needs to be clearly defined as to purpose, programmatic options, and desired outcome. The degree to which academic advising differs from and is similar to other programs offered to students must be described in a clear statement of purpose that shows how the activity fits into a broader institutional perspective on student development.

2. Judicious use of computer technology to assist in advising, both as a record keeping mechanism for staff and as an interactive and information-retrieval approach for students is critical. The informational needs of students are considerable; however, the interpretation of this information is a crucial role for an advising program to play. From the standpoint of record keeping, Kramer, Peterson, and Spencer (1984) indicate that quality and accuracy can be improved with use of computers for such things as keeping track of degree requirements and reducing the clerical tasks for monitoring student progress.

3. Careful identification and collection of information about students prior to entrance and throughout their college years can add significantly to an advising program when incorporated into information exchanges that can enhance program planning. The development of advising tools for students that provide ways for students to become actively engaged in their own program planning, such as feedback of information they have contributed at various points in their academic careers, strengthens the developmental nature of an advising program. As pointed out in the 1984 report from the Study Group on the Conditions of Excellence in American Higher Education, the data collected on students needs to be used in useful ways ". . . that enhance student learning and lead to improvements in programs, teaching practices, and the environment in which teaching and learning take place" (p. 21).

4. Identifying factors associated with why students select different fields of study (Jackson, Holden, Locklin, & Marks, 1984) can contribute considerably to the advising program. Developing a perspective of the nature of the curriculum (Ford & Pugno, 1964; Hursh, Haas, & Moore, 1983) can add to approaches taken with students to help them to understand better the choices they are making. These areas of consideration require not only using the scholarly and research resources on campus but also academic support services such as career planning as tools in the advising process.

5. Continuous evaluation of programs designed to provide academic advising to students will be essential to justify programs that range beyond the minimal record keeping functions of academic advising (Greenwood, 1984). Establishing mechanisms that build student feedback into the evaluation process can keep advisors current to the needs of their constituencies.

REFERENCES

Aitken, C.E., & Conrad, C.F. (1977). Improving academic advising through computerization. *College and University, 53*(1), 115-123.

Astin, A.W. (1977). *Four critical years: Effects of college on beliefs, attitudes, and knowledge.* San Francisco: Jossey-Bass.

Barman, C.R., & Benson, P.A. (1981). Peer advising: A working model. *National Academic Advising Association (NACADA) Journal, 1*(20), 33-40.

Beatty, J.D., Davis, B.B., & White, B.J. (1983). Open option advising at Iowa State University: An integrated advising and career planning model. *National Academic Advising Association (NACADA) Journal, 3*(1), 39-48.

Borgard, J.H. (1981). Toward a pragmatic philosophy of academic advising. *National Academic Advising Association (NACADA) Journal, 1*(1), 1-7.

Boyer, E.L. (1987). *College: The undergraduate experience.* New York: Harper & Row.

Brubacher, J.S., & Rudy, R. (1968). *Higher education in transition.* New York: Harper & Row.

Carstensen, D.J., & Silberhorn, C.A. (1979). *A national survey of academic advising, final report.* Iowa City: American College Testing Program.

Clayton, B. (1982). Minority advising resources: An example of consultative services. *National Academic Advising Association (NACADA) Journal, 2*(2), 30-34.

Council for the Advancement of Standards for Student Services/Developmental Programs. (1986). Standards and guidelines for academic advising. *National Academic Advising Association (NACADA) Journal, 6*(2), 63-66.

Creamer, D.G. (1980). Educational advising for student retention: An institutional perspective. *Community College Review, 7,* 11-18.

Crockett, D.S. (Ed.). (1978a). *Academic advising: A resource document.* Iowa City: American College Testing Program.

Crockett, D.S. (1978b). Academic advising: A cornerstone of student retention. In L. Noel (Ed.), *New directions for student services: No. 3. Reducing the dropout rate* (pp. 29-35). San Francisco: Jossey-Bass.

Crockett, D.S. (Ed.). (1979). *Academic advising: A resource document* (1979 Supplement). Iowa City: American College Testing Program.

Crockett, D.S. (1982). Academic advising delivery systems. In R.B. Winston, S.C. Ender, & T.K. Miller (Eds.), *New directions for student services: No. 17. Developmental approaches to academic advising* (pp. 39-53). San Francisco: Jossey-Bass.

Crockett, D.S. (1984). ACT as a strategic resource in enhancing the advising process. *National Academic Advising Association (NACADA) Journal, 4*(2), 1-11.

Crockett, D.S. (1986). Academic advising. In L. Noel, R. Levitz, D. Saluri, & Associates (Eds.), *Increasing student retention.* San Francisco: Jossey-Bass.

Crockett, D.S., & Levitz, R. (1984). Current advising practices in colleges and universities. In R.B. Winston, Jr., T.K. Miller, S.C. Ender, T.J. Grites, & Associates (Eds.), *Developmental academic advising* (pp. 35-63). San Francisco: Jossey-Bass.

Crookston, B.B. (1972). A developmental view of academic advising as teaching. *Journal of College Student Personnel, 13,* 12-27.

Elliott, E.S. (1985). Academic advising with peer advisors and college freshmen. *National Academic Advising Association (NACADA) Journal, 5*(1), 1-9.

Ender, S.C., Winston, R.B., Jr., & Miller, T.K. (1982). Academic advising as student development. In R.B. Winston, Jr., S.C. Ender, & T.K. Miller, *New directions for student services: No. 17. Developmental approaches to academic advising* (pp. 3-18). San Francisco: Jossey-Bass.

Feldman, K.A., & Newcomb, T.A. (1969). *The impact of college on students.* San Francisco: Jossey-Bass.

Ford, G.W., & Pugno, L. (Eds.). (1964). *The structure of knowledge and the curriculum.* Chicago: Rand McNally.

Gardner, J.N. (1982). *Proceedings of the national conference on the freshman orientation course/freshman seminar concept.* Columbia, SC: University of South Carolina.

Gerlach, M.E. (1983). Academic advising centers. In P.J. Gallagher & G.D. Demos (Eds.), *Handbook of counseling in higher education* (pp. 180-189). New York: Praeger.

Glennen, R.E. (1976). Intrusive college counseling. *The School Counselor, 24,* 48-50.

Goetz, J.J., & White, R.E. (1986). A survey of graduate programs addressing the preparation of professional academic advisors. *National Academic Advising Association (NACADA) Journal, 6*(2), 43-47.

Gordon, V.N. (1980). Training academic advisers: Content and method. *Journal of College Student Personnel, 21,* 334-340.

Gordon, V.N. (1983). Meeting the career needs of undecided honors students. *Journal of College Student Personnel, 24,* 82-83.

Gordon, V.N. (1984). *The undecided college students: An academic and career advising challenge.* Springfield, IL: Charles C Thomas.

Gordon, V.N., & Grites, T.J. (1984). The freshman seminar course: Helping students succeed. *Journal of College Student Personnel, 25,* 315-320.

Gordon, V.N., & Polson, C.L. (1985). Students needing academic alternative advising: A national survey. *National Academic Advising Association (NACADA) Journal, 5*(2), 77-84.

Greenwood, J. (1984). Academic advising and institutional goals. In R.B. Winston, Jr., T.K. Miller, S.C. Ender, T.J. Grites, & Associates, *Developmental academic advising* (pp. 64-68). San Francisco: Jossey-Bass.

Grites, T.J. (1979). *Academic advising: Getting us through the eighties* (Report No. 7). Washington, D.C.: American Association for Higher Education-Educational Resource Information Center.

Grites, T.J. (1981, September). Being "undecided" might be the best decision they could make. *The School Counselor,* 41-45.

Grites, T.J. (1982). Advising for special populations. In R.B. Winston, Jr., S.C. Ender, & T.K. Miller (Eds.), *New directions for student services: No. 17. Developmental approaches to academic advising* (pp. 67-83). San Francisco: Jossey-Bass.

Grites, T.J. (1984). Noteworthy academic advising programs. In R.B. Winston, Jr., T.K. Miller, S.C. Ender, T.J. Grites, & Associates, *Developmental academic advising* (pp. 469-537). San Francisco: Jossey-Bass.

Habley, W.R. (1979). The advantages and disadvantages of using students as academic advisors. *National Association of Student Personnel Administrators (NASPA) Journal, 17,* 46-51.

Habley, W.R. (1981). Academic advisement: The critical link in student retention. *National Association of Student Personnel Administrators (NASPA) Journal, 18*(4), 45-50.

Habley, W.R. (1984). Integrating academic advising and career planning. In R.B. Winston, Jr., T.K. Miller, S.C. Ender, T.J. Grites, & Associates, *Developmental academic advising* (pp. 147-172). San Francisco: Jossey-Bass.

Hardee, M.D. (1962). Faculty advising in contemporary higher education. *Educational Record, 42,* 112-116.

Hardee, M.D. (1970). *Faculty advising in colleges and universities.* Washington, D.C.: American College Personnel Association.

Higginson, L.C., Moore, L.V., & White, E.R. (1981). A new role for orientation: Getting down to academics. *National Association of Student Personnel Administrators (NASPA) Journal, 19*(1), 21-28.

Hursch, B., Haas, P., & Moore, M. (1983). An interdisciplinary model to implement general education. *Journal of Higher Education, 54*(1), 42-59.

Jackson, D.N., Holden, R.R., Locklin, R.H., & Marks, E. (1984). Taxonomy of vocational interests of academic major areas. *Journal of Educational Measurement, 21*(3), 261-275.

Jacob, P.E. (1957). *Changing values in college.* New York: Harper.

Johnson, J., & Sprandel, K. (1975). Centralized academic advising at the departmental level: A model. *University College Quarterly (Michigan State University), 21*(1), 16-20.

Kramer, G.L., & Mergerian, A. (1985). Using computer technology to aid faculty advising. *National Academic Advising Association (NACADA) Journal, 5*(2), 51-61.

Kramer, G.L., Peterson, E.D., & Spencer, R.W. (1984). Using computers in academic advising. In R.B. Winston, Jr., T.K. Miller, S.C. Ender, T.J. Grites, & Associates, *Developmental academic advising* (pp. 226-249). San Francisco: Jossey-Bass.

Kramer, H.C., & Gardner, R.E. (1977). *Advising by faculty.* Washington, D.C.: National Education Association.

Kramer, H.C., & Gardner, R.E. (1977). *Advising by faculty* (2nd ed.). Washington, D.C.: National Education Association.

Levine, A. (1978). *Handbook of undergraduate curriculum.* San Francisco: Jossey-Bass.

Light, D. (1974). Introduction: The structure of the academic professions. *Sociology of Education, 47,* 2-28.

McKeachie, W.J. (1978). *Teaching tips: A guidebook for the beginning college teacher* (7th ed.). Lexington, MA: Heath.

Moore, K.M. (1976). Faculty advising: Panacea or placebo? *Journal of College Student Personnel, 17,* 371-375.

Mueller, K.H. (1961). *Student personnel work in higher education.* Boston: Houghton-Mifflin.

National Academic Advising Association (NACADA) Journal. (1986). *6*(1).

O'Banion, T. (1971). *Student personnel monograph series: No. 15. New directions in community college student personnel programs.* Washington, D.C.: American College Personnel Association.

O'Banion, T. (1972). An academic advising model. *Junior College Journal, 44,* 62-69.

Parsons, T., & Platt, G.M. (1973). *The American university.* Cambridge, MA: Harvard University Press.

Pascarella, E.T. (1980). Student-faculty informal contact and college outcomes. *Review of Educational Research, 50,* 545-595.

Pascarella, E.T., & Terenzini, P.T. (1977). Patterns of student-faculty informal interaction beyond the classroom and voluntary freshman attrition. *Journal of Higher Education, 48,* 540-552.

Peterson, L., & McDonough, E. (1985). Developmental advising of undeclared students using an integrated model of student growth. *National Academic Advising Association (NACADA) Journal, 15*(1), 61-69.

Polson, C.J., & Cashin, W.E. (1981). Research priorities for academic advising: Results of a survey of NACADA membership. *National Academic Advising Association (NACADA) Journal, 1*(1), 34-43.

Polson, C.J., & Jurich, A.P. (1979). The departmental academic advising center: An alternative to faculty advising. *Journal of College Student Personnel, 20,* 249-253.

Rudolph, R. (1962). *The American college and university.* New York: Random House.

Schneider, L.D. (1977). Junior college services, In. W.T. Packwood (Ed.), *College student personnel services* (pp. 450-486). Springfield, IL: Charles C Thomas.

Spencer, R.W., Peterson, E.D., & Kramer, G.L. (1982). Utilizing college advising centers to facilitate and revitalize academic advising. *National Academic Advising Association (NACADA) Journal, 2*(1), 13-23.

Study Group on the Conditions of Excellence in American Higher Education. (1984). *Involvement in learning: Realizing the potential of American higher education.* Washington, D.C.: National Institute of Education.

Terenzini, P.T., Pascarella, E.T., & Lorgan, W.G. (1982). An assessment of the academic and social influences on freshman year educational outcomes. *Review of Higher Education, 5*(2), 86-109.

Thomas, R.E., & Chickering, A.W. (1984). Foundations for academic advising. In R.B. Winston, Jr., T.K. Miller, S.C. Ender, T.J. Grites, & Associates, *Developmental academic advising* (pp. 89-117). San Francisco: Jossey-Bass.

Tinto, V. (1982). Limits to theory and practice in student attrition. *Journal of Higher Education, 53,* 687-700.

Trombley, T.B. (1984). An analysis of the complexity of academic advising tasks. *Journal of College Student Personnel, 25*(4), 234-239.

Upcraft, M.L. (1971). Undergraduate students as academic advisers. *Personnel and Guidance Journal, 49,* 827-831.

Vreeland, R.S., & Bidwell, C.E. (1966). Classifying university departments: An approach to the analysis of their effects upon undergraduates' values and attitudes. *Sociology of Education, 39*(3), 237-254.

Ware, N.C., Steckler, N.A., & Leserman, J. (1985). Undergraduate women: Who chooses a science major? *Journal of Higher Education, 56,* 73-84.

Weaver, F.S. (1981, Summer). Academic disciplines and undergraduate liberal arts education. *Liberal Education,* 151-165.

Winston, R.B., Jr., Grites, T.J., Miller, T.K., Ender, S.C. (1984). Epilogue: Improving academic advising. In R.B. Winston, Jr., T.K. Miller, S.C. Ender, T.J. Grites, & Associates, *Developmental academic advising* (pp. 538-550). San Francisco: Jossey-Bass.

Wiebe, R.H. (1967). *The search for order: 1877-1920.* New York: Hill & Wang.

CHAPTER 3

ADMISSIONS AND
ENROLLMENT MANAGEMENT

DON HOSSLER

INTRODUCTION

BOTH THE 1937 and 1949 *Student Personnel Point of View* place the function of the admissions office within the purview of student affairs. It is appropriate that this chapter appear near the beginning of this book for the admissions office is usually the institution's first contact with prospective students, the student affairs division, as well as the entire campus. On many campuses, however, the admissions office is not located in the student affairs division. Frequently, admissions offices are housed in divisions of academic affairs or institutional advancement. This may be unfortunate because student affairs should be directly involved in all aspects of the students' college experience from the point of initial contact to the point of graduation.

The purpose of this chapter is to examine the development of the field of admissions and to describe the emerging concept of enrollment management. While the admissions function has been interested in attracting and admitting college students, enrollment management is concerned with the entire college experience. The first part of this chapter defines admissions and presents its history. The second part of this chapter defines enrollment management and explores this emerging concept.

ADMISSIONS

A Definition

Kuh (1977) defines admissions as:

> those policies and procedures which provide for students' transitions from secondary to postsecondary education. All admissions policies are based on the inherent belief that the educational experience offered by the institution will benefit certain individuals. Faculty determined admissions policies and academic qualifications, considered the institution's most important expression of educational philosophy, are translated into action by the admissions office. (p. 6).

The purpose of admissions is to help students make a successful transition from high school to college (Munger & Zucker, 1982) and to recruit students for specific colleges and universities (Shaffer & Martinson, 1966). Thus it is important for admissions officers to understand the needs of traditional and non-traditional college students and to know the institution by whom they are employed. In this way admissions officers can help students make the best college choice decision possible while at the same time recruiting students well-suited to the specific institution the admissions officer represents. Like most functional areas in student affairs, the admissions function has been a part of American higher education for a long time but has a relatively short formal history.

HISTORICAL DEVELOPMENT

Gatekeeper or Salesman — The Image of the Admissions Officer

The history of admissions in American colleges and universities is difficult to unravel. This is because our understanding of the field has been shaped by two competing images of the admissions officer. On one hand, the image of the admissions officer is that of the "ivy league" admissions officer who, along with a faculty admissions committee, decides who will receive the coveted offers of admissions on "Bloody Monday."[1] They decide who will be able to "join the club." The other image is that of the salesman, attempting to attract prospective students to

---

[1]This is the term used to describe the Monday in April on which all highly selective colleges send out their notices of acceptance or rejection to all applicants.

a college or university so that the institution's budget will be balanced, the doors will be open and the faculty will be happy. Depending upon the image one holds, the history of the admissions function might look quite different. Thelin (1982) has labeled these two contrasting images of admissions as the gatekeeper and headhunter images. Actually, both images are accurate descriptions of periods of time in American higher education, as well as of various types of institutions.

Early American colleges trace the role of the admissions office to that of the "major beadle" in the medieval university (Smerling, 1960). The "major beadle" was succeeded by the office of the archivist (Lindsay & Holland, 1930) and later by the office of the registrar. The role of faculty members or administrators in these positions was to record student progress while enrolled in college, and to determine whether prospective students had the "right background" for admission to the institution. For the early American college, the right background frequently meant that the student could speak the English language with some modicum of proficiency and was of good moral character. At more selective institutions, students were expected to have some knowledge of Latin and Greek (Broome, 1903; Rudolph, 1962). In any case, most early colleges also had preparatory schools attached to them so that students who did not meet the admissions requirements could acquire the necessary skills for admission (Brubacher & Rudy, 1968; Rudolph, 1962).

Not all colleges, however, were able to sit passively and wait for students to arrive to complete an admissions test. Part of the American dream included equal access to education and upward mobility. During the expansion westward in the nineteenth century, every town aspired to greatness. The presence of a college in a town was viewed as a clear signal to current and prospective residents that the town was going to become a major center and a good place to live. As a result, colleges were created at a rapid rate. For example, in the early 1870's, England had four universities for a population of 23,000,000. The state of Ohio had 37 colleges for a population of 3,000,000 (Rudolph, 1962, p. 48).

In these institutions, however, we find the forerunner of the other image of the admissions officer, the salesman. Early American colleges did not have many faculty and staff members and frequently consisted of the president and one or two additional faculty. The president taught classes, and in addition, performed all of the roles now associated with positions such as the chief fund raiser, the academic dean, the dean of students, and the registrar. Rudolph's history of American higher education (1962) is replete with stories of college presidents traveling through the countryside trying to attract the sons during most of the eighteenth and nineteenth centuries of farmers and the emerging merchant class.

There were not enough potential college students to support the large number and variety of colleges that had been established in the United States. As a result, many institutions of higher education had to be creative in devising new ways to attract students. Frequently, new professionals in student affairs view some of the current marketing efforts and financial aid strategies, such as telemarketing, pre-purchase tuition plans, or guaranteed cost plans, as new ideas emerging as the result of current rising college costs and competition for students. However, many early American colleges also had to devise creative marketing and recruitment strategies. In the nineteenth century, several colleges sold tuition payments in advance to families. This was done to attract revenues that could be invested in endowments to support faculty and instruction, thus reducing current, as well as future instructional costs. Unfortunately, these early colleges could not afford to invest the money, but were forced to spend the money on current needs. Thus, when these new pre-paid students arrived, the money was gone and in some cases the colleges were also gone, because of bankruptcy. For those that survived, institutions such as Dickinson and DePauw lost large amounts of money, ranging in excess of more than two dollars for each dollar that had been raised (Rudolph, 1962).

The mass marketing techniques of today are not entirely new. In 1893 one state university had sufficient funds and political clout to mail brochures describing the virtues of attending the institution to every school superintendent in the state. Any high school that did not post the brochures was assessed a $50 fine being levied against the local school superintendent (Thelin, 1982). Although the first Dean of Admissions was not appointed until the early part of the twentieth century, the activities of these struggling colleges to attract students are part of the history of the salesman image of the admissions field.

The Emergence of Admissions

Tension between the images of gatekeeper and salesman continued into the twentieth century. Prior to the actual appointment of the first Deans of Admissions in the 1920's two important trends emerged that shaped the role of the admissions officer. By the end of the nineteenth century, many higher education institutions began to decry the lack of standardization in the academic preparation of high school students. As a result, administrators within institutions of higher education could make few assumptions about the skills and academic training of prospective students.

In 1870, in response to this problem, the University of Michigan began to send teams of faculty to visit high schools to improve both the level of instruction and articulation between colleges and high schools. Other states followed suit and in 1894 the North Central Association was formed to standardize high school curriculum within that geographical region. Although the University of Michigan is often credited as the first university to employ this process, the precedent for regional associations was set in the 1880's with the creation of the New England Association of Colleges and Preparatory Schools (Brubacher & Rudy, 1968).

In addition to the creation of associations to improve education at the high school level, standardized testing emerged as a way to improve high school education and to standardize "chaotic entrance requirements" (Brubacher & Rudy, 1968, p. 245) employed by colleges and universities. The Regents exam created in 1878 was the first such effort. In the 1890's a meeting of the Association of the Colleges and Secondary Schools of the Middle States and Maryland led to the establishment of the College Entrance Examination Board (The College Board). The development of standardized tests by the College Entrance Examination Board caused many colleges and universities to slowly abandon their own admissions tests and rely on a single standardized instrument.

The emergence of accreditation associations and standardized testing had a significant impact on the admissions function. It was now easier to determine who was prepared for college, even though the criteria for admissions varied widely and to compare the quality of entering students. Standardization forever changed the dialogue on institutional quality and prestige and formalized the tension between the role of the gatekeeper and the salesman. Now admissions officers could use objective criteria to compare not only the number of students enrolled, but the quality of those students enrolled.

The use of a full time admissions director did not become widespread until the 1930's when the concept of selective admissions was formally articulated (Thresher, 1966). Selective admissions helped to further entrench the concept of institutional prestige based upon selectivity. As Thelin (1982) noted, the competition for talented students and faculty has always been closely interwoven with institutional prestige.

However, the emergence of elite, highly selective institutions such as Harvard, Yale, and Stanford are still a relatively recent phenomenon.

Consequently, the current image of the admissions gatekeeper as one who sits and selects from among as many as seven to ten applicants for each freshman class slot is also a relatively new development. The Depression years resulted in a decrease in the number of college applicants. As a result, the 1930's was an era of the salesman, rather than the gatekeeper. The United States involvement in World War II also depressed college applications. It was not until the 1950's that admissions officers at highly selective institutions were able to truly function as gatekeepers.

Because of the large numbers of World War II veterans returning to college and the subsequent rise in enrollments due to the "baby boomers," the 1960's and 1970's are often referred to as the "Golden Age" of American higher education (Jencks & Reisman, 1969). During this year some admissions officers at many well-known, but less prestigious private colleges and universities, as well as many public institutions, were able to function as gatekeepers. Nevertheless, it would be a mistake to think of this as an era of gatekeeping for all admissions officers. The rapid growth of public four year and two year colleges had a major impact on admissions officers at smaller and lesser known private institutions. As a result, many private colleges and universities had to market themselves aggressively and recruit students to maintain enrollments (Thresher, 1966).

The Admissions Officer of Today

By the beginning of the 1970's colleges and universities were preparing for a predicted decrease of traditional age college students that could reach 42 percent (Crossland, 1980) before the end of this century. As college administrators shifted from the "bullish" student enrollment market of the 1950's and 1960's to the "bear" market of the 1980's and 1990's, institutions began to look to external agencies for techniques to maintain or increase student enrollments. This set the stage for the emergence of the admissions officer of today. Currently, admissions officers have, in many cases, become hybrids of both the gatekeeper and the salesman. At non-selective institutions, admissions officers continue to function primarily as salesmen, however, even at the most selective institutions, where gatekeeping remains an important role, admissions officers have had to become salesmen to attract sufficient numbers of high ability students with specific attributes desired by prestigious colleges and universities (geographical representation, minority representation, and music, leadership, athletic and other special skills).

Thelin (1982) described the present time period for admissions officers as the era of marketing. In the 1970's, offices of admissions began to use marketing techniques such as: improved publication materials; targeted mailing strategies; and telemarketing techniques to attract larger numbers of students. At the same time, senior level administrators began to utilize strategic planning techniques borrowed from business. Strategic planning incorporates market research to help organizations better understand their clients and the organization's position in relation to its competitors. This emphasis on marketing created the foundation for the concept of enrollment management which is discussed later in this chapter.

Marketing techniques forced admissions officers to do a better job of tracking and communicating with prospective students. Targeted mailing and telemarketing techniques require that admissions officers are able to analyze the background and attitudinal characteristics of students in order to identify the best potential markets. Personalized communication techniques are also hallmarks of modern marketing techniques. These developments required admissions officers to become (1) more analytical; and (2) able to use computer assisted technology. For admissions officers serving as salesmen, the adoption of these techniques and skills became essential for institutional well-being.

The modern admissions office, with its emphasis on marketing and computer technology, has separated admissions officers from other student affairs areas which have a stronger counseling or student development orientation. As a result, many professionals in the field of admissions do not consider themselves as student affairs professionals (Hossler, 1986). However, as admissions and student affairs staff have become part of institutional enrollment management efforts, the connections between admissions and student affairs work are once again becoming apparent.

ENROLLMENT MANAGEMENT

An Introduction

Predicted declines in traditional age college students caused college and university administrators to become interested in student retention, as well as student recruitment. Student attrition became a frequent topic of inquiry (Bean, 1980, 1983, 1985, 1986; Noel, 1979, 1985; Pascarella,

1985; Pascarella & Terenzini, 1980, 1981; and Tinto, 1987). Student affairs administrators often found themselves assigned the responsibility of developing institutional retention programs.

Converging interests in attracting and retaining new students led to the evolution of the enrollment management concept. Enrollment management provided an integrated framework for institutional efforts to more directly influence their student enrollments. On some campuses, student affairs divisions began to assume key roles in enrollment management activities. Since enrollment management, as a formal concept is new, its history is limited and thus more emphasis will be given to describing and analyzing enrollment management.

A number of conceptual frameworks were suggested as the organizational basis for student affairs divisions (Delworth & Hanson, 1980). Enrollment management can be viewed as yet another framework for organizing student affairs divisions. To accomplish this, many student affairs professionals will have to become knowledgeable about enrollment management activities. The subsequent section of this chapter will describe enrollment management, the evolution of enrollment management, enrollment management as a concept, enrollment management as a profess, four archetypal enrollment management models, the role of student affairs in enrollment management, ethical issues related to enrollment management, the professional preparation needs of enrollment managers and the future of enrollment management.

Defining Enrollment Management

If student affairs professionals are to utilize the enrollment management concept, they must first understand it. On many campuses, the term has developed a potent image as a systematic institutional response to issues related to student enrollments. At most institutions, enrollment management has become associated with a diverse set of activities being employed by colleges and universities as they attempt to exert more control over the characteristics of their enrolled student body, or the size of their enrolled student body. In one sense, the images of the gatekeeper and salesman in admissions are still relevant. From an enrollment management perspective, however, institutions are not only concened about the characteristics and the total number of new students, but about the characteristics and total number of all enrolled students.

Enrollment management has been defined in a number of ways, but consistently students remain the fundamental unit of analysis. Enrollment management is a process that involves the entire campus. A number of definitions of enrollment management have been suggested (Hossler, 1984; Kemerer, Baldridge, & Green, 1982; Muston, 1985). A definition of enrollment management which synthesizes previous definitions is:

> Enrollment management is both an organizational concept as well as a systematic set of activities designed to enable educational institutions to exert more influence over their student enrollments. This is accomplished by the use of institutional research in the areas of student college choice, student attrition, and student outcomes to guide institutional practices in the areas of new student recruitment and financial aid, student support services, as well as curriculum development and other academic areas which affect the enrollment and persistence of students.

The Emergence of Enrollment Management

The term, and perhaps the concept, of a comprehensive enrollment management system is new. However, as a process, enrollment management has been developing for several years. An examination of the evolution of offices of admissions and financial aid, along with other areas of student affairs, non-profit marketing in higher education, research on student college choice and student persistence demonstrates that the enrollment management concept represents the convergence of developments in each of these areas.

It is difficult to determine whether the competitive nature of college admissions during the last three decades has caused the advances made in marketing techniques or whether the emergence of non-profit marketing has made possible the increasing sophistication of collegiate recruitment activities. It is equally difficult to determine whether the emergence of differentiated financial aid and pricing activities are the products of competition for students or if research on student college choice and the effects of aid and price on college choice have resulted in more effective aid and pricing policies. Research on student attrition, the impact of college on students, and student-institution fit have produced institutional retention programs tailored to meet the needs of specific student populations such as non-traditional adult learners, transfer students, or minority students.

It may be difficult to determine the precise genesis of the enrollment management concept. The declining numbers of traditional age students, along with the overbuilding of colleges and universities to accommodate the veterans and baby boomers of the 1950's and 60's, have created a set of internal and external constraints that require college administrators to be more attentive to student enrollments. Thus, the emergence of enrollment management is tied to the environmental press to which institutions of higher education have been forced to respond. What makes the enrollment management concept new is not the development of new marketing techniques nor new retention strategies. Rather it is the organizational integration of functions such as academic advising, admissions, financial aid, and orientation into a comprehensive institutional approach designed to enable college and university administrators to exert greater influence over the factors which shape their enrollments.

In 1976, the term enrollment management was used to describe efforts to attract and retain students at Boston College (Maguire, 1976). One of the first times the term enrollment management formally appears in the literature is in a 1980 *College Board Review* article by Kreutner and Godfrey that describes a matrix approach to managing enrollments developed at California State University at Long Beach. Several books and monographs followed including: *Strategies for Effective Enrollment Management* (Kemerer, Baldridge, & Green, 1982), *Enrollment Management: An Integrated Approach* (Hossler, 1984), *Marketing and Enrollment Management in State Universities* (Muston, 1985) and *Creating Effective Enrollment Management Systems* (Hossler, 1986). This formalizing process appears to have lent legitimacy to these new ways of influencing enrollments and have been at least partially responsible for the increased interest in the concept of enrollment management.

Institutions such as Boston College, Bradley University, California State University at Long Beach, Carnegie-Mellon University, and Northwestern University are generally credited as the first colleges and universities to develop comprehensive enrollment management systems. Even among these institutions, however, there was great variation in the scope and sophistication of their systems. Among these early systems, Hossler (1986) suggests that common characteristics exist:

1. A continual analysis of the institution's image in the student market place.
2. Attention to the connections between recruitment and financial aid policies.
3. An early willingness to adopt sound marketing principles in their recruitment activities;
4. A recognition of the importance of gathering and utilizing of infor-

mation to guide institutional practices and policies. Hossler, 1986, p. viii.

The concept and process of enrollment management is still emerging. As enrollment management systems mature, they continue to focus on marketing and recruitment. In addition, institutions begin to give more attention to student retention and student outcomes (Hossler, 1986). Undoubtedly enrollment management systems will continue to change and develop in response to the needs of individual institutions.

Enrollment Management as a Concept

Although definitions and a sense of the history of enrollment management provide some perspective on this concept, they are not sufficient. To better understand this evolving concept, the metaphor of a lens is useful. Three lenses which can be used: (1) the organizational lens, (2) the student lens, and (3) the institutional lens. Each one provides a different perspective of enrollment management systems.

The Organizational Lens

Weick (1976) suggested that educational organizations can be described as "loosely coupled." By this he means that administrative and departmental units operate with a great deal of autonomy. Such organizations have difficulty agreeing upon goals, acting consensually, or moving in common directions to achieve organizational purposes. Until recently, the attempts of most institutions to influence their enrollments might be described as loosely coupled. Offices such as orientation, admissions and financial aid seldom act in a coordinated fashion and all too often act in ways which are counterproductive.

Examples of loose coupling abound in the anecdotal records of most colleges and universities. For example, at one urban campus, which is perceived to be in a threatening neighborhood, the orientation committee sent a notice home about rape prevention to all new students just before they were supposed to sign and return their housing contracts. On another campus, the financial aid office waited until May 15 to send their financial aid packages out because it was more efficient. In the meantime, the institution's competitors sent their awards notices out on April 1. In both cases, institutions experienced enrollment declines.

Although many students of organizational theory in higher education have come to accept loose coupling as normative, the challenge for enrollment managers is to create more tightly coupled structure among the offices and administrators who are in a position to influence student enrollments. Although there are a number of organizational models for enrollment management, that may be more important than the specific model is the degree of communication and cooperation that is created. The organizational lens calls our attention to these issues.

The Student Lens

The student lens provides another view. It attempts to see the college experience from the students' perspective. The student lens is a wide angle lens that views the student experience in its entirety. From the point of initial inquiry, to a student's graduation and career path, the student lens seeks to understand every aspect of the student experience.

The student lens draws primarily on three types of research on college students: (1) student college choice; (2) student persistence; and (3) student outcomes. This knowledge base provides a basis for policy decisions in areas such as marketing activities; orientation programs; and the activities of the career planning and placement office. College student research findings also raise new questions about students and their experiences with the college. This in turn leads to a new round of research, creating an iterative process in which some questions are answered and new ones are raised.

Research on student college choice tells enrollment managers why students select one institution over another. It enables campus administrators to determine what prospective students consider important when they select a college or university to attend. The college choice research of Litten, Sullivan, & Brodigan (1983), conducted for Carleton College, demonstrates how such information can be used to help institutions make internal changes necessary to improve their image, as well as enabling them to improve recruitment strategies.

Student persistence research provides information about the students' experiences while they are enrolled. Retention studies, such as those conducted by Bean (1980, 1983, 1985, 1986), Noel (1979, 1985), Pascarella and Terenzini (1980, 1981) and Tinto (1987) help enrollment managers to understand how the campus enhances student-institution "fit" and also how the "fit" is affected negatively. Programmatic interventions can then be initiated to increase student persistence.

Student educational outcomes research provides information about student growth and maturation during their college experience.[2] It also tracks students after they graduate, tracking the career paths and life style of alumni. This can be useful information for marketing the institution. Educational outcomes information can also be used to guide curricular and co-curricular policies. For instance, if institutional outcome studies reveal that most students do not become very involved in campus activities or use the library very much, policies may be developed to increase student use and involvement.

The Institutional Lens

The institutional lens is the reverse image of the student lens. Rather than using research to better understand students' experiences, it is used to provide a more accurate picture of the institution. Many college administrators and faculty are unable to see their own college or university accurately because they have invested too much of themselves in the campus to be able to acknowledge its shortcomings (and in some cases their own shortcomings). Thus student choice, persistence, and outcomes research can be viewed as means to see the campus as others perceive it.

Market research may show that prospective students rate the residence halls unfavorably when compared to other institutions. Market research may also reveal that currently enrolled students may give a low rating to the quality of instruction in the math department. Some may argue that on "objective criteria" these perceptions are inaccurate. Objectivity, however, is not as relevant as subjective perceptions because students will make decisions to enroll or to persist on the basis of their perceptions. Thus, viewing student research as an institutional lens can become a powerful impetus to bring about change. Understanding how prospective and current students view the institution can be extremely useful information for strategic planning and goal setting.

Both the student and institutional lenses are research driven. Effective enrollment management systems are dependent upon a competent institutional research capability. Most large campuses maintain institutional research offices. Smaller campuses may not be able to afford a full-time institutional research office, but they may be able to free a faculty member from full-time teaching in order to conduct some of the necessary research.

---

[2]See for example Astin's discussion of student outcomes research at Northeast Missouri State University (Astin, 1985).

The organizational lens, the student lens, and the institutional lens each provide a different perspective on the enrollment management concept. Enrollment management, however, is not only a series of lens, it is also a set of organization activities. It is a process designed to enable colleges and universities to exert more influence over their enrollments.

Enrollment Management as a Process

To develop a comprehensive enrollment management system, a diverse set of functions and activities must be formally or informally linked. Functional areas ranging from admissions, financial aid, career planning and placement and student orientation must be linked. Equally important are activities such as student outcome assessments and retention efforts which must be used to inform policy decisions in areas like admissions, financial aid, or curriculum decisions.

Planning and Research

As a process, enrollment management begins with institutional planning. Planning begins with a discussion of the institution's mission statement. Following this discussion, most authors on strategic planning call for an objective assessment of the external and internal environment (see Cope, 1981; Keller, 1984). That is, colleges and universities must carefully assess external social trends, such as reductions in state and federal student financial aid or an increasing number of adults enrolling in higher education, as well as internal strengths and weaknesses such as the need for new buildings on campus, the skills of some administrators, or the lack of an academic major that is popular among high school graduates. Following an environmental assessment, planning involves the development of goals and objectives that take into consideration both the mission of the institution, its strengths and weaknesses, as well as the external environment.

Muston's (1984) study of midwestern public colleges and universities shows that successful enrollment management efforts are more frequently found at institutions that have integrated recruitment and retention goals into the planning process. Clearly articulated goals for the number and academic quality of new students, as well as clear retention goals were positively related to increases in new students and improved retention rates.

Once these enrollment related goals have been articulated, institutional objectives are developed.

The objectives should reflect links between areas such as marketing, recruitment and financial aid. These linkages should help answer the following questions: (1) What kinds of students are we interested in attracting? (2) Where can we find these students? (3) What do we need to do to attract these students? (4) What do we need to do to retain these students? (Hossler, 1986)

Attracting Applicants and Matriculants

Although data from an institution's research office provides needed information, marketing and recruitment are typically located in the admissions office. Knowledge of student characteristics helps an admissions office determine what types of potential students are most likely to be interested in coming to the campus. Marketing research provides insights into the type of information desired by most students and parents. Tuition levels and financial aid packages plan an important role in determining whether a student will apply to an institution and matriculate (Hossler, 1984; Jackson, 1982). As a result, the office of financial aid is also important. The financial aid and admissions offices should coordinate financial aid wards with other "courtship" activities to attract the quality and number of students the institution seeks to enroll. The admissions and financial aid offices represent the admissions management subsystem of an enrollment management system.

Influencing the Collegiate Experience

In an enrollment management system, once students arrive on campus, attention shifts to the students' collegiate experiences. The comprehensive nature of enrollment management systems means that they are concerned with the students' experience during their entire tenure at the institution. An enrollment management system advocates that admissions officers be as concerned about student-institution fit as they are about the number of students recruited. Bean (1986) suggests that admissions officers be evaluated on the basis of how many matriculants persist rather than on the number of students recruited. An enrollment management system encourages student affairs officers to be responsible for creating a more attractive campus environment that will help to retain more students. Astin (1985) recommends that student affairs administrators strive to facilitate student involvement in all facets of the college experience. Faculty also have an impact on students during the college choice process and during the years spent in college. Academic quality is the single most important determinant of where students go to college (Chapman & Jackson, 1987; Litten, Sullivan, & Brodigan, 1983), which makes the instructional and research activities of the faculty very important to the ability of colleges and universities to attract students. Pascarella (1985) provides evidence that formal and informal faculty contact has a positive impact on student satisfaction and student perceptions of the college environment. Both administrators and faculty have roles to play in an enrollment management system.

Orientation

Orientation programs are an important part of an enrollment management system. They should help students adjust to the intellectual norms, the social norms, and the physical layout of the campus. Pascarella (1985) recommends that orientation be viewed as an opportunity for "anticipatory socialization." Orientation should create new student expectations which more closely approximate the campus environment and norms. In this way students are more likely to find meaning and satisfaction in their collegiate environment. A study conducted by Bean (1985) shows that students whose level of fit is improving during the freshman year are more likely to persist. Orientation can help enhance student-institution fit. Pascarella (1985) reports that participation in orientation has a small, but significant indirect positive effect on student persistence.

Academic Advising

In addition to orientation, academic advising is also important for new students. For many students their first advising session takes place during orientation. Academic advising is also an excellent place to encourage more student involvement with faculty. Several campuses have begun to take advantage of the linkages between orientation and advising to develop extended orientation/advising programs. "University 101," an orientation and advising course offered at the University of South Carolina, is an example of an approach linking advising and orientation. Using faculty in these extended orientation/advising programs, or in small freshman seminars, can be used to encourage student-faculty interaction.

Course Placement

In addition to academic advising and orientation, students also interact with their new environments through course placement. The first interactions students have with their new environment revolve around academic advising, course placement and orientation. The diversity of today's college students has resulted in wide variations in student interests, experiences and skills. This is especially true in two year colleges and in open admission four year institutions where some matriculants enter with minimal academic skills while other new students are eligible for honors programs. This has increased the importance of academic advising and course placement. An enrollment management system should include academic assessment tests which will increase the likelihood of appropriate course placement. Helping students to select the courses which will challenge them, but not overwhelm them, is a function of orientation and advising during the critical freshman year. Students who do not fare well academically are less likely to persist.

Student Retention

Successful integration into the campus environment should have a positive impact upon student satisfaction and persistence. Student retention research and retention programs should be part of an enrollment management plan. Unlike functional areas like admissions or orientation, retention is usually not the direct responsibility of one office. Retention cuts away many functional areas and divisions within the institution. Nevertheless, it is precisely because of the many organizational variables which can affect student attrition that student retention research and programming should be assigned to one administrative office. Usually, retention activities are assigned to a commitee which ensures that retention will not receive adequate attention. As new members rotate in and out of the committee, it becomes difficult to develop an ongoing set of retention activities. The importance of student attrition in maintaining enrollments requires that it be assigned as the responsibility of a specific office, just as admissions or student activities are the assigned task of identifiable administrators. This will ensure that data will be collected and programs will be planned, implemented, and evaluated. The retention officer should not be held personally accountable for attrition rates, the issue is too complex for one office to monitor or "control." Nevertheless, creating an administrative office to monitor student attrition and develop retention programs assures that the institution will continue to address student persistence. The retention officer is an integral element within the enrollment management system.

Learning Assistance

Learning assistance offices should also be a part of retention efforts. Many colleges continue to admit underprepared students. To help these students succeed academically, campuses have established learning assistance offices. These offices offer a wide range of services including: (1) study skills workshops; (2) reading assistance; (3) writing labs; (4) test taking workshops; and (5) tutoring in specific subject areas. Professionals in this area are also part of the enrollment management staff. The admissions office usually identifies underprepared students during the admissions process. The admissions office is in the best position to inform the learning assistance office of the particular academic needs of these students. Completing the feedback cycle, learning assistance offices should monitor the academic success of students. This places them in a unique position to provide continual feedback to the admissions office regarding student success. If few underprepared students are succeeding, then the institution may not be spending its recruiting and financial aid dollars wisely, or it may not be providing adequate academic support services.

Career Planning and Placement

An important part of the college experience is preparation for a career. Career concerns have become one of the most important considerations for college students from the time they select an institution until they graduate. Students are aware of the competitive nature of the job market. Institutions which are perceived as helping to place their graduates in good jobs after graduation will not only be in a better position to attract new students, but also to retain current students. Part of the job turnover model of student attrition developed by Bean (1980; 1983) posits that the practical value of a college degree—the likelihood of getting a desirable job after graduation—has a positive effect on student persistence. A successful career planning and placement office should help students in establishing linkages between their academic and vocational goals. In an enrollment management system, the career planning office should play a central role in helping students secure desirable positions after graduation.

The Role of Other Student Affairs Functions

Functions like student activities, career planning, learning assistance, and orientation, are present on most college and university campuses.

They are usually part of the student affairs division. Depending upon whether the campus is residential or not, intramural and intercollegiate athletics, residence life, and Greek affairs can contribute substantially to the quality of campus life.

In addition, student participation in intramurals, student government, or Greek affairs may also enhance student development and student persistence. Astin (1985) asserts that student involvement in co-curricular and extracurricular activities determines the quality of student educational outcomes, as well as influencing student persistence. The work of Astin (1985) and Pace (1984) suggests that the goals of facilitating student development and managing student enrollments may not be in conflict, but instead mutually reinforce goals in some areas of student life. The theory of student involvement provides a theoretical basis for strategies to facilitate student development. Student affairs officers, through careful planning and evaluation, can promote programs which encourage student involvement in order to enhance development and increase student persistence.

This discussion of enrollment management began with planning and research and then moved to marketing and recruiting students and was followed by an examination of the student collegiate experience. This brings the discussion to graduation. A comprehensive enrollment management plan, however, does not stop with graduation. This is where enrollment management demonstrates it cyclical nature. Student educational outcome studies should include regular assessments of alumni. Their experiences and attitudes can provide institutions with useful information about students themselves. From an enrollment management systems perspective, this brings us back to the imagery of the wide-angle lens which enables us to see and understand the entire collegiate experience.

The Faculty Role in Enrollment Management

The faculty plays an important role and it is a mistake for any enrollment manager to neglect the role of the faculty. For example, the academic quality of programs is the most important factor in determining where a student will go to college (Chapman & Jackson, 1987). It is difficult, however, for administrators to speak directly to issues of academic quality. At best they are likely to be disregarded and at worst administrators will alienate themselves from the faculty and reduce their effectiveness. Faculty, however, should be aware of the impact they have upon student enrollments.

In the areas of marketing and student recruitment, the academic image of an institution and individual majors can influence students' decisions about where they go to college. Marketing research can be used to create an institutional lens that lets faculty see how they are viewed by prospective students. In some cases, faculty discover that the negative image that students hold of academic programs discourages students from enrolling. Information such as this can create an impetus for changes in academic programs which would be difficult for administrators to require of the faculty.

Student-faculty interaction can have a significant impact on student outcomes and student persistence. Enrollment managers should plan an educative role with the faculty in this area. On many campuses the connection between enrollment and institutional health are already understood by the faculty. On these campuses acquainting faculty with research that establishes the impact of faculty upon students and the role of academic programs in college choice is likely to create a receptive audience for enrollment management activities. However, many commuter institutions, as well as research universities, do not have a strong tradition of faculty involvement with students. At institutions where the faculty are not concerned about student enrollments, it will be more difficult to convince them to seek out more opportunities for student faculty-interaction. Students at these institutions can also benefit from more contact with faculty.

A Comprehensive System

Successful enrollment management systems must include an organizational structure that enhances communication and cooperation among academic departments and administrative units. For example, a new honors program must be marketed by the admissions office. A new writing test initiated by the faculty will frequently be administered by the academic advising unit which must also then recommend course placements based upon the test results. These two examples illustrate the cooperation that is fostered by an enrollment management system. A sound organizational framework will enable colleges and universities to address both the conceptual and process elements of enrollment management.

Although many campuses appear to be adopting some type of enrollment management system, in many cases the director of admissions is simply taking on a new title while the responsibilities remain the same.

Figure One
The Enrollment Management Continuum

Admissions Management		*Enrollment Management*
marketing	marketing and	strategic planning
recruitment	choice research	institutional research and evaluation
	recruitment	marketing
	financial aid	recruitment
		financial aid
		academic advising and course placement
		orientation
		student retention programs
		learning assistance
		career planning and placement
		other student services

(Source: Hossler, 1986, p. 12)

Huddleston (1984) distinguishes between enrollment management and "admissions management." As Figure One indicates, enrollment management is concerned with more than just the admissions of students.

Kemerer, Baldridge and Green (1982) describe four archetypal enrollment management models: the enrollment management committee, the enrollment management coordinator, the enrollment management matrix, and the enrollment management division. Each model has its own strengths and weaknesses and will be briefly described.

The Enrollment Management Committee

The enrollment management committee is often the first part of an enrollment management system created. The committee may begin with a focus on marketing and admissions, student retention, or with a comprehensive view of student enrollments that includes marketing, retention, and monitoring student outcomes. Committee membership usually includes key faculty members, mid-level administrators like admissions, financial aid, student activities, and perhaps a senior officer, such as the vice president for student affairs, or the vice president of academic affairs.

Most committees begin with unclear goals and are comprised primarily of members who have little knowledge of the complex set of factors that influence student enrollments. In addition, the membership of committees changes regularly, which makes it difficult for members to follow through on agenda items developed. Most committees have no formal authority and often no direct way to influence institutional policy making. Such a description would seem to suggest that the committee approach has little to offer, but this is not necessarily the case.

The committee can serve as a means of educating a large group of people about enrollment related issues. Since most members will not have a background in these areas, they all start at a basic level and need to learn a good deal about such issues as market segments, need versus merit aid, and student persistence. Committee members then become advocates for enrollment related issues and resources. An effective committee can help activate the campus.

The Enrollment Management Coordinator

The enrollment management coordinator is usually a mid-level administrator, often the director of admissions. The coordinator is assigned responsibilities for coordinating and monitoring the enrollment management activities of the institution. On many campuses, the term enrollment management is used, but in reality the coordinator is the "admissions manager."

The weaknesses of this approach are that the coodinator seldom has the influence and authority to change administrative practices and procedures. Equally important, the coordinator may be separated by one or more layers of administrative bureaucracy from senior level administrators. As a result the enrollment management agenda may not be heard by those administrators with the authority to change structures and allocate resources.

Nevertheless, the coordinator's role can be effective if the coordinator is well respected within the organization. In addition, if the coordinator has a proven record of effectiveness, the coordinator may have needed credibility to be able to exercise leadership in the organization without formal institutional authority.

The Enrollment Management Matrix

In the matrix model, key administrators in financial aid, career planning, and admissions who have the most direct influence on student enrollments are brought together regularly under the direction of a senior level vice-president. It is unlikely that all of these middle managers will report directly to this senior administrator. This results in a matrix where some campus managers report to more than one supervisor. The senior level manager functions somewhat like the enrollment management coordinator, because he/she must rely more upon cooperation and persuasion and less upon the organizational hierarchy.

This model has several advantages. For one, a senior level administrator now takes direct resonsibility for enrollment management programs. This ensures a greater impact on organizational structure and resources. Cooperation and communication among the appropriate offices will increase. Finally, the head of this matrix will become enmeshed in all elements of an enrollment management system. This process is likely to educate the administrator and create a well informed advocate in senior level administrative circles.

This model also has some disadvantages. In most circumstances the senior administrator may not have the time that enrollment related issues require. This may cause the system to become ineffective. In addition, this creates a more centralized enrollment management system which may have political reverberations that reduce the effectiveness of enrollment management activities. Finally, the time required to educate the senior level administrator may use valuable time of all of those involved.

The Enrollment Management Division

The enrollment management division is the most centralized enrollment management system. In this model, the major offices connected with enrollment management efforts are brought together under the authority of one senior level administrator. The advantages of such a system appeal to many college and university administrators. Each of the components of the system can be directed by one vice president. Also, cooperation, communication, and resource allocation can be dealt with from a system wide perspective. In addition, the vice president speaks with formal authority on enrollment issues in all policy decisions.

The primary problem with this model is administrative turf and organizational politics. Other vice presidents do not gladly relinquish their control over offices which are part of their responsibilities. On many campuses, philosophical differences make it difficult for areas such as career planning or student activities to find themselves reporting to someone who carries the title of enrollment manager. Such a title doesn't sound "very developmental." Even a presidential decision does not easily change existing patterns and politics. In addition, Bowen (1980) noted that the number of administrators at colleges and universities has increased during the last five decades, while the number of faculty members has remained constant. Many faculty are concerned about the growth of administrative "empires" and would react negatively to the creation of a new vice president. Thus, the potential benefits and liabilities of an enrollment management division should be weighted carefully before implementing this model.

Because of the specific needs of each campus, no one ideal enrollment management system exists, whether it is directed by a vice president or a committee. The system that emerges on each campus is usually the product of unique characteristics of each institution. An enrollment management system should adopt a view of the student experience which links new student matriculation, new student adaptation, student persistence, and student outcomes. By closely coupling an array of offices with sound planning and a research evaluation component, colleges and universities can exert more influence over their enrollments. Nevertheless, they cannot actually "manage" their enrollments. The factors that determine student enrollments are far too complex to be "managed." Through thoughtful planning and the coordination of programs, however, institutions of higher education can exert more influence over their enrollments. Student affairs professionals can play an integral part of enrollment management efforts.

The Role of Student Affairs

Just as the expertise of a biologist is living organisms, the specialized expertise of student affairs personnel should be students. The unit of analysis in student affairs work and enrollment management is students.

In classical models of student affairs organizations, the administrative elements of an enrollment management system (excluding curriculum decisions and teaching) fall under the student affairs umbrella. Admissions, financial aid, orientation, career planning and placement, and student activities are traditionally part of student affairs divisions. Although some offices, especially admissions and financial aid, are frequently housed in areas outside of student affairs, there can be little doubt that student affairs professionals can play an important role in an enrollment management system. At Bradley University and Drake University, the student affairs division is the enrollment management division. On other campuses, student affairs staff members may be responsible for student retention, or for conducting student outcomes research.

Conversely, on some campuses, student affairs divisions have included admissions; financial aid; and registration and records for many years. Often times, these areas have felt unwanted. With the emergence of student development as the "raison d' etre" for most student affairs divisions, these offices sometimes felt unwanted because they did not have a developmental orientation. The enrollment management concept, however, can provide an administrative framework that makes these offices an important part of a student affairs division.

Student affairs professionals on some campuses may see the marketing emphasis which accompanies the enrollment management concept as incompatible with a student development perspective. However, if we accept the assertion that student development results in increased student growth and satisfaction, then enrollment management and student development need not be in conflict. Marketing efforts grounded in sound student college choice research should help students to better understand the college or university they have chosen to attend, thus enhancing student-institution fit. Increasing student development and involvement should enhance student persistence. The enrollment management concept need not replace existing philosophies for student affairs divisions, it can, in fact, be used along with other frameworks within a comprehensive student affairs division.

Ethical Issues

Although enrollment management need not conflict with or create ethical dilemmas with the traditional goals of student affairs divisions, a number of ethical issues are inherent in attempts to influence student enrollments. During the recruitment process and after students matriculate there are also opportunities for unethical practices.

During the recruitment process, institutions should be careful to portray their campus accurately. Written publications should accurately describe the location of the campus, the academic offerings, and the nature of the student body. Admissions folklore is replete with stories of admissions representatives that have told prospective students that they could earn a degree in a major that the campus did not offer, or the campus that used aerial photographs to make a campus that was 45 minutes from the ocean appear as if it was almost "on the beach." Deceptive recruitment is unfair to students and in the long run harms both the institution as well as the entire higher education system. Students and the public can lose confidence in the mission and purpose of American higher education.

A related admissions issue is the admission decision itself. As colleges and universities have struggled to maintain enrollments, some institutions have admitted more underprepared students, along with unprepared international students. Unless these institutions have strong academic support systems such as learning support systems, English as a Second Language, and advising systems in place when students arrive, it is likely that such students will fail academically.

Financial aid offices will sometimes use aid as a recruitment device, offering large sums of non-renewable money to freshmen students. In such cases the student may not be told that the award is non-renewable and the student may be unable to return to the same institution the following year because he/she can no longer afford the tuition costs. The code of ethics of the National Association of Student Financial Aid Administrators advises against such practices, but some colleges and universities continue to do so.

The growing practice of awarding merit, "no-need," scholarship to students is a more subtle ethical question. While there are no professional standards which prohibit these types of awards, financial aid is a "fixed-pie." That is, there is a finite amount of financial aid which can be awarded. Gillespie and Carlson (1983) have documented the declining value of financial aid in real dollars. In addition, the percentage of minority students enrolled in higher education has been declining (Hossler, 1986). Some observers have suggested the declining enrollment rates of minority students are the result of smaller financial aid awards. The use of scarce institutional aid dollars for no-need scholarships may not be defensible if it reduces the amount of money available to help assure access to American higher education.

The other area rife for unethical practices is in the area of student retention programs. Tinto (1987) indicates that for many students who withdraw, the decision to drop out is a positive decision that is in the student's long term best interests. To the extent to which we use early warning systems and retention programs to try to "talk students into staying," students are not served well. Although enrollment management is a viable concept for student affairs divisions to adopt, student affairs professionals must be careful to carry out their responsibilities with integrity and be sensitive to the potential ethical conflicts.

Preparation and Training

At the moment there are no preparation programs specifically designed to prepare enrollment managers. There is a combination of experiences and coursework that would help to prepare professionals who are interested in this field. Coursework that includes the study of the American college student, non-profit marketing, student attrition, and student development would be useful. Research methods and program evaluation skills are also valuable. In addition, work or internship experiences in admissions, financial aid, orientation, institutional research and student retention officers would be beneficial.

Leadership positions in enrollment management systems typically are assigned to mid-level or senior level administrators. These administrators may have been the chief student affairs officer, director of admissions or financial aid. Occasionally, the position is filled by a faculty member or a director of institutional research. Entry level student affairs professionals should attempt to have a range of experiences in the work areas already outlined. The enrollment management concept appears to be gaining in recognition and acceptance and it is difficult to find professionals with the necessary skills and background. Career opportunities in this area, as well as in related entry level areas such as admissions and financial aid, should continue to be strong for the foreseeable future.

The enrollment management concept is too new to make assertive predictions too far into the future. Given the predicted numbers of traditional age students, competition for college students and the knowledge that student enrollments account for 60 to 80 percent of all revenues on most campuses, enrollment management is probably here to stay. Even student affairs professionals who are not attracted to the concept should be aware of it because so many of the functional areas within a student affairs division are potentially part of an enrollment management system. In the future, student affairs professionals may find themselves in leadership roles or in support roles on many campuses. Student affairs divisions that choose to become involved with this new concept can be an important element of any enrollment management system.

REFERENCES

Astin, A.W. (1985). *Achieving educational excellence.* San Francisco: Jossey-Bass.

Bean, J.P. (1980). Dropouts and turnover: The synthesis and test of a causal model of student attrition. *Research in Higher Education, 12,* 155-182.

Bean, J.P. (1983). The application of a model of job turnover in work organizations to the student attrition process. *Review of Higher Education, 6,* 129-148.

Bean, J.P. (1985). *The comparative selection effects of socialization and selection on college student attrition.* Paper presented at the Annual Meeting of the American Association of Educational Research, Chicago.

Bean, J.P. (1986). Assessing and reducing attrition. In D. Hossler (Ed.), *New directions in higher education: Managing college enrollments* (pp. 47-62). San Francisco: Jossey-Bass.

Bowen, H.R. (1980). *The costs of higher education.* San Francisco: Jossey-Bass.

Broome, E.C. (1903). *A historical and critical discussion of college admissions requirements.* New York: Macmillan.

Brubacher, J.S., & Rudy, W. (1968). *Higher education in transition: A history of American colleges and universities, 1636-1976.* New York: Harper & Row.

Chapman, R.G., & Jackson, R. (1987). *College choices of academically able students: The influence of no-need financial aid and other factors.* New York: The College Board.

Cope, R.G. (1981). *Strategic planning, management, and decision making.* Washington, D.C.: American Association of Higher Education.

Crossland, F. (1980). Learning to cope with the downward slope. *Change Magazine, 12*(5), 18-25.

Delworth, U., & Hanson, G.H. (Eds.). (1980). *Student services: A handbook for the profession.* San Francisco: Jossey-Bass.

Gillespie, D.A., & Carlson, N. (1983). *Trends in financial aid: 1963 to 1983.* New York: College Entrance Examination Board.

Hossler, D. (1984). *Enrollment management: An integrated approach.* New York: The College Board.

Hossler, D. (1986). *Creating effective enrollment management systems.* New York: The College Board.

Huddleston, T. (1984). *Effective organizational structures for enrollment management.* Paper presented at First Annual Conference on Leadership for Enrollment Management: An Integrated Strategy for Institutional Vitality, Conference sponsored by The Midwest Region of The College Board and Loyola University of Chicago, Chicago.

Jackson, G. (1982). Public efficiency and private choice in higher education. *Educational evaluation and policy analysis, 4*(2), 237-247.

Jencks, C., & Resiman, D. (1969). *The academic revolution.* Garden City, NY: Doubleday.

Keller, G. (1983). *Academic strategy: The management revolution in higher education.* Baltimore: Johns Hopkins University Press.

Kemerer, F.R., Baldridge, J.V., & Green, K.C. (1982). *Strategies for effective enrollment management.* Washington, D.C.: American Association of State Colleges and Universities.

Kreutner, L., & Godfrey, E.S. (1981, Fall/Winter). Enrollment management: A new vehicle for institutional renewal. *The College Board Review,* 6-9, 29.

Kuh, G.D. (1977). Admissions. In W.T. Packwood (Ed.), *College student personnel services.* Springfield, IL: Charles C Thomas.

Lindsay, E.E., & Holland, O.C. (1930). *College and university administration*. New York: Macmillan.

Litten, L.H., Sullivan, D., & Brodigan, D. (1983). *Applying market research to college admissions*. New York: The College Board.

Manski, C.F., & Wise, D.A. (1983). *College choice in America*. Cambridge, MA: Harvard University Press.

Maguire, J. (1976, Fall). To the organized go the students. *Bridge Magazine,* 6-10.

Munger, S.C., & Zucker, R.F. (1982). Discerning the basis for college counseling in the eighties. In W. Lowery & Associates, *College admissions: A handbook for the profession.* San Francisco: Jossey-Bass.

Muston, R. (1984). *Enrollment strategies among selected state universities.* Paper presented at the Annual Meeting of the Association for the Study of Higher Education, Chicago.

Muston, R. (1985). *Marketing and enrollment management in state universities.* Forest City, IA: The American College Testing Program.

Noel, L. (Ed.). (1979). *Preventing students from dropping out.* San Francisco: Jossey-Bass.

Noel, L., Levitz, R., Saluri, D., & Associates. (1985). *Increasing student retention.* San Francisco: Jossey-Bass.

Pace, C.R. (1984). *Measuring the quality of the college student experience.* Los Angeles: Higher Education Research Institute, University of California at Los Angeles.

Pascarella, E.T. (1985). *A program for research and policy development on student persistence at the institutional level.* Paper presented at the Second Annual Chicago Conference on Enrollment Management: An Integrated Strategy for Institutional Vitality, sponsored by The Midwest Region of The College Board and Loyola University of Chicago, Chicago.

Pascarella, E.T., Duby, P., Miller, V., & Rasher, S. (1981). Preenrollment variables and academic performance as predictors of freshman year persistence, early withdrawal, and stop-out behavior in an urban, non-residential university. *Research in Higher Education, 15,* 329-349.

Pascarella, E.T., & Terenzini, P.T. (1980). Patterns of student-faculty interaction beyond the classroom. *Journal of Higher Education, 48,* 540-552.

Rudolph, F. (1962). *The American college and university: A history.* New York: Vintage.

Shaffer, R.F., & Martinson, W.D. (1966). *Student personnel services in higher education.* New York: Center for Applied Research in Education.

Smerling, W.H. (1960). The registrar: Changing aspects. *College and University, 35,* 180-186.

Thelin, J.R. (1982). *Higher education and its useful past: Applied history in research and planning.* Cambridge, MA: Schenkman.

Thresher, B.A. (1966). *College admissions and the public interest.* New York: The College Entrance Examination Board.

Tinto, V. (1987). *Leaving college: Rethinking the causes of student attrition.* Chicago: University of Chicago Pres.

Weick, K.E. (1976). Education organizations as loosely coupled systems. *Administrative Science Quarterly, 21*(1), 1-19.

CHAPTER 4

CAREER PLANNING AND PLACEMENT

JOANN KROLL AND AUDREY L. RENTZ

The focus of the Career Planning and Placement Services is upon the student not only immediately before and after graduation, but during the earlier undergraduate years in the quest for self-understanding, appraisal of interest and abilities, and efforts to determine vocational objectives which are most meaningful and satisfying.

College Placement Council

INTRODUCTION

THE AREAS of career planning and placement have traditionally functioned as distinct entities supervised by different student affairs administrators and located in separate offices. The Counseling Center was responsible for career planning activities while the Placement Office was responsible for skill activities associated with the job-search process, such as interviewing and resume writing. Consequently, early writers viewed the Placement Office as business-related and the Counseling Center as clinic-oriented (McLaughlin, 1973). Since the early 1900's, placement functions have evolved from a philosophy that stressed job-matching and an assessment of individual needs by trait-and-factor analyses to a more humanistic emphasis on counseling and the application of student development theories in the 1980's.

Career planning evolved as the popularity of developmental theories describing vocational choice and career search behavior were applied by vocational counselors in the late 1960's and 1970's. Specific stages were identified within the developmental process that culminates in securing an employment position. These stages were self-awareness or assessment, exploration, decision-making, preparation and employment.

During the late 1960's and early 1970's, many institutions of higher education implemented an organizational model within student affairs that integrated career planning and placement resources. Career planning's emergence as an integral part of career development and its association with lifelong learning began to unite these two closely related student affairs units. Although many institutions retain the traditional separation model, the authors describe the integrated organizational structure in this chapter.

HISTORICAL DEVELOPMENT

The development of the modern placement office has been, at times, attributed to the efforts of individuals such as George Washington, George Steinmetz, and George Westinghouse (Boynton, 1949; Lansner, 1967). Each of these men recruited, interviewed, and subsequently employed new personnel within their respective work forces. However, student affairs professionals usually do not view these informal placement activities, initiated during the eighteenth and early nineteenth centuries, as representatives of the early stages of placement programs. Rather, Oxford University's Committee on Appointments, created in 1899 in England, is considered the precursor of the modern American placement office (Wrenn, 1951).

During the Colonial Era, faculty members or dons frequently assumed the institutions' responsibility for assisting male graduates to secure ministerial positions with local churches. This early placement practice continued until the mission of American higher education was broadened from an elitist model to an egalitarian model. The establishment of separate professional and specialty schools (agriculture, business, and engineering) created needs unable to be satisfied by the traditional, narrowly focused practice involving a student and his don.

Placement offices, as a separate function within institutions of higher education, became a reality when Yale University established an office in 1919. This office was staffed with professionals trained in vocational guidance to advise and counsel students (Teal & Herrick, 1962). During the early 1900's, this student affairs unit assumed responsibility for matching college students with employment positions during the academic year, the summer months and after graduation. As employer and student needs for services increased, employment offices or bureaus of occupation were established on many campuses. Their goal was to "aid young people in choosing an occupation, preparing themselves for it, and building up a career of efficiency and success" (Brewer, 1942, p. 61). Frequently, college and university personnel coordinated these offices assisted by faculty members working in cooperation with alumni (Lorick, 1987). Record keeping was a major function because lists were required of the numbers and types of degrees earned, by whom, and the numbers and types of jobs available.

Dramatic changes in placement services took place during the beginning of the twentieth century. Professionals incorporated into their practice concepts emerging from the vocational guidance movement which was gaining popularity among psychologists, sociologists and educators. Specialists in vocational guidance and psychometrics increasingly accepted individual differences and the potential for human growth through work and love (*arbeiten unt lieben*) as basic needs. The works of Binet and Cattell, attempting to assess and predict individual abilities, brought psychological thought in closer communication with the educational process. In *Choosing a Vocation,* Parsons (1908), the founder of the vocational guidance movement, presented the first major analysis of job-search behavior. He conceptualized decision-making as the central element within the complex process of vocational choice. His three-part model includes the following:

> (1) a clear understanding of yourself, your aptitudes, abilities, interests, ambitions, resources, limitations, and their courses; (2) a knowledge of the requirements and conditions of success, advantages and disadvantages, compensation, opportunities, and prospects in difficult lines of work; and (3) true reasoning on the relations of these two groups of facts (p. 5).

Other changes in placement services occurred early in this century. The World War I years were associated with dramatic changes in the evolution of contemporary placement services and programs. Manpower demands in the early 1900's and the need to improve the effectiveness of matching individuals to specific jobs provided the impetus for the development of several personnel assessment instruments. An early application of psychometric principles was the Army Alpha General Classification Test. By administering this test to draftees, the Army more effectively assigned some draftees to leadership and other training specialty programs.

This new and objective method of personnel matching was soon generalized to college and university campuses. Similar surveys were designed to identify the attributes of entering students. Several years later, the administration of assessment instruments was required during freshman orientation and registration programs. These activities helped new students select courses, pre-professional or technical curricula and undergraduate degree programs.

However, during the 1920's and 1930's, the placement of graduates required minimal services on the part of many institutions. Most students, who were from upperclass socio-economic families, either joined the family business or decided to enroll in professional schools. The availability of jobs following the Stock Market Crash in 1929 and the Depression of the 1930's was at an all time low.

A dramatic reversal occurred after World War II. Employment recruiters were eager to visit campuses. Memberships in professional regional associations swelled as representatives of the work world joined to establish relationships with college and university placement professionals. Federal funding for the Vocational Rehabilitation and Educational Counseling Program and the creation of the Veteran's Administration resulted in a contract in 1944 involving 429 institutions of higher education. These institutions were to provide job-related counseling services and programs for returning veterans (Blaska & Schmidt, 1977) who required assistance in securing educational counseling and skills needed to re-enter the job market. As the previous war defense economy shifted its focus to the manufacture of consumer products, the emphasis on industrialization resulted in an increased need for engineers, managers, educators and other professionals. These years witnessed the largest expansion phase within the history of placement services (Wrenn, 1951).

During the Vietnam War days in the 1960's, many students decided to pursue graduate and professional education rather than remain subject to the military draft system or seek employment with corporations which were perceived as impersonal and dehumanized. The need for on-campus recruiting efforts decreased significantly. The popularity and funding of placement activities in institutions of higher education, state legislatures and the business world declined dramatically. An economic recession in the 1970's forced administrators in colleges and universities to operate on reduced budget allocations. Job market supply and demand needs became relatively balanced as the numbers of college graduates increased. Reduced job availability caused many employment recruiters to restrict their on-campus interviews to diverse student populations at large universities. The demand for elementary and secondary teachers declined and hiring freezes were enacted in many governmental agencies. Recruiting efforts were redirected toward such specialties as engineering, science, accounting and other business-related fields. Students often "camped out," sleeping outside placement buildings to be among the first to register for limited open interview schedules. These limited placement conditions forced many students to apply directly to employers.

By the late 1970's and early 1980's, interest in career decision-making skills and strategies to assist with the job search increased not only among academic administrators and placement professionals, but students as well. For many students, getting a better job became their first priority after college admission (Astin, 1976). The "Me" student generation of the 1980's, which Levine (1979) characterized as "passengers on a sinking ship, a Titanic . . . called the United States . . ." have "decided that as long as they are doomed, they ought to at least 'go first class' " (p. 104-5). A wave of careerism began to sweep through higher education as students shifted away from learning for learning's sake and equated a college diploma with a ticket to "the good life."

PROFESSIONAL ASSOCIATIONS

As the expansion of placement services continued throughout the United States and the numbers of professionals so employed increased, efforts to improve the coordination of placement activities and planning led to the creation of regional placement associations. The 1926, five charter members of the Eastern College Placement Officers (ECPO) sought to facilitate "professional improvement for the members through an interchange of information on common problems" (Powell & Kirts, 1980; Stephens, 1970). Other regional associations followed: the Rocky Mountain College Placement Association in 1947, the Southern College Placement Association and the Middle Atlantic Placement Associations in 1948. The 1949 membership in the largest of these conferences consisted of representatives of business, industry and education. Today this organization is the Midwest College Placement Association. The last regional association to be formalized was the Western College Placement Association, chartered in 1951. These seven regional groupings continue to provide professional development activities for members and were motivating forces in the subsequent establishment of a national organization for placement professionals.

As memberships increased in regional associations, a more effective means of communication among practitioners was needed. Discussions led to the publication of a national journal. The Director of Placement at the University of Pennsylvania initiated *School and College Placement* in 1940. The journal was renamed the *Journal of College Placement* in 1950 and is known today as the *Journal of Career Planning and Employment* (Shingleton & Fitzpatrick, 1985).

Responding to a need for increased dissemination of information, the presidents of the regional placement associations convened a national advisory board which became the College Placement Council (CPC) in 1957. It was created to serve as a clearinghouse for placement publications and to encourage research efforts among professional members. With headquarters in Bethlehem, Pennsylvania, the CPC continues to provide information through monographs, research reports, handbooks describing services and the *Journal of Career Planning and Employment.*

DEFINITION

Initially, placement services were needed to achieve the goal of matching individual students to employment positions. In 1937 vocational guidance was defined as the process of assisting an individual to choose, prepare for and advance in a vocation (the National Vocational Guidance Association). Professional staff were expected to assume responsibility for soliciting jobs, registering students, scheduling of recruiter interviews, and reporting the number of job placements (Blaska & Schmidt, 1977; Mohs, 1962). As the influence of developmental theories of vocational development spread, career planning evolved as an educational process by which students come to understand the relationship between their capabilities and interests, their university experiences, and professional opportunities, as well as the steps to prepare for those opportunities" (Seeloff, 1984, p. 16). Powell and Kirts (1984) described placement services as the integration of an individual's self-concept and existing career options.

Since 1970 an emphasis on the teaching of career planning skills related to the job search process has changed the image of the placement professional. Today, most practitioners believe they contribute to the total education of students. Their function is to assist in the overall education of students rather than to offer a single service in an area separated from the academic mission of the institution (Lorick, 1987). Their influence on student learning encompasses gaining an understanding of self, interests, abilities, values, and needs; determining occupational or career goals; and learning strategies to help obtain employment (Stephens, 1970).

MISSION

In an attempt to standardize practice within this student affairs specialty area, the Council for the Advancement of Standards in 1986 published a document entitled *Guidelines for Student Services/Development Programs*. This document contained a set of criteria to be used when developing or evaluating services or programs. The Council defined the primary purpose of career planning and placement as aiding "students in developing, evaluating, and effectively initiating and implementing career plans" (p. 15). Specifically, the Council recommended that career planning and placement programs assist students to "(1) engage in self-assessment, (2) obtain occupational information, (3) explore the full range of employment opportunities and/or graduate study, (4) present themselves effectively as candidates, and (5) obtain optimal placement in employment or further professional preparation" (p. 15). To achieve this mission, a list of behavioral objectives was developed by the Council for each of the two major program emphases: (1) career counseling, and (2) placement counseling and referral programs. Students involved in career counseling should be assisted in analyzing their own interests, aptitudes, abilities, previous work experience, personal traits, and desired life style to better understand the interrelationship between self-awareness and career choice. Additionally, they should be helped in obtaining occupational information including, where possible, exploratory experiences such as cooperative education, internships, externships, and summer and part-time jobs; in making reasoned, well-informed career choices free of race/sex stereotypes and setting short and long range goals (Council for the Advancement of Standards, 1986, p. 15). Programs focusing on placement counseling and referral, should be designed to assist students as they learn to:

(1) clarify objectives and establish goals; (2) explore the full range of life/work possibilities including graduate and professional preparation; (3) prepare for the job search or further professional preparation; (4) present themselves effectively as candidates for employment or further study; and lastly, (5) make the transition from education to the world of work (p. 15).

THE EMERGENCE OF CAREER PLANNING

Several forces influenced higher education during the decade of the 1960's. Student activism, the Civil Rights Movement, and the Vietnam War had a profound effect, not only on students, but college and university administrators and faculty as well. Student sub groups or sub-cultures emerged. While many students enrolled in colleges and universities to avoid being subject to the draft, others dropped out of academia and "the Establishment society" to pursue a personal goal of self-fulfillment. Still other students remaining on campuses, argued against prescribed degree requirements and policies that were perceived as restricting student behavior. The new emphasis on actualizing one's potential as a goal of life affected basic values and attitudes toward education and the role of work. Both education and employment were now viewed as means of facilitating individual self-expression and self-fulfillment. Much of the existing collegiate curriculum was perceived as irrelevant by many college students, both to the process of self-actualization and to the solution of societal problems.

As a result of an economic recession and reduced financial support from state subsidies during the 1960's, institutional budgets were reduced and a new concept, accountability, was applied to higher education. Adapted from the corporate sector, the management concept known as accountability caused many administrators to examine the cost effectiveness of student affairs services and professionals. Funding levels as well as the continued existence of student affairs services and programs were being questioned. Student affairs administrators compiled quantitative data to satisfy budget administrators and at the same time struggled to describe the qualitative outcomes of their interaction with students.

Other changes occurred within society. As the process of enhancing self-awareness and the goal of self-fulfillment gained support in society, changes occurred in the relationship that had existed between the educational community and the world of work. The traditional loose relationship between these two previously separate institutions of society was tightened. Educators recognized that an integration of classroom learning with the off-campus community would benefit not only students, but also the labor force. Increased communication between business and industry and education would lead to more effective job recruitment and career placement because graduates would possess academic preparation more consistent with employer's needs.

To achieve the goal of integrating education and the employment world and to ease an individual's progress through the complex job choice and seeking phases, interest in studying job vocational choice behavior increased. Vocational development theorists supported the notion that work was "the primary purpose of a person's life" (Warnath, 1975, p. 422). Vocational counselors believed that with appropriate motivation, information, and assistance, each person could progress smoothly through the educational process and attain employment that would permit the expression of their personality, thus facilitating self-actualization.

Career development emerged as the major developmental process that could guide an individual through the sequential stages of education, career choice, and the subsequent attainment of employment. The essential element in career development was decision-making. The purpose and the components of the decision-making process were provided by Jepsen and Dilley (1974):

> A decision-making conceptual framework assumes the presence of a decision-maker both from within and outside the person. The information is arranged into decision-making concepts according to the function it serves. Two or more alternatives are considered and several outcomes or consequences are anticipated from each action. Each outcome has two characteristics . . . likelihood of occurrence in the future, and . . . relative importance to the decision-maker. (p. 333)

However, the process of career development also focused on the decision-maker and the developmental tasks encountered throughout life. Distinct stages within career development were identified. These included: (1) self-awareness; (2) career exploration; (3) career choice; (4) reality testing; and (5) job-seeking.

While vocational counselors applied decision-making models, theorists described the need for an appropriate degree of congruence or fit between the individual and the working environment to facilitate self-actualization or fulfillment. Given the appropriate fit, the individual could experience maximum growth and development and facilitate self-actualization.

Many directors of placement services changed their titles to Career Planning and Placement or Career Development Services, which symbolized the increasing popularity of career development (Bishop, 1966). These titles were meant to convey, to members of the campus community, the new importance assigned to career counseling and career planning activities. Ultimately, this emphasis on career development led to a deemphasis of one of the traditional placement functions, campus recruiting. In addition, the allocation of resources shifted toward the goal of dissemination of occupational information and the development of career counseling programs.

Although career development evolved from a concept of career education initially created to focus on grades K-12, it soon became apparent that similar career-related needs existed on many college and university campuses. By assessing entering students' needs in the areas of job skills, information about specific careers, campus resources and insight into themselves and career compatibility, colleges and universities identified a large number of students requiring assistance (Ard & Hyder, 1978; Lawson & Felstehausen, 1978; Michigan State University, 1981; Walters & Saddlemire, 1979). Surveys of older, non-traditional and graduate students revealed similar needs for career development programs and services (Kasworm, 1980; Lance, Lourie, & Mayo, 1979; Swain & Walton, 1980; Smallwood, 1980).

The achievement of career development goals was assisted by the development of a five stage process model: (1) self-awareness, (2) exploration, (3) decision-making, (4) preparation, and (5) employment (Issacson, 1977). Assumptions associated with these stages conceived career development as a dynamic and lifelong process. Skills developed within each stage would be applied repeatedly during a person's lifetime as the individual strives toward the goal of self-actualization through their career lifetime. Successful career choices were seen as the fulfillment of a person's self-concept (Scott, 1983).

The first three stages of career development became known as career planning. Career planning professionals design programs to teach skills necessary for the completion of the self-awareness, exploration, and decision-making stages. The awareness stage requires the gathering of information about the self (interests, goals, values, attitudes, and motivations). The exploration stage involves learning about the characteristics associated with the multiplicity of occupations, environments and people in the work world. Techniques for seeking and securing employment are elements of the employment stage and emphasize skills related to resume writing and effective interviewing (Issacson, 1977). Workshops and structured credit courses were developed to assist students in learning and applying skills required for the assessment of individual differences, clarification of values, establishing short and long range goals, and gaining an understanding of the nature of the world of work.

The goal of career planning was to help students learn to: (1) identify and transfer career interests to a plan of action, (2) relate interests and goals to opportunities, (3) relate career plans to life goals, and (4) evaluate progress toward career goals through academic preparation (Sovilla, 1972).

Models of career planning were based on vocational development theories categorized by their emphasis on one of the following approaches: trait-and-factor analysis; client-centered perspective; psychoanalytic orientation; or a developmental or behavioral viewpoint. Each model assumed a somewhat different view of the individual and suggested different roles played by the various factors involved in career choice behavior. A description of each of these models is beyond the scope of this chapter. Common to all career choice models was the continuous nature of decision-making as a behavior "extending from late childhood to at least early adulthood and sometimes to midlife" (Crites, 1981).

ROLES AND RESPONSIBILITIES TO CONSTITUENCIES

Cappeto (1980) identified four unique roles for the career planning and placement professional: (1) advisor, (2) evaluator, (3) intermediary, and (4) advocate. As advisors, staff members teach students how to make realistic career decisions. By helping students assess their own interests, values, needs, and personal traits in relation to available academic and employment options, staff act as impartial evaluators. The role of intermediary requires staff to serve as both an arbitrator and mediator when resolving disputes and promoting negotiations among students, parents or faculty. Last, the professional staff must market their services and programs to students and faculty while continually serving as advocates for career planning and placement (Cappeto, 1980).

The Career Planning and Placement Office is the connecting link between the academic community and the world of work. Demands and expectations from different segments within the institution as well as those external to the campus constantly confront career planning and placement directors. Students and alumni, faculty and administrators, employers, and the general public are the primary constituent groups served by practitioners in this area. Balancing the complex and often competing demands made by each of these groups is essential to a successful career planning and placement program.

Today's professionals are torn between a need to emphasize traditional placement services while at the same time feeling compelled to provide effective career planning programs. As Stokes (1980) noted, "on the one hand, placement's quantitative results, such as the faculty/administration interest in placement, the high proportion of use of services by seniors, the placement school of thought, and the director's view of the placement orientation of other centralized offices, tug toward the placement perspective" (p. 65). Conversely, the expected increase of service use by underclassmen, the demands of faculty members and staff, the career planning school of thought, and the inclination to increase career planning if the success rate of either placement or career planning diminishes, push the staff toward an emphasis on career planning (Stokes, 1980).

To resolve this dilemma, directors should examine their own attitudes and orientation toward both career planning and placement. They should design evaluation instruments to gather objective data describing the direct relationship between involvement in career planning activities and a successful job search. In addition, directors should acknowledge that different groups on campus have special needs that must be met by the career planning and placement process. For example, students are also paraprofessionals; faculty may want to serve as co-trainers of workshops and seminars; and alumni may both need advice and be able to give advice about careers (Stokes, 1980). Responsibilities and roles of career planning and the placement professionals to each of the groups described will be explained in the following section.

Responsibility to Students

Practitioners have been encouraged to involve students in planned programs and services not only during the senior year but throughout the college years. Career planning and placement professionals should initiate communication during the freshman year and build a relationship "that will extend through initial job placement and continue into the graduates' later life and career" (Robb, 1976, p. 41). Students also should maintain a close relationship with these staff members, so that students "will define themselves in terms of their major or seek a formula that matches their major to a career or job. Students will learn that . . . they cannot wait until their senior year . . . 'to get a job' " (Seeloff, 1984, p. 16). By adopting a more proactive approach and deemphasizing crisis management, staff members can improve their delivery system of services and change the "senior-year-only" perspective of many students.

Freshmen and sophomores who are exposed to career counseling and career resource material are more likely to make well informed career decisions (Shingleton, 1978).

In addition to fostering good relationships with students, professionals should promote the value of internships, cooperative education experiences, and summer and part-time jobs as methods of helping students explore career options and experiment with tentative career choices. Staff should increase their communication with academic departments as well as with personnel at prospective field sites.

Planning a career and securing the right job requires knowledge and persistence. Career planning and placement professionals must help students prepare for the competitive job market and implement action plans to achieve their goals. Practitioners should be prepared to "provide information on current and projected employment opportunities and employers, including policies, products, locations, typical career paths and corporate financial reports" (Council for the Advancement of Standards, 1986, p. 16). Taylor's (1984) research revealed that students need to rely on a vast network of professional organizations, friends, relatives, and direct applications to companies. Expanding the number and types of networking activities has become increasingly important for students.

Responsibility to Alumni

Past graduates of the institution have unique needs for services from career planning and placement professionals. Effectively satisfying the needs of this constituency often leads to increases in alumni financial support and alumni involvement with the institution (Cappeto, 1980). The need to increase the number of specialized services for alumni has been linked to specific sociological trends. Greater numbers of alumni are seeking employment or career changes. Because of a desire or need for lifelong learning, an increasingly mobile society, more mature women entering or re-entering the job market, mid-life career changes, and early or partial retirement, more alumni need information, counseling, and career planning activities (Shingleton, 1978). Adults in transition expressed needs for specific information on jobs, careers and educational opportunities (Arbeiter, 1978).

To meet these needs of alumni, directors should offer services within the geographical area surrounding their campus. Among the recommended services are: (1) a bibliography of career and occupational information and trend line data, (2) a career counseling course, (3) a weekend workshop for adults, (4) resume referral services supported by fees, and (5) job fairs for alumni and community people (Arbeiter, 1978).

Responsibility to the Institution and Its Faculty

Regardless of the diverse demands placed by different constituencies and the competing pressures from the distinct orientations toward placement and career planning, the professional staff must be committed to the values, philosophies and mission of their institution (Cappeto, 1980). Given the nature of the academic environment within which they work, practitioners have an obligation to help educate faculty and staff colleagues about the availability and value of services offered. In addition, staff need to assume responsibility for improving their campus visibility by initiating contacts with individual faculty members, department chairs, deans, and members of the central administration; designing activities to educate faculty about the world of work and its current expectations; defining career orientation or planning activities so as not to threaten academic standards or alienate faculty; and helping faculty increase the marketability of their specific academic majors (Smith, 1979). The necessity of collecting data describing supply and demand market trends and recording career path experiences of previous graduates is assumed. Stengthening the lines of communication between the career planning and placement office and members of the faculty, administration and board of trustees is an obligation most professionals do not overlook.

Professional staff should provide current information about the nature of employment positions and the expectations of employers if they are to assist faculty in assessing and redesigning curricula. Because of their constant contact with professionals in business and industry, practitioners are in an advantageous position to educate faculty about changing trends in the marketplace and predicted areas of need (Robb, 1976; Swanson, 1980).

Results from a national survey conducted by Scott (1983) revealed that presidents, chief academic affairs officers and chief student affairs officers were in agreement concerning the role career planning and placement should assume within the academic community. More than 95 percent of the respondents indicated that this student affairs area should play an integral role in the total academic process. However, when asked if career planning and placement professionals were assuming an integral role, 89 percent of the presidents and 80 percent of the chief academic affairs officers responded affirmatively, while only 78 percent of the chief student affairs officers did so. The three groups of respondents most frequently cited developing and/or integrating all aspects of a comprehensive program and expanding the developmental aspects of the program as the single activity in which career planning and placement practitioners should be involved.

Responsibility to Employers

Since 1982 dramatic changes occurring in college recruitment and forced recruiting organizations to control, reduce and justify costs; do more with fewer staff; increase the interview-hire ratio; and adapt to a high rate of turnover in recruiting personnel. To help secure the best candidates, professionals must expand cooperative education experiences, internships and other on-site learning situations (Yost, 1985). It is becoming increasingly important for practitioners to "understand the recruiters' environment and . . . (to) attempt to understand the constraints and needs being placed upon the recruiters" (Smith, 1979, p. 25). To be successful in this area, professional staff must be flexible and able to respond to last minute changes and requests from recruiters. By recognizing campus recruiters through award ceremonies on campus or by sending letters to their supervisors, practitioners can enhance the recruiter's position within his/her employing institution.

Seeloff (1984) also advises career planning and placement professionals to spend more time with employers to become aware of new career opportunities and needs, gather reliable information for students, and develop additional employment options for graduates.

Responsibility to the General Public

Of all the constituent groups, members of the general public are the individuals to whom the professional must devote additional time and effort. Staff members must be heard and seen talking about the world of work and its opportunities before the media, parents, public school teachers, and governmental agencies. To do this, professionals can publish reports describing surveys of employers, salary ranges of certain positions and predicted changes in market demands. This area of responsibility may also include being involved in the writing of state and federal legislation pertaining to college student employment, and assisting high school personnel in the placement locations and conducting research by identifying future employment needs (Shingleton, 1978; Shingleton & Fitzpatrick, 1985; Smith, 1979).

TYPES OF SERVICES

Throughout its long history, placement professionals, and now career planning and placement staff have provided students with a variety of services to help them in the process of choosing and working toward their career goals. National surveys of employers from business, industry, government and education, as well as career planning and placement administrators, reveal support for the following types of services: (1) on-campus recruiting; (2) full-time employment; (3) employer literature; (4) career information centers; (5) student employment; (6) vacancy listings; (7) job campaign assistance; (8) career planning and advising; (9) recruiting trends; (10) resume referrals; (11) career fairs; (12) alumni services; (13) occupational and employer information libraries; and (14) experienced candidate programs (Scott, 1983; Shingleton & Sheetz, 1985). Data from these surveys reflected the greatest gain in sponsorship of programs in the following three areas from 1976 to 1982: (1) cooperative education, internship and experiential services; (2) vocational testing; and (3) academic counseling (Weber, 1982).

The following services: (1) on-campus recruiting; (2) sign-up procedures; (3) preselection; (4) student credentials; (5) resume referrals; (6) occupational and employer information libraries; and (7) educational programs are considered essential to an effective career planning and placement program and will be described in the next section.

On-Campus Recruiting Services

Professional staff offer students opportunities to interview with prospective employers from business, industry, non-profit organizations, human service agencies, public schools and government agencies. Generally 30 minutes long, the on-campus interview is designed to help the employment recruiter gather information about the student's career goals, academic preparation, co-curricular activities, relevant work experiences and job-related skills.

On-campus recruiting is an efficient and cost effective method of bringing recruiters and student applicants together. For students this process is ideal, because "campus interviewing is the most convenient, most efficient, and least expensive method of making contact with potential employers . . ." (Powell & Kirts, 1980, p. 201). However, the college or university pays for these interviewing sessions. Costs to the institution traditionally include printing brochures and related materials as well as travel and entertainment expenses for recruiters. Consequently, small institutions usually are unable to allocate the necessary funds to implement this program on a large scale.

When recruiters select campuses to visit, they are influenced by several factors. These include location, academic reputation and relevance to the available jobs, strength of the faculty, size of the graduating class, past performance of previous graduates hired and the quality of career planning and placement services.

In general, recruiting schedules are determined six to 12 months in advance of the on-campus interview. Approximately six weeks prior to the on-campus interview, the staff gather information describing the positions available and the specific academic majors sought by the employer. This material is then distributed to students and faculty. Students self-select companies or organizations of interest and then follow prescribed sign-up procedures to schedule interviews.

When recruiters visit the campus, they usually are guided by a three stage interviewing process: (1) planning; (2) conducting; and (3) evaluating. During the initial stage, the interviewer decides which information from the student's resume will be explored during the interview, which selection criteria will be used to evaluate the student and which questions will be asked of the student. Once the student is comfortable in the interview situation, the recruiter explains the procedure and clarifies incomplete data from the resume. The interviewer then begins to use one of four techniques to gather needed information. These include using open-ended questions designed to encourage expansive responses; asking closed-ended questions to limit responses; using silence to allow the student the opportunity to formulate a response before sharing it; and encouraging comments to help the student feel at ease and willing to respond freely and fully.

At the end of the interview, the employment recruiter may invite the applicant for an on-site interview with other members of the employment institution. This day-long session often includes pre-employment testing. Once this in-depth interview is completed, the recruiter may extend an offer of employment to the student.

Sign-Up Procedures

Most institutions employ one of three types of sign-up procedures, depending on the philosophy and objectives of the career planning and placement director and the condition of the economy. These sign-up procedures are: (1) the traditional "first-come, first-served" approach which is used frequently on relatively small campuses; (2) a computerized process that allows students to participate in a rank order, bidding or lottery system to schedule interviews; and (3) a service that combines a first-come, first served method with an educationally-based system. For example, at Bowling Green State University, students who complete six hours of training in interviewing, resume writing and job hunting techniques receive priority during the sign-up period. This innovative program ensures that most students involved in the interviewing process possess basic skills that enhance their effectiveness as job applicants.

Preselection

A related practice used by many professional staffs permits employers to preselect candidates for on-campus interviews. Credentials of all students expressing an interest in a specific organization are sent to employers. Candidates who are selected by the recruiter are extended an invitation to interview during the recruiter's on-campus visit. Although this is an extremely popular method with employers, many institutions have resisted employers' requests because specific performance indicators such as grade point average are not always good predictors of students' employment potential. In addition, students who have not performed well academically are excluded from the interview process. During periods of economic recession and limited hiring in entry-level positions, many employers persuaded practitioners to permit this procedure. An obvious advantage of this approach is the employer's ability to improve their interview-to-hire ratio and conserve time and effort. However, in better economic times, other interview procedures are preferred.

Student Credential Files

Because recruiters need to evaluate each candidate's credentials in a short time, practitioners have developed standard data sheets or forms, which are used by all students. The credential form, the basis of the credential file, usually contains a statement signed by the student authorizing the professional staff to release information to prospective employers or to graduate admissions officers.

Prior to the Buckley Amendment of 1975, all student records were considered confidential. Since that time, students have the right to review contents of all institutional records. Students may waive these rights and consequently will be unable to read letters of recommendation requested from faculty or staff members. Generally, a career planning and placement staff member will review the letters and then advise the student about retaining or deleting them from the credential file.

Resume Referrals

Employers may identify candidates for immediate employment openings through resume referral. In this process the professional nominates qualified applicants by sending copies of their credential files or resumes to the employer for review and consideration. Although the procedure sounds simple, it can present the professional with a difficult situation.

Under Title VII of the Civil Rights Act of 1964, college placement offices are considered as employment agencies and are prohibited from failing or refusing to refer an individual for employment or from classifying or referring an individual on the basis of race, sex, color, religion, or national origin (Powell & Kirts, 1980). In a 1975 case, an employment agency received a request to refer only women to an employer who had under-utilized women in the workforce and was attempting to remedy the situation through affirmative action procedures. The Equal Employment Opportunity Commission noted only one exception allowed under Title VII: "exclusive referrals of applicants may be possible under Title VII in the very limited circumstances where there exists a bona fide occupational qualification on the basis of religion, sex, or national origin . . ." (Decision of Equal Employment Opportunity Commission, Decision No. 75-268, May 30, 1975). As might be expected, few employment positions meet these limited circumstances. To minimize possible violations of Title VII, career planning and placement professionals should refer all qualified candidates regardless of group status. Questions regarding the legal aspects of resume referrals should be addressed to the institution's legal counsel.

Occupational and Employer Information Libraries

A comprehensive library is one of the essential elements of a career planning and placement service. Material available to students should include the full array of occupations, training or educational requirements, and references to and profiles of employing organizations or agencies. Two annotated bibliographies assist the staff in selecting appropriate materials for their library: *What Shall I Order for the Career Planning and Placement Library* and *Career Information for College Graduates* (College Placement Council). Several volumes are generally found within most libraries. Some standard references are a set of *College Placement Annuals;* Petersen's Guides to *Engineering, Science and Computer Jobs,* and *Business and Management Jobs; Encyclopedia of Careers and Vocational Guidance; Occupational Outlook Handbook; The Professional Resume and Job Search Guide; What Color is Your Parachute?;* and *Sweaty Palms: The Neglected Art of Being Interviewed.*

Although a universal library classification system has not been developed, most staff members organize their materials by using one of the following schemes: (1) stages of the career development process (self-assessment, career exploration and placement); (2) the numerical system of the *Dictionary of Occupational Titles;* or (3) the general themes of the Strong-Campbell Interest Inventory.

Career and Job Fairs

A central mission of career planning and placement offices is facilitating student and employer contacts. Career days and job fairs enable students to gather valuable career information, make initial contacts with employers, and in some cases, interview directly with many employers at a single location. Employers appreciate the opportunity to meet with students in an informal atmosphere, interact with faculty and placement personnel and gain visibility for their organizations on campus.

Student Publications

By publishing a comprehensive guide to programs, procedures and policies, staff can effectively inform students of their services. Frequently the costs incurred for publications are underwritten by employer advertisements. To stimulate student participation in career planning and placement activities, many offices publish a monthly supplement to the campus newspaper in addition to the traditional placement manual.

EDUCATIONAL PROGRAMS

Career Planning Courses

Career planning courses designed for freshmen and sophomores help many students "to identify their own interests, to examine a number of majors, and to confront many basic values and priorities which contribute to their effectiveness in planning long-term goals" (Shingleton & Fitzpatrick, 1987, p. 79). In structured courses students learn by interacting in small group discussions, keeping a journal reflecting their feelings about materials they have read and conducting informational interviews with individuals working in the students' immediate major area. Assessment instruments, such as the Strong-Campbell Interest Inventory and the Kuder Occupational Interest Inventory, and interactive computerized programs, Discover and System of Interactive Guidance and Information (SIGI), help students during the self-assessment and early decision-making stages (Bruce, Varelas, & Shuman, 1982).

The objectives of a career planning and placement course are to provide students with a greater understanding and awareness of the career development process and to develop student attitudes and competencies needed to make career decisions. Parts or stages of the career development process are sometimes the subjects of workshops. A career exploration workshop, for example, would focus on students who have already completed several self-assessment tasks and understand employment needs and expectations. The workshop then would assist students in examining appropriate career options compatible with their values and skills (Shumate, 1983).

Counseling

Although courses and workshops are efficient ways to reach large numbers of students, many students prefer individual counseling appointments with the professional staff. Therefore, staff members must be proficient in counseling skills, career and human development theory, knowledgeable about the employment market and the world of work and competent in job search techniques. Providing realistic, accurate information is critical in helping students make career decisions that will enhance their career satisfaction. In counseling sessions, staff often use computerized guidance systems, vocational interest inventories and self-help exercises to assist students through the career planning process.

Individual counseling sessions also involve career planning discussions, resume critiques, mock interviews and an evaluation of employment offers. Strong communication links with academic advisors and departmental faculty increase the effectiveness of these referrals.

Workshops

Career planning and placement workshops, seminars and credit courses are designed to teach skills necessary for interviewing, resume writing and conducting an effective job search campaign. In addition, students' levels of anxiety are often reduced by participation in such structured learning experiences. Topics for these educational programs often include employer interviews and techniques, applicant questioning, follow-up procedures, job search correspondence, resume writing, skill identification and networking. At a minimum, students should be prepared to present themselves in an effective manner during the interview. This requires the ability to write a resume and to conduct a satisfactory job search.

Employment recruiters are usually more than willing to participate in workshops to help students identify career opportunities or to discuss career adjustment issues. These sessions generally focus on dual career marriages, professional image, and the transition from the academic world to the work world.

ADMINISTRATIVE AND ORGANIZATIONAL MODELS

As the popularity of the career planning perspective continued throughout the 1960's and 1970's, administrative relationships involving career planning and placement offices changed. In the late 1960's, 30 percent of career planning and placement directors reported directly to the president of their institution, 30 percent to the Dean of Students and 27 percent to the Chief Academic Officer (Herrick, 1975). By 1981, however, Weber (1981) found that most directors reported to the Chief Student Affairs Officer. Although the *Standards and Guidelines for Career Planning and Placement* recommends that "career planning and placement should be organized as part of or closely related to the academic structure to increase faculty/staff awareness of the career development process and the current employment trends" (Council for the Advancement of Standards, 1986, p. 16), only one-fifth of the directors responded that they were supervised by an academic officer. In a few rare cases, the Director of Career Planning and Placement reported to the Chief Financial Officer of the institution (Crouch & Tolle, 1982).

Organizational Models

The advantages and disadvantages of various organizational models for career planning and placement have been the subject of numerous articles (Babbush, Hawley, & Zeran, 1986; Boynton, 1949; Chervenik, Nord, & Aldridge, 1982; Herrick, 1976; Lentz, 1984; Robb, 1979; Shingleton, 1978; Swaim, 1968; Wrenn, 1951). Of all these models, the three organizational models implemented most frequently are: (1) a centralized program for the entire institution, (2) a decentralized program within various colleges or schools within the institution, and (3) a combination program utilizing centralized and decentralized approaches within a single institution (Shingleton & Fitzpatrick, 1985).

The goal of developing one model to fit all institutional types seems unrealistic. To determine the appropriate organizational structure, organizational planners have found that they must analyze the institution's physical layout, its academic offerings, a demographic profile of the student body, and the types of employment solicited by recruiters visiting the campus (Babbush, Hawley, & Zevan, 1986).

Results of the College Placements Council's national survey of career planning and placement officers supported the popularity of the centralized organizational model. Of the more than 700 respondents, 85 percent maintained all programs, services, networks of employer contacts, staff and records within a physically and administratively centralized operation. Decentralized models were used by only 14 percent of the directors surveyed (Scott, 1983).

More recently, Magoon, Saddoris, and Settle (1987) completed a national survey of organizational structures by institutional size and concluded that the popularity of the centralized approach has remained constant. On campuses with less than 10,000 students, 88 percent of the directors administered a single career planning and placement unit. Even when student enrollment exceeded 10,000, 76 percent of the directors reported supervising centralized operations, while decentralized offices were reported by an equivalent minority of 14 percent of the directors.

Frequently cited advantages of the centralized model include more efficient use of staff, office space, and equipment; reduced recruiting program costs; convenience for students; simplified patterns of employer contacts; greater emphasis on career planning and better coordination of student employment, volunteer programs, internships, and co-op programs. Perhaps the most important rationale for the centralized model is that it conveys to the rest of the campus community the integration of career planning and placement within the institution's broad educational goals (Boynton, 1949). However, certain disadvantages of the model also have been noted. Most often, staff members experience a tendency to become isolated from academic departments, faculty, and students. In addition, employment recruiters perceive their access to individual faculty as more limited. (Babbush, Hawley, & Zevan, 1986; Herrick, 1975; Shingleton & Fitzpatrick, 1985).

Advocates of the decentralized model base their opinions on the value derived by each specialty area on campus (college or school) having their own career planning and placement office and staff team readily accessible. Satellite offices are thought to provide more personalized service because they deal with fewer students and can promote more frequent interaction between faculty and recruiters (Teal & Herrick, 1962). Frequently, the decentralized model is found within the specialized collegiate units of business and engineering. Another positive outcome of decentralization is the availability of more specific career and academic advising for undergraduate and graduate students (Crouch & Tolle, 1982; Shingleton & Fitzpatrick, 1985). Negative outcomes are usually related to increased recruiting costs; duplication of efforts, facilities, and staff; and the fact that compartmentalization tends to hamper students from a broad based exploration of choices across academic disciplines.

PERSONNEL

During the 1950's and 1960's, most career planning and placement personnel were not graduates of preparation programs with an emphasis in college student personnel. Instead, personnel moved to these positions from other assignments within their institution. In some cases staff members had prior work experience in governmental agencies, business corporations, or teaching (Bishop, 1966; Calvert & Menske, 1967; Windle, Van Mondfrans, & Kay, 1972).

Since then, however, the profile of the typical director has remained rather constant. Women continue to constitute the minority of office directors (40%), although their number has increased by almost 12 percent since 1975. The director generally is in his mid-forties and possesses a Masters degree either in guidance and counseling or higher education with a concentration in college student personnel (Calvert & Menske, 1967; Crouch & Tolle, 1982; Herrick, 1975; Vokac, 1959). The percentage of directors with doctorates has been stable at 13 percent.

Among the characteristics considered essential for career planning and placement practitioners are previous business and/or teaching experience; knowledge of job availability and manpower supply and demand information; ability and skills to work effectively with people; a graduate degree with a concentration in counseling, guidance, or college student personnel; and practicum or internship responsibilities. Recent trends have suggested a decreased emphasis on prior business or industrial work experience and a greater significance placed on Master's degree work in counseling and career planning skills and theories within the context of college student personnel administration (Vokac, 1959; Stevens, 1965; McLaughlin, 1973; Commission VI of the American College Personnel Association, Council for the Advancement of Standards, 1986). Such a pattern represents the transition from the earlier philosophy of matching and record keeping to the more student-centered counseling and human development perspective.

When asked to suggest the courses that should constitute a graduate preparation program for individuals interested in career planning and placement activities, most directors suggested an emphasis on career counseling and planning, counseling and guidance, and business and job search skills. The undergraduate fields viewed as being of greatest value to the future director were psychology, English, business, and education (Crouch & Tolle, 1982).

RESPONDING TO THE CHANGING NEEDS OF STUDENTS IN THE FUTURE

Numerous authors in the late 1970's and early 1980's described changes not only in the nature of the work force but changes in the values of college students as well (Hoehn, 1982; Levine, 1980; Smith, 1979; Swanson, 1980; Thain, 1977; Yost, 1985). In *When Dreams and Heroes Died,* Levine (1980) categorizes students of the 1980's as more career-oriented than those of past decades. He noted that "when undergraduates were asked in 1969 what was most essential for them to get out of college, they ranked learning to get along with people first and formulating values and goals for their lives second. Seven years later . . . these aims fell to third and fourth place, being replaced by getting a detailed grasp of a special field and obtaining training and skills for an occupation. Top among the reasons freshmen give for attending college is to get a better job" (Levine, 1980, p. 60-61).

According to Koehn (1982), the underlying theme in this changing pattern of student values and attitudes "is a belief in the entitlement ethic and the concept of a risk-free life. Baby boom individuals believe they are entitled to affluence and happiness . . . (which should be) acquired without taking chances financially or emotionally. The younger end of this group even seems to have rediscovered the work ethic" (Koehn, 1982, p. 31).

Bachman and Johnson (1979) support the view that today students expect to go first class and realize that to do so requires money. Associated with going first class are a "status profession, personal recognition, professional acclaim, and an opportunity to make decisions and manage a staff" (Levine, 1980, p. 111).

Students in the 1980's seem primarily interested in careers. In addition, these students have acquired life style values that were not possible in the post-Depression or post-World War II eras (Swanson, 1980). These students have been characterized as expecting open and honest communication in the work place and in the home, seeking greater involvement in managerial decisions and being unwilling to support authoritarian rules in their lives (Koehn, 1982).

As the number of traditional college aged students declines, more non-traditional students are enrolling in colleges and universities. As non-traditional students move into the job market, the composition of the work force will change dramatically. One author projects "fewer entry-level workers; more senior citizens demanding age-neutral, non-traditional involvement; more women demanding sex-neutral employment and remuneration; and dramatically more ethnicity." (Koehn, 1982, p. 31).

What effects will these changing enrollment and value patterns have on the work place in the decades ahead? Predictions include an increase in employment opportunities for women and minorities, greater demands for non-technical personnel, importing workers from other countries to offset labor shortages, and greater demands for postgraduate education (Smith, 1985).

In light of the above information, the future for the career planning and placement professional promises to be one of both support from institutions and challenges from students and the work world.

REFERENCES

Arbeiter, S. (1978). Adults in transition. *Journal of College Placement, 38,* 54-58.

Ard, R.F., & Hyder, L.L., Jr. (1978). Career planning objectives of college students and activities perceived as instrument in their achievement. *Journal of College Student Personnel, 19*(1), 48-54.

Astin, A. (1976). *Four critical years.* San Francisco: Jossey-Bass.

Babbush, H.E., Hawley, W.W., & Zeran, J. (1986). The best of both worlds. *Journal of Career Planning and Employment, 46,* 49-53.

Bachman, J. & Johnson, L.D. (1979). The freshman, 1979. *Psychology Today, 13*(4), 79-87.

Bishop, J.F. (1966). Portents in college placement. In G.J. Klopf (Ed.), *College student personnel work in years ahead.* Student personnel monograph series, no. 7. Washington, D.C.: American Personnel and Guidance Association.

Blaska, B., & Schmidt, M.R. (1977). Placement. In W.T. Packwood (Ed.), *College student personnel services* (pp. 368-421). Springfield, IL: Charles C Thomas.

Boynton, P.W. (1949). *Selecting the new employee.* New York: Harper.

Brewer, J. (1942). *History of vocational guidance* (p. 61). New York: Harper.

Bruce, R.C., Varelas, E., & Shuman, R.S. (1982). Technology in career planning and placement. *Journal of College Placement, 42,* 35-37.

CPC Foundation. (1985, June). *The current status of, and reactions to, the issues of prescreening, preselection, and prerecruiting.* Bethlehem, PA.

Calvert, R., Jr., & Menke, R.F. (1967). Placement. *Journal of College Placement, 27*(4), 29-31; 119-121; 123; 125-126; 129; 131; 135.

Cappeto, M.A. (1980). The career services professional. *Journal of College Placement, 40,* 43-47.

Chervenik, E., Nord, D., & Aldridge, M. (1982). Putting career planning and placement together. *Journal of College Placement, 42,* 48-51.

Council for the Advancement of Standards for Student Services/Development Programs. (1986). *CAS standards and guidelines for student services/development programs.*

Crites, J.O. (1981). *Career counseling: Models, methods and materials.* New York: McGraw-Hill.

Crouch, L.R., & Tolle, D.J. (1982). The placement director of the '80's: A profile. *Journal of College Placement, 42,* 43-46.

Dempsey, F.K., Jr. (1970). College recruitment — a reassessment. *Personnel Journal, 49,* 746-749.

Decision of Equal Employment Opportunity Commission, Decision No. 75-268. (1975, May 30).

Hackamack, L.C., & Iannone, C.R. (1969). Selecting, recruiting, retaining today's college graduate. *Personnel Journal, 48,* 988-991.

Herrick, R.F. (1976). *Career planning and placement in the mid-seventies: An operational profile.* Bethlehem, PA: College Placement Council.

Issacson, L.E. (1977). *Career information in counseling and teaching* (3rd ed.). Boston: Allyn & Bacon.

Kasworm, C. (1980). Student services for the older undergraduate students. *Journal of College Student Personnel, 21,* 163-169.

Koehn, H.E. (1982). The changing work force. *Journal of College Placement, 42,* 31-33.

Lance, M., Louri, J., & Mayo, C. (1979). Needs of reentry students. *Journal of College Student Personnel, 20,* 479-485.

Lansner, L.A. (1967). Evening college placement. In M.L. Farmer (Ed.), *Student personnel services for adults in higher education.* Metuchen, NJ: Scarecrow.

Lawson, D., & Felstehausen, J. (1978). *A study of staff and student awareness, use and need for career education services and resources at Eastern Illinois University.* Occupational Teacher Education Committee, Eastern Illinois University.

Leonard, E.A. (1956). *Origins of personnel services in American higher education.* Minneapolis: University of Minnesota Press.

Lentz, G.F. (1984). Combining cooperative education and placement. *Journal of College Placement, 44,* 43-47.

Levine, A. (1980). *When dreams and heroes died.* San Francisco: Jossey-Bass.

Lorick, B.A. (1987). Career planning and placement services. In J.L. Amprey, Jr. (Ed.), *Student development on the small campus* (pp. 92-126). National Association of Personnel Workers.

Magoon, T.M., Saddoris, A.M., & Settle, W.H. (1987). *Career centers pilot data bank.* Unpublished.

Marland, S.P. (1972). Career education now. *Vocational Guidance Quarterly, 293,* 188-192.

Marland, S.P. (1974). *Career education.* New York: McGraw-Hill.

McEanery, T.J. (1973). On campus recruiting. In P.W. Dunphy (Ed.), *Career development for the college student* (pp. 55-77). Cranston: Carroll.

McLoughlin, W.L. (1973). Placement's emerging role. *Journal of College Placement, 33,* 79-82.

Michigan State University. (1981). *Career development: A model for post-secondary education.* East Lansing: Career Planning and Placement Council.

Mohs, M.C. (1962). *Service through placement in the junior college.* Washington, D.C.: American Association of Junior Colleges.

National Advisory Council on Vocational Education. (1972). *Career preparation for everyone, 29*(3), 1983-87.

Parsons, F. (1909). *Choosing a vocation.* Boston: Houghton-Mifflin.

Powell, C.R., & Kirts, D.K. (1980). *Career services today.* (p. 201). Bethlehem, PA: College Placement Council.

Robb, F.D. (1976). Fallback, regroup and charge! *Journal of College Placement, 37,* 38-41.

Robb, W.D. (1979). Counseling—placmeent, must they be separate entities? *Journal of College Placement, 39,* 67-71.

Ryan, T.A. (1974). A systems approach to career education. *Vocational Guidance Quarterly, 22*(3), 172-179.

Scott, G.J. (1983). *Career planning and placement office: Implications for the future.* Bethlehem, PA: College Placement Council Foundation.

Seeloff, E.R. (1984). Integrated career planning and placement: New lyrics to an old tune. *Journal of College Placement, 45,* 16-18.

Shartle, C.L. (1959). *Occupational information: Its development and application.* Englewood Cliffs, NJ: Prentice-Hall.

Shingleton, J.D. (1978). The three R's of placement. *Journal of College Placement, 38,* 33-38.

Shingleton, J.D., & Sheetz, L.P. (1985). *Recruiting trends, 1985-86.* A study of businesses, industries, governmental agencies, and educational institutions employing new college graduates. East Lansing, MI: Michigan State University Placement Services.

Shumate, S.E. (1983). *Career exploration course workbook.* Kent, OH: Kent State University, Career Planning and Placement.

Smallwood, K. (1980). What do adult women college students really need? *Journal of College Student Personnel, 21,* 64-73.

Smith, J.M. (1979). The professional's role in a changing environment. *Journal of College Placement, 39,* 21-26.

Smith, J.M. (1985). The challenge of our changing demographics. *Journal of College Placement, 45,* 3, 6.

Sovilla, E.S. (1972). A new functional balance for career planning activities in the '70s. *Journal of College Placement, 33*(1), 62-66.

Steele, E.W. (1978). College relations: A bright future if we know what we're talking about. *Journal of College Placement, 38,* 37-41.

Stephens, E.W. (1970). *Career counseling and placement in higher education: A student personnel function.* Bethlehem, PA: College Placement Council.

Stevens, N.D. (1965). A changing concept of college placement. *Journal of College Student Personnel, 6,* 27-32.

Stokes, R.D. (1980). The dilemma of career services professionals. *Journal of College Placement, 41,* 63-67.

Straus, J.C., & Magee, J.E. (1979). Federal equal employment opportunity law: An overview. *Journal of College Placement, 39,* 33.

Swaim, R. (1968). Centralization or decentralization: Two approaches to placement receive an up-to-date review. *Journal of College Placement, 28*(3), 117-128.

Swain, R., & Walton, F. (1980). *Career planning needs of UIUC graduate students in the humanities and social sciences.* Career Development and Placement Center, University of Illinois, Urbana-Champaign.

Swanson, D.S. (1980). Forecast for the '80's. *Journal of College Placement, 40,* 57-60.

Taylor, M.S. (1984). Strategies and sources in the student job search. *Journal of College Placement, 45,* 40-45.

Teal, E.A., & Herrick, R.F. (Eds.). (1962). *The fundamentals of college placement.* Bethlehem, PA: College Placement Council.

Thain, R.J. (1977). What lies ahead? *Journal of College Placement, 38,* 34-46.

Vokac, R.B. (1959). Directors suggest their own qualifications. *Journal of College Placement, 19*(3), 71-78.

Walters, L., & Saddlemire, G. (1979). Career planning needs of college freshmen and their perceptions of career planning. *Journal of College Student Personnel, 20,* 224-229.

Weber, D.W. (1982). *The status of career planning and placement.* Bethlehem, PA: The College Placement Council.

Windle, J.L., Van Mondfrans, A.P., & Kay, R.S. (1972). *Review of research: Career planning and development, placement and recruitment of college-trained personnel.* Bethlehem, PA: The College Placement Council.

Wrenn, C.G. (1951). *Student personnel work in college.* New York: Ronald.

Yost, A.E. (1985). Warning: A bear might be shaking your tree. *Journal of Career Planning and Employment, 46,* 29-32.

CHAPTER 5

COUNSELING

ELIZABETH YARRIS

CASE I

IT IS 11:30 Sunday night. A Resident Advisor who has been alternating between studying and worrying about Monday's Chemistry exam is interrupted by one of the residents on his floor. Jim is concerned about his roommate, Harry. Harry has just returned to the room, has obviously been drinking and is upset because he saw his girlfriend with someone else at a party. Jim overheard Harry say that so many things had gone wrong lately he "just wanted out." Jim was afraid that Harry wanted to kill himself. The RA went to the room with Jim where they discovered that Harry was asleep and appeared to be in no danger as a result of his alcohol consumption. Jim agreed to stay with Harry until the next day when the RA returned and the three of them discussed the situation. Harry did not deny that he was feeling depressed about his girlfriend, his parents pending divorce and financial problems. He admitted that he had been drinking more than usual and not eating or sleeping regularly. His grades were beginning to suffer. In fact, he hadn't been attending all of his classes which was new for him. When asked about his remark about "wanting out" Harry also admitted that he sometimes thought about killing himself as a solution to his problems—but he also said he did not really want to die and did not have any intention of harming himself in spite of feeling pretty miserable and scared about failing out of college. The RA suggested that it might be helpful for Harry to talk to one of the counselors at the Counseling Center so that he could look for some new options that would help with his academic and personal difficulties. Although Harry was at first reluctant to agree to go, he was reassured by the RA's explanation of the services as confidential and available to all students no matter what their concerns. Harry began to understand that using the college counseling center did not mean he was "crazy" and together the RA and Harry called to schedule an appointment with a counselor. Upon leaving Harry's room the RA immediately went to talk to his supervisor. Although his supervisor assured him he had handled the situation well, the RA continued to feel anxious. Not only was he feeling overwhelmed with the responsibilities of his residence hall position but he was afraid that he would not pass his Chemistry test. It didn't take much encouragement from the supervisor to get the RA to agree to go talk to someone at the Counseling Center! Although the RA had always thought of himself as someone who "had it all together" he also remembered some of the things he was told during his RA Training Class. Staff members from the Counseling Center talked about the stresses of their jobs and the importance of seeking help for themselves when dealing with difficult situations such as suicide intervention.

CASE II

On a large urban campus a faculty member has noticed that one of the students in her 9:00 section of English 101 has been either late or absent from class with increasing frequency. She observed that the student—a woman who appears to be around 30 years old and who probably is enrolled part-time—appears to be tired with dark circles evident under her eyes. The faculty member is considering asking the woman if anything is wrong and offering some suggestions to make up missed assignments. However, she is uncertain if that is her role and is also somewhat unsure of how to approach the discussion with the student. The faculty member is aware of the Student Counseling and Consultation Center on campus and decides to call to talk over the situation with one of the counselors at the center. She receives advice on how to discuss her concerns with the student, how to make a referral to the Counseling Center or some other service if needed and also receives support and encouragement for her personal attention to students. As a result of the faculty member's intervention the student was referred to a professional counselor to address the fact that her husband had become quite angry at the woman's return to school and had begun to physically abuse her.

INTRODUCTION

Counseling services have played an important role on college and university campuses for over 50 years. Since the early 1970s there has been an increase in the many roles and functions that counseling services have assumed in higher education (Garni, et al., 1982) and as Leona Tyler has summarized, "counseling centers are no longer regarded as interesting innovations but as indispensable parts of the administrative structure" (1969, p. 3).

The purpose of a counseling center is to assist students to define and accomplish personal and academic goals which are congruent with the overall mission statement of the university (Stimpson, 1986). The activities of a counseling center can be seen as serving five broad institutional goals: (1) a counseling center makes a distinct contribution to the quality of life of the entire institution; (2) a counseling center assesses and responds to developmental needs of students and faculty; (3) counselors contribute to mental health by working with people who have psychological difficulties which interfere with satisfaction and academic pursuits; (4) a counseling center provides campus consultation for a variety of situations; and (5) counseling centers are involved in a variety of activities designed to encourage student retention (The Counseling Center, 1984).

Although the "counseling role" is one that is inherent in all student affairs and historically has been the basis for work in student personnel (Betz, 1980; Hedahl, 1978), some students have complex problems which may be highly personal so that help in one or two obvious areas is not sufficient (Demos & Swan, 1970). Counseling centers are unique in that they do not have a functional specialty, such as Financial Aid, and a holistic assessment of both the student and the situation may be made. Staff are trained in counseling and psychology with specialized knowledge of the psychological characteristics and development of college students. While specialists in the assessment of and intervention with both normal and abnormal human development, counseling services usually maintain a "generalist" perspective. Generalist refers to the diversity of the approaches and the issues addressed in the counseling process (Demos & Mead, 1983; Demos & Swan, 1970). Most universities expect that a modern counseling center will deal with the broad areas of personal-social, educational and vocational development (Aiken, 1982).

In order to accomplish its mission the goals and professional responsibilities of counseling services include: (1) individual and group counseling for students who may be experiencing psychological or behavioral difficulties; (2) programming focused on the developmental needs of college students; (3) consultative services to the institution to make the environment beneficial to the students (Stimpson, 1986); (4) research and evaluation of services; and (5) involvement in the training of new professionals (Garni, et al., 1982).

The example of the RA who was concerned about a potentially suicidal student illustrates that counseling services have moved beyond a merely remedial role (assisting the student who was depressed; assisting the RA with his test anxiety) to one that includes both preventive and developmental activities (RA training on both suicide prevention and how to combat burnout to be a more successful Resident Advisor). Further, the efforts to maintain the grade point and academic standing of both the depressed student and the Resident Advisor are common examples of the role of the counseling center in student retention.

The report of a faculty member concerned about the woman who had been abused illustrates the consultative role of the counseling center and also gives an example of the increase in problems related to violence which are being seen on college campuses (Crime on campus, 1985; Roark, 1987).

This chapter is divided into three major sections. The first will provide an overview of the historical development of the university and college counseling center with an expanded account of how the goals of the counseling center have changed and broadened to be congruent with the mission and goals described in this introduction. Next the administration and organization of the counseling center will be presented, including financial support, staffing patterns, physical facilities, professional and ethical issues, models of functions, patterns of use by students, types of problems experienced by students, and types of interventions provided by counseling centers. The third and final section will give more specific information concerning the programs and services provided by the contemporary counseling center with a description of and speculation on present and future trends for college and university counseling centers.

HISTORICAL DEVELOPMENT

The Early Years

The earliest college counselors were the college faculty and presidents (Gibson, Mitchell, & Higgins, 1983). A variety of influences led to the need for more specialized "counselors," student personnel workers of the late nineteenth and early twentieth century. Colleges and universities had expanded both in number and in type of institution with the development of land-grant colleges, the elective curriculum and a renewed emphasis on technological and scientific education. An influx of American Ph.D.'s who had been trained in Germany in a more impersonal and intellectualized approach to education reduced the amount of student-faculty interaction. Finally the disproportionate increase of the extracurriculum over the curriculum led to the need for colleges and universities to employ "special staff" who would attend to the development of the total student (Gibson, Mitchell, & Higgins, 1983). The first formal recognition that institutions of higher education had the obligation to provide a specifically designated "counseling service" for students may have been the appointments of a "Chief of Advisors" at Johns Hopkins University in 1889 and of a "Dean of Student Relations" at Harvard in 1890 (Gibson, Mitchell, & Higgins, 1983).

Professionally trained counselors began to appear on a few college campuses after World War I as a result of the development of assessment techniques and other psychological advances (Schneider, 1977). In addition to the development of psychometrics during World War I, two other major influences led to the rise of the counseling profession and to a counseling center specialty area within student personnel work (Berk, 1983; Hedahl, 1978; Tyler, 1969). First, the 1909 publication of Clifford Beers' *A Mind That Found Itself* is cited as the beginning of the Mental Hygiene movement with attention to both prevention and cure of less serious as well as more serious emotional difficulties (Tyler, 1969). The second influence was Frank Parsons whose work in the Boston YMCA after World War I began counseling as an organized service in the public school system (Williamson, 1961, cited in Schneider, 1977). Parsons' 1906 publication of *Choosing a Vocation* proposed a model of counseling which focuses on the need for helping young people to find suitable places in the world of work (Tyler, 1969).

The vocational guidance model and the Mental Hygiene movement, along with the use of psychometrics, were the historical influences on the two essential functions of counseling: to facilitate wise choices and decisions and to promote adjustment or mental health (Tyler, 1969). College and university counseling services began with a major focus on vocational choices and decisions but have expanded to include personal counseling, which includes helping clients' "adjustment to self and others" (Berk, 1983, p. 60).

The University Testing Bureau established in 1932 at the University of Minnesota appears to be the earliest separate unit organized to offer professional educational and vocational guidance (Hedahl, 1978). However, most colleges had no professional counselors on campus until after World War II when the Veterans Administration funded guidance bureaus to monitor the large population of veterans who were attending college with government subsidies. As the numbers of veterans on campus declined, many colleges and universities took over the budgetary and administrative support of what became the forerunners of the modern counseling center. However roles, functions, and standards were very ambiguous (Warnath, 1971).

Heppner and Neal (1983) view the years from 1945 to 1955 as ones of "transition and professionalism." In the early 1950s, counseling center directors began to meet annually to discuss mutual problems and concerns. Some of the growth and development during this period and into the 1960s parallelled changes within the field of counseling psychology (Whitely, 1980, 1984). The phasing out of Veterans Administration support of counseling centers coincided with the development of counseling psychology as a specialty area within the American Psychological Association. If a counseling faculty existed on campus, they typically were involved in the further growth of the counseling center (McKinley, 1980). Both counseling psychology and counseling centers followed a trend away from exclusively vocational guidance to a broad developmental form of "personal" counseling (Berk, 1983, p. 59).

1960-1980

The decade of 1960-1970 was a time of social unrest, "encounter groups" and draft counseling. For college and university counseling centers it was a time of expansion and consolidation (Heppner and Neal, 1983; Lamb, Garni, & Gelwick, 1983). However, the call for universities to be more relevant to social concerns led administrators to ask counseling services to be more relevant to the goals of higher education and to be prepared to do so on lower budgets (Foreman, 1977). From within the profession, Warnath (1971, 1973) called counseling centers to task for practicing in a medical model, the student viewed as "Sick" and "in need of treatment," and serving only a small select group of students. He objected to counselors behaving as private practitioners who focused on individual therapy isolated from the university community (Berk, 1983). As a result, the 1970s was a period of reassessment of the role of counseling centers (Lamb et al., 1983). However, ground work had already begun for constructive change. In 1968 Morrill, Ivey, and Oetting (cited in McKinley, 1980) provided a major stimulus for change in function by proposing that the counseling center become a center for student development which would (1) move out into the campus to create programs to prevent problems; (2) mobilize community resources for mental health; and (3) redefine the counseling center role within a developmental framework (McKinley, 1980). A task force of counseling center directors had developed guidelines for university and college counseling centers (Kirk et al., 1971) which distinguished between "remedial" and "developmental/preventive" services. This distinction among services and the concept of a human development center was given direction by the "cube" (Morrill, Oetting, & Hurst, 1974). This conceptual scheme for organizing the expanding view of the role of counselors on a college campus specified targets (individual, primary group, associational group and institution or community), purposes (remedial, preventive, or developmental), and methods (direct, consultation and training, or media) for intervention on a college campus (McKinley, 1980). A related concept which emerged during the 1970s is that of "campus ecology" which emphasizes the interrelationship between students and their environment (e.g., Aulepp & Delworth, 1976; Conyne, 1983; Conyne et al., 1979; Conyne & Lamb, 1978; WICHE, 1973).

Additional influences toward redesigning the role of counseling services during the seventies were the counseling center directors themselves, external accrediting bodies and professional organization, and legal requirements (Lamb et al., 1983). The annual Director's Conferences have been used to establish guidelines, review accountability issues, develop clearinghouses for the dissemination of innovative counseling programs and to formulate constructive responses to the legitimate challenges facing counseling centers. External accrediting bodies (e.g., International Association of Counseling Services, American Psychological Association) have helped to establish, maintain, and enhance standards within counseling centers (Fretz & Mills, 1980). Professional organizations such as the Association of Counseling Center Training Agencies and the American College Personnel Association (ACPA) also encourage continual assessment of the role and functions of the counseling center. Finally, legal requirements for licensing or certification of psychologists and counselors affected the changing role of counseling centers in the 1970s. As services expanded and issues of consumer rights became more visable counseling centers also increased their attention to the avoidance of malpractice claims.

Present

By 1980, counseling centers were functioning in broader and more comprehensive roles with constricted budgets. Preventive and outreach programs had increased but the most frequent intervention schema involved direct, remedial, and individual approaches (Heppner & Neal, 1983). An increasingly heterogeneous group of students required the development of programs to meet the needs of diverse populations.

The accepted mission and goals of the counseling center of the 1980s are described in the introduction to this chapter. An illustration of possible controversies concerning the functions of a modern counseling center is the comparison of selected sections of two sets of "general principles for university counseling centers." Leventhal and Magoon (1979) state that "counseling or psychotherapy in the counseling center is based upon an educational model of behavior rather than a model of disease" (p. 350), "consultation services are of equal importance to counseling/psychotherapeutic services" (p. 360), and "the counseling center implements alternatives to its traditional individual and group services" (p. 362). In a modification of these principles, Demos and Mead (1983) state that "Personal counseling and therapy should be based on a developmental and clinical foundation — that is, counselors should be well-versed in both developmental psychology and diagnosis and assessment procedures. Since a focus on any single theoretical background is too narrow, professional staff should be diverse in their training and background. Consultation services are important, but they are supplementary to counseling services, which are the primary function of the center" (p. 6). Demos and Mead (1983) clearly state that "A direct contact of students and counselors in counseling interactions, individual or group, is the major function of the psychological counseling center" (p. 7).

ADMINISTRATION AND ORGANIZATION

Financial Support

Most counseling centers are funded by the institution (Magoon, 1984) with some receiving financial support through student fees (Gallagher, 1986). A very small percentage of centers charge students for counseling but an increasing number charge if faculty, alumni, or community members use the services (Gallagher, 1986). Nearly two-thirds of the centers that provide testing services generate some income through those services (Weissberg, 1987).

Administration

A major variable in the administration and organization of a counseling center is the size of the institution with which it is affiliated. Among colleges and universities conferring the bachelor's degree, the larger the institution the more likely there will be a counseling facility (Oetting, Ivey, & Weigel, 1970), with 96 percent of institutions of over 10,000 and approximately 55 percent of those with enrollments of less than 2,000 reporting the existence of a counseling center. In a more recent survey of four-year colleges with enrollments of less than 5,000, similar characteristics were reported, with an overall increase in the number of colleges reporting a counseling center on campus (Richardson, Seim, Eddy, & Brindley, 1985). Overall, 83 percent reported existence of a center with 73 percent of institutions under 1,000 students and 94 percent of colleges with enrollments of 2,000 to 5,000 reporting organized counseling centers. In one survey of community colleges, more than 85 percent of the responding colleges had organized counseling services (Goodman & Beard, 1976).

Regardless of size, most directors of counseling centers report to the administrative unit of student affairs and frequently to the Chief Student Affairs Officer (Richardson et al., 1985; Oetting et al., 1970). In smaller colleges, the organizational structure is generally less formal (Richardson et al., 1985), the counseling programs more diverse, with multiple roles for the director or other counselors (Oetting et al., 1970). Most community college counseling appears to be administered through the Division of Student Affairs, counselors are likely to serve in a variety of roles and more time is spent in academic advising (Paradise & Long, 1981; Wolf & Aguren, 1978). As an ideal arrangement, Preston (1978) recommends that the director of the center report directly to the president of the university. Although this rarely occurs, his rationale is sound advice:

> The position of the counseling center and its director in the organizational nexus of the university is decisive in determining its effectiveness as a resource for students and as a change agent for the institution.

Its effectiveness will depend on how the administration sees it, how the faculty see it, and how the students see it. These perceptions of the center will determine its resources, its referrals (both their number and their nature), the use made of the counseling center, and its impact in the university community (p. 72).

The counseling center must be seen as administratively neutral and should not be linked to units that are directly involved in making academic, disciplinary, admission or other matriculation decisions (Garni et al., 1982; Stimpson, 1986).

Staffing

In a survey distributed to the 250 individuals who attended the 1978-79 National Directors' Conference, 80 respondents reported that most (90%) counseling centers with a staff of three or more have a director and 18 percent report an assistant or associate director (Aiken, 1982). The majority of counseling center directors hold the doctoral degree, especially in larger institutions (Oetting et al., 1970). The training and credentialing of counseling center directors and staff is driven by various professional standards. Guidelines for Accreditation by the International Association of Counseling Services (IACS) state that the director should have an earned doctorate in counseling psychology, clinical psychology, or other related discipline and be eligible for state licensure. Equivalency criteria are recommended for nondoctorate directors (Garni et al., 1982). Those centers with a pre-doctoral internship training program must have a Training Director and many larger centers delegate responsibilities to Directors of Clinical Services, Evaluation & Research, Career Services, Consultation or Programming.

The change in name of Commission VII of ACPA from "Counseling" to "Counseling and Psychological Services" in 1986 reflects the fact that many college counseling centers provide services which are psychological in nature. Thus, the staff providing the services must be trained and credentialed as psychologists or be appropriately supervised by psychologists (American Psychological Association, 1977, 1981b, 1987).

In 1985, approximately 50 percent of counseling centers in four-year institutions of less than 5,000 had no full time doctoral level staff (Richardson et al., 1985). In 1965 only 19 percent of such centers had doctoral level staff (Oetting et al., 1970) suggesting a trend toward higher degrees for staff in these centers.

Within larger centers the specialty and level of training among staff ranges from paraprofessional through doctorate with most of the latter being Ph.D. rather than Ed.D. and Counseling Psychology, followed by Clinical Psychology, the most frequent specialty area at that level (Oetting, et al., 1970; Aiken, 1982). Large ($>$10,000) centers report a median full-time-equivalent professional staff at 8.6 with 5 being the median number of doctoral level staff (Magoon, 1984). Small centers ($<$10,000) report a median of 3.7 total staff and 2 doctoral.

About half of the counseling centers with a staff of three or more employ at least one social worker and one psychiatrist. Those which do have a psychiatrist on the staff are likely to have more than one. More than half of these counseling centers employ a psychometrist or test officer and about half have a statistician, programmer, or analyst (Aiken, 1982). In a survey of 180 community and junior colleges there were 116 questionnaires returned, the majority from public institutions with enrollments between 1,000 and 5,000 (Higgins, 1981). The mean number of professional staff reported was 5.7 with the majority (64.7%) employing two to six professional counselors. Most indicated some staff with at least a master's degree, over one-half had at least one doctoral level staff member and nearly one-fourth reported some staff with only a bachelor's degree.

From his annual national survey of counseling centers, Magoon (1984) reported a median ration of one professional staff member for every 1,909 equivalent full-time students in large universities ($>$10,000) and median ratio of one professional for every 1,172 equivalent full-time students in smaller universities ($<$10,000).

Some counseling center staff hold faculty rank and may have a joint appointment with an academic department such as psychology, counseling psychology or counseling and guidance. There are advantages and disadvantages to these joint appointments, some disadvantages being the time taken from counseling to pursue academic activities, disputes over salaries and conflicts with other student affairs professionals who do not hold faculty rank (Schneider, 1977). However, IACS guidelines (Garni et al., 1982) state that "professional staff members holding an appropriate terminal academic degree or its equivalent should be accorded all the responsibilities, rights, and privileges of other university faculty, including the opportunity to secure academic rank, tenure, and representation on university governing bodies" (p. 119). Also, it is recommended that counseling centers should have close relationships with academic departments for joint programming and use of resources especially in time of tight budgets (Aiken, 1982; L. Douce, personal communication, September 18, 1987).

Support staff should be selected carefully. They play an important role in the students' impressions of the service and must sometimes make some preliminary decisions concerning response to a student request (Garni et al., 1982). In the case of a crisis or an emergency, the receptionist is often the first person to be aware of the situation (Quintana, 1974). Clerical staff must maintain the confidential nature of all records and client contacts.

Physical Facilities

Counseling Centers should be centrally located and readily accessible to all students. Both the reception area and the offices must provide comfort and privacy. There must be lockable storage facilities for records and adequate equipment such as telephones and audio recording equipment. Some centers require additional equipment for training purposes (e.g., observation rooms, video recording facilities). There should be adequate space for testing, groups, and a professional library (Garni et al., 1982; Iwai, Churchill, & Cummings, 1983).

Professional and Ethical Issues

Some of the professional affiliations and their influence on counseling centers have already been mentioned. Others include: Association of University and Counseling Center Directors (for directors of four-year institutions with three or more full-time professional staff); Association of Psychology Internship Centers and Association of Counseling Center Training Agents (for centers providing pre-doctoral internship training); Commission VII (Counseling and Psychological Services) and other Commissions and Task Forces of the ACPA; Division 17 (Counseling) and 12 (Clinical) of the APA; the Council for the Advancement of Standards. Many states have organizations and conferences for all centers in the state or a portion of the state or for the smaller centers. There are also regional conferences such as that of the Big Ten Counseling Centers. Some counseling center staff members are active in their state psychological or college personnel associations.

The professional and legal guidelines of the above organizations affect the functioning of a college counseling center by suggesting or requiring standards for professional practice and by providing a forum for self-evaluation, exchange of ideas and professional development. Recent attention has been given to insure fair treatment of diverse populations by the IACS/AUCCCD Joint Task Force on Equity Statement on Counseling Center services (Carlson et al., 1986) and the Division 17 Principles Concerning the Counseling/Psychotherapy of Women (Fitzgerald & Nutt, 1986).

Counseling Centers must follow the ethical principles of the American Psychological Association, the American Association of Counseling and Development and other equivalent organizations. The welfare of the client is the basis for standards which address the competencies and responsibilities of the counselor. The legal and ethical issue which is most frequently discussed in counseling services is that of confidentiality. In many states there is a legal privileged communication between client and psychologist and there is always an ethical obligation to keep confidential client information, including records. The rare exceptions to this caveat are those situations where someone is potentially harmful to self or others. Even in these dangerous situations protection must be provided in a sensitive manner (American Psychological Association, 1981a). How a counseling center handles issues of confidentiality can greatly impact its reputation and relationships on campus. On the one hand the students must be able to trust that, for example, parents will not be informed of declining grades or an acquaintance rape. On the other hand, parents' phone calls must be handled diplomatically and appropriate permission must be obtained from the client to consult with cooperating services such as the Health Service and Campus Police to help a rape victim.

Models

The model of a counseling center is interrelated to the types of programs and services, to the size of the institution and to the philosophy of the director. Issues include: whether or not there are other counseling, psychological, and psychiatric services on campus or in the community; the relationship between the Health Center and the Counseling Center; the existence of a Placement Center or Career Planning Center and its relationship to the Counseling Center; whether a campus has centralized or decentralized counseling and advising services; whether counseling center staff are viewed as generalists or specialists.

A survey in the 1960s (Oetting et al., 1970) revealed a number of types of counseling centers. The *vocational guidance model* is historically the "original counseling center" and in the 1960s this model was the most prevalent (Oetting et al., 1970). In the vocational guidance model testing and vocational choice counseling are the primary functions. In the 1980s, this type of counseling is more often referred to as career counseling, is more likely to be one of many types of counseling offered in a counseling center and it may be available in settings other than the counseling center, such as a Career Planning and/or Placement Office. Preliminary results of a survey to determine the location of career counseling on campuses in the mid-1980s revealed heterogeneous models of Career Centers with overlapping services among agencies on campus (T.M. Magoon, personal communication, September 16, 1987). For example, on some campuses all career counseling is done through the Placement Office and in other locations there is very little career counseling provided in the Placement Office.

The **personnel services model** is a counseling service that functions as an entire personnel service (e.g., including such responsibilities as financial aids and disciplinary referrals) and it is usually found only in smaller schools (Oetting et al., 1970). Current practice recommends that the counseling service not be linked to units involved in disciplinary, admission, or other matriculation decisions (Garni et al., 1982; Stimpson, 1986).

Another infrequent model which was found also had the disadvantage of close ties to administrative decisions. The **academic affairs model** is a counseling service which functions almost entirely in an academic role with counselors being assigned to each student for academic and other advisement (Oetting et al., 1970).

The **psychotherapy model** considers the treatment of emotional problems as its primary function. There is little vocational guidance and the focus is on long-term individual therapy for a few students (Oetting et al., 1970).

The **training model** counseling center is probably a training clinic for an academic department in psychology or education. Most of the clients are seen by students under this model (Oetting et al., 1970).

The **consultation model** counseling center serves as mental health consultant to the campus and has a strong emphasis on prevention of problems before they occur (Oetting et al., 1970).

The **research model** was found in one center which for a time devoted most of its efforts toward data collection (Oetting et al., 1970).

The **traditional counseling model** was found among those centers whose directors had formed the original counseling center directors' organization. The service functions as a separate campus agency and provides vocational counseling, short-term treatment of emotional problems and some longer term counseling. Service to clients is the primary orientation, although some intern and practicum training experiences exist (Oetting et al., 1970).

Research subsequent to the Oetting et al. survey frequently refers to their models. Gelso, Birk, Utz, and Silver (1977) found the "traditional model" was evaluated most positively by counselors, resident assistants, faculty, students, and "administrators" while student personnel administrators preferred a "consultant" model. Others have recommended the consultant role (Bosmajian & Mattson, 1980) or criticized it (Cannon, 1982).

Student Development Center

In reality it is difficult to depict counseling center roles accurately because of the diversity among centers, particularly between training and service-only centers (Heppner & Neal, 1983). Some generalizations can be made, however. There is an increase in emphasis on personal counseling, and continuation of vocational counseling—now usually called career counseling. Prevention, outreach, training, and environmental design programs continue to increase, with a wide variety of programs offered (Heppner & Neal, 1983). Staff members are involved in a diversity of tasks and frequently report having to deal with more seriously disturbed clients and crisis-oriented situations (Robbins, May, & Corazzini, 1985). Clearly, counseling centers have assumed multiple roles and function with demonstrated progress toward a model of a student development center (Harmon & Baron, 1982; Morrill et al., 1968; Morrill et al., 1974).

Patterns of Use

Research on patterns of use indicate that between 10 percent and 25 percent of students utilize the Counseling Center (Heppner & Neal, 1983). Earlier reports indicated that students were more likely to come to the center for career planning, negotiating the system and coping with financial and academic concerns (Carney, Savitz, & Weiskott, 1979). More recently students view the counseling center as an appropriate place to discuss personal and interpersonal concerns (Altmaier & Rapaport, 1984; Heppner & Neal, 1983; Tryon, 1980). The essential components of a student seeking counseling include the availability of the service, the reason the student needs the service and the availability of alternative resources (Altmaier & Rapaport, 1984). Lack of information and concerns about confidentiality may keep students away from counseling centers (Tryon, 1980). Since many seek counseling on the recommendation of another (Altmaier & Rapaport, 1984), it is extremely important that all members of the college/university community be informed about the center and referral procedures.

Types of Problems

The types of problems which students experience and bring to a counseling center may vary with year in school, age, gender, academic major, or race. The fact that the college years are stressful is well documented (e.g., Bloom, 1975). Many of the concerns seen in a counseling center are related to the expected developmental tasks of the college student: (1) adjusting to a new environment; (2) choosing a major and planning for a future career; (3) establishing an identity separate from parents; (4) learning time management and study skills appropriate to higher education; (5) establishing intimate relations; (6) exploring sexual identity; and (7) sexuality and values clarification. Unexpected crisis events also happen to college students, and professional staff at the counseling center are available to attempt to deal with the immediate concern and to promote growth as a result of the experience. Examples include: (1) death or suicide of a family member or friend; (2) chronic illness in a family member, friend or self (AIDS is a particularly devastating current example; however, some college students must deal with a parent who is terminally ill with cancer or chronically ill with diseases such as multiple sclerosis); (3) parents' divorce and remarriage; (4) rape; (5) legal problems with possible pending jail terms; (6) severe loss of self esteem which is frequently related to loss of academic standing or loss of loved one resulting in a suicide attempt; and (7) disability from a car accident. Finally, there are more chronic problems which some students bring with them to college: (1) a history of repeated sexual, physical, or emotional abuse; (2) an inherited biochemical imbalance which results in major depression or hallucination if not treated with the proper medication; (3) chemical dependency in self or family members; (4) learning disabilities; and (5) eating disorders which result in either self-starvation or an habitual pattern of overeating followed by self-induced vomiting or laxative abuse.

Intervention: Direct, Indirect, Environmental

For these concerns the main "target of intervention" (Morrill, Oetting, & Hurst, 1974) frequently is the individual. However, counseling center staff may also consult with faculty, staff, or other students for any of these problems. A frequent example is a request for consultation from the instructor of a course which requires a personal journal or papers which may contain information about problems in the student's life. Some problems such as depression, substance abuse, eating disorders, and victims of abuse need the intervention of a caring other to encourage help-seeking behavior. The counseling center can help another plan for such an intervention. Another example of indicted service is when professional staff are called to a residence hall to meet with students when a crisis has occurred, a death, or a rape. There are also educational programs designed to prevent problems such as substance abuse, acquaintance rape, and test anxiety.

Finally, some counseling centers attempt to provide proactive services to the campus environment by assessing areas of stress and difficulty and designing interventions which will benefit the entire campus. A student satisfaction study by the Directors of the Counseling and Career Development Center was the beginning of this ecological perspective within Student Affairs at Southern Illinois University (Coffman & Paratore, 1987). A more traditional manner in which counseling services staff serve the campus is involvement in college and university-wide action-oriented committees such as Retention, Non-traditional Student Advisory Board, Affirmative Action, and Career Network.

Many counseling center staff are involved in service to the profession through contributions to the professional literature and organizations. One notable example is the Counseling Center Data Bank, a survey of information conducted and disseminated annually by Dr. Tom Magoon at the University of Maryland.

PROGRAMS AND SERVICES

The programs and services offered will depend upon the size and type of institution, the model of the center, the orientation of the director, and other services offered elsewhere on campus. For example, some small liberal arts colleges have a high staff to student ratio and can provide more in-depth long-term individual counseling and therapy. This emphasis is evident in the Journal of College Student Psychotherapy which was begun by the director of Swarthmore College Psychological Services in 1986. Some other examples of types of counseling centers can be found in a description of the formation of a counseling center emphasizing health rather than illness at Brandeis University (Hanfmann, 1978), the merger of a traditional counseling center with a traditional student health center at Indiana University (Foster, 1982) and the development of a multidisciplinary service at Duke (Talley & Rockwell, 1985).

An observation of services offered by counseling centers if provided by a vice president of student affairs:

> . . . the predominant pattern in contemporary counseling centers is one of maintaining the focus on "outreach" and similar interventions. That philosophical commitment is subject to erosion when the alligators are snapping. It **is** difficult to sustain the more abstract — if the more productive — focus when one is fretting over a couple of potential suicides and assorted other clients who are maintaining only marginal control (Canon, 1982, p. 58).

The services which are offered in a college or university counseling center can be illustrated from a day in the life of a counseling center staff member. An average day might consist of: (1) three individual counseling sessions (one student being seen for the third and final time concerning his decision to change his major from vocal performance to music education; a non-traditional student who is feeling overwhelmed by the environment of the university; the eighth session with a socially withdrawn freshman who has finally admitted to the counselor that she was sexually abused by her father); (2) one intake interview with an International Student who was referred by the Office of International Programs because he seemed excessively depressed over his difficulties with grades; (3) one telephone consult with a coach concerning the possibility that a student athlete might be using drugs; (4) one call from a parent worried that her daughter has bulimia and requesting information on referral sources; (5) an hour spent reviewing audio tapes of a group counseling session led by a graduate student supervisee; (6) a brief look at the mail which contains an anxiously-awaited report from a neurologist concerning a student who experiences episodes of amnesia, a journal reporting recent counseling research, advertisements for workshops and a large bill for professional liability insurance; (7) the time allotted to prepare for tomorrow's presentation at the Off Campus Student Center on stress management was interrupted by the need to serve as back-up consultant to another staff member who was working with a student who appeared to be seriously suicidal; (8) hospitalization was arranged for this student just in time to attend a meeting with Residence Hall Directors to plan for some para-professional staff training.

In a survey of four-year public institutions, it was found that over half of the counselors' time was spent on vocational, education, and personal counseling (Lewing & Cowger, 1982). Overall, among the types of counseling, the greatest amount of time (27%) was spent on personal counseling (marital, parental, developmental, and interpersonal relationship problems); 16.5 percent of the time was spent on academic and educational counseling (selecting major and courses; developing study habits); 13 percent on vocational counseling (providing literature, familiarizing with vocational opportunities); 13 percent on administrative duties (preparing interviews and reports, updating files, staff meetings, staff and faculty contacts, correspondence); 8 percent on administration and interpretation of tests; 7 percent on teaching; 6 percent on professional development; 6 percent on supervision and training (including outreach programs); and 3 percent on research. Larger (greater than 15,000) institutions reported smaller percentages of academic counseling, educational counseling and testing, and larger percentages of supervision, training, and research than the smaller colleges.

Most colleges and universities counseling centers offer counseling and therapy groups, structured groups, workshops and alternative treatment modes (Magoon, 1985). In a survey of 115 large (over 10,000, mostly four-year public universities) and 140 small (less than 10,000; about half public and half private four-year colleges and universities) college and university counseling centers the following median numbers of clients/participants/consultees were served with the first number referring to the large institutions and the second to the small institutions; 400 and 150 for vocational-educational, 654 and 262 for emotional-social, 60 and 35 for reading and study skills, and 382 and 190 in structured groups and alternative treatment modes (Magoon, 1984).

The Counseling Centers Annual Data Bank collects information on Innovative or Novel Functions Performed by counseling centers. Some examples include: Hispanic Mentoring Program at Boston College, program for parents during freshmen pre-registration at Bowling Green State University, conferences on domestic violence at California State University-Fresno, peer career counselors at Denison University, Coping with College, a series of weekly articles in the student newspapers at

Illinois State University, an experimental course for students on academic probation at Kent State. Many counseling centers report groups or structured workshops focused on rape or assault victims, adult children of alcoholics, those involved with alcohol or drug related disciplinary offenses and for those with eating disorders (Magoon, 1985).

Some counseling centers develop formalized consultation programs as a means to provide more outreach services to the campus (e.g., Domke, Winkelpleck, & Westefeld, 1980; Rademacher, May, & Throckmorton, 1980).

Other innovative approaches which have been used to reach large numbers of students are self-help brochures (Allen & Sipich, 1987), self-help tapes (Chiauzzi & Carroll, 1982; Thurman, Baron, & Klein, 1979), peer counseling (D'Andrea, 1987; Delworth, 1978; Giddan & Austin, 1982), and the use of computers (Ekstrom & Johnson, 1984; Wagman & Kerber, 1980). The latter are most frequently used as career guidance and information systems (e.g., Heppner & Johnston, 1985). Some counseling centers such as the Counseling and Career Development Center at Bowling Green State University are involved in the teaching of undergraduate courses in career and life planning and have a career resource library available for student use.

Although there has been a decrease in the number of counseling centers providing national (e.g., GRE, SAT) and university-wide (e.g., orientation testing, placement and proficiency tests) testing, 40 to 50 percent of those centers responding to a survey are providing such non-counseling-related testing services (Weissberg, 1987).

An important program, especially among larger counseling centers, is that of training. In addition to the training of paraprofessionals many centers are involved in pre-professional training programs. These may include practicum placement for M.A. and Ph.D. graduate students in fields such as Counseling Psychology, Clinical Psychology, Counseling and Guidance and College Student Personnel. A more formal and structured training program exists in centers providing a pre-doctoral internship in professional psychology, especially if the training program is approved by the American Psychological Association. Provision of a quality training program within an agency that is primarily service-oriented is time-consuming but provides a variety of rewards: contribution to the development of new professionals and the profession, fresh insight gained from students of academic programs throughout the country, national recognition, the enriching experience of supervision for senior staff and the provision of quality service at relatively low cost

(Holloway & Roehlke, 1987).

An important training component of any counseling center is the professional development of the entire staff. According to IACS (Garni et al., 1982), a continuous in-service training program is required along with opportunities for staff members to attend local, state, and national seminars, workshops, and professional meetings.

PRESENT AND FUTURE TRENDS

There is disagreement over whether there are data to support the purported increase in "more serious" cases recently seen in counseling centers (Magoon, Cook, Jones, & Jenks, 1987). However, there is some consensus concerning current relevant problems on the college and university campus which are reflected in the work of the counseling services: the debate over mandatory withdrawal of students with mental disorders (Pavela, G., 1983-83; 1985); the issue of how or if disciplinary referrals for counseling should be handled; the increased referrals for victims of crime and other abuse; issues related to AIDS (support for those dealing with death and dying, counseling for those who may have the virus, informed consent for testing, teaching safe sex); the need for counseling for those from dysfunctional families (adult children of alcoholics, traumatically blended families, "latch-key kids"); issues of retention; the continuing number of women and increasing number of men with eating disorders; and the needs to respond to those with learning disabilities (L. Douce, personal communication, September 18, 1987; Jenks, 1986; Magoon et al., 1987; Pascale, Hattauer, Sommers, Wilson, & Evans, 1987).

Other predictions for the future include: an increased number of requests for special needs; an increase in part-time specialists; an increase in staff members training in clinical psychology; more joint appointments with academic departments such as counseling and psychology; an increase in on-campus helping agencies (e.g., career planning centers) resulting in "turf issues;" an increase in the number of directors who are women or minorities; and an increase in credentialism (Magoon, 1987). These trends are not viewed as major changes but counseling centers are cautioned to maintain their diversity of services, to remain generalists, to evaluate the effectiveness of services and to attempt to maintain the personal attention to students which is available at college and university counseling centers.

REFERENCES

Aiken, J. (1982). Shifting priorities: College counseling centers in the eighties. *NASPA Journal, 19,* 15-22.

Allen, D.R., & Sipich, J.F. (1987). Developing a self-help brochure series: Costs and benefits. *Journal of Counseling and Development, 65,* 257-258.

Altmaier, E.M., & Rapaport, R.J. (1984). An examination of student use of a counseling service. *Journal of College Student Personnel, 25,* 453-458.

American Psychological Association. (1977). Standards for providers of psychological services. *American Psychologist, 32,* 495-505.

American Psychological Association. (1981a). Ethical principles of psychologists. *American Psychologist, 36,* 633-638.

American Psychological Association. (1981b). Specialty guidelines for the delivery of services by clinical (counseling, industrial/organizational, and school) psychologists. *American Psychologist, 36,* 639-681.

American Psychological Association. (1987). General guidelines for providers of psychological services. *American Psychologist, 42,* 712-723.

Aulepp, L., & Delworth, U. (1976). *Training manual for an ecosystem model: Assessing and designing campus environments.* Boulder, CO: Western Interstate Commission for Higher Education.

Berk, S.E. (1983). Origins and historical development of university and college counseling. In P.J. Gallagher & G.D. Demos (Eds.), *Handbook of counseling in higher education* (pp. 50-71). New York: Praeger.

Betz, E. (1980). The counselor role. In U. Delworth & G.R. Hanson (Eds.), *Student services: A handbook for the profession* (pp. 175-190). San Francisco: Jossey-Bass.

Bloom, B.L. (Ed.). (1975). *Psychological stress in the campus community: Theory, research, and action. Community Psychology Series, Vol. 3, American Psychological Association, Division 37.* New York: Behavioral Publications.

Bosmajian, C.P., & Mattson, R.E. (1980). A controlled study of variables related to counseling center use. *Journal of Counseling Psychology, 27,* 510-519.

Canon, H.J. (1982). The future of college and university counseling centers: One vice president's view. *Counseling Psychologist, 10,* 57-61.

Carlson, N., Southwick, R., Farsleff, L., Gelwick, B.P., Gallagher, R., Hughes, M., & Lacy, O.W. (1986). IACS/AUCCCD Joint Task Force on Equity Statement on Counseling Center Services. *Proceedings of 35th Annual Conference of the Association of University and College Counseling Center Directors* (pp. 1-2). San Diego, CA.

Carney, C.G., Savitz, C.J., & Weiskott, G.N. (1979). Students' evaluations of a university counseling center and their intentions to use its programs. *Journal of Counseling Psychology, 26,* 242-249.

Chiauzzi, E., & Carroll, B.P. (1982). Self-help tapes as an adjunct to hotline counseling services: A preliminary analysis. *Journal of College Student Personnel, 23,* 25-28.

Coffman, J., & Paratore, J. (1987). Operationalizing the ecological perspective: The Southern Illinois University experience. *The Campus Ecologist, 5,* 1-2.

Conyne, R.K. (1983). Campus environmental design for counseling centers. *Journal of College Student Personnel, 24,* 433-437.

Conyne, R.K., Banning, J.H., Clack, R.J., Corazzini, J.G., Huebner, L.A., Keating,

L.A., & Wrenn, R.L. (1979). The campus environment as client: A new direction for college counselors. *Journal of College Student Personnel, 20,* 437-442.

Conyne, R.K., & Lamb, D.H. (1978). A role for the professional psychologist in campus environmental change. *Professional psychology, 9,* 301-307.

Crime on campus: Is violence growing? (1985, March 11). *National On Campus Report, 13,* p. 2-5.

D'Andrea, V.J. (1987). Peer counseling in colleges and universities. A developmental viewpoint. *Journal of College Student Psychotherapy, 1,* 39-55.

Delworth, U. (Ed.). (1978). *New directions for student services: Training competent staff.* San Francisco: Jossey-Bass.

Demos, G.D., & Mead, T.M. (1983). The psychological counseling center: Models and functions. In P.J. Gallagher & G.D. Demos (Eds.), *Handbook of counseling in higher education* (pp. 1-22). New York: Praeger.

Demos, G.D., & Swan, R.J. (1970). The psychological counseling center—A point of view. In P.J. Gallagher & G.D. Demos (Eds.), *The counseling center in higher education* (pp. 3-11). Springfield, IL: Charles C Thomas.

Domke, J.A., Winkelpleck, J.M., & Westefeld, J. (1980). Consultation and outreach: Implementation at a university counseling center. *Journal of College Student Personnel, 21,* 211-214.

Ekstrom, R., & Johnson, C. (Eds.). (1984). Computers in counseling and development (Special issues). *Journal of Counseling and Development, 63* (3).

Fisher, K. (1987, October). National conference provides push to accredit postdoctoral interns. *APA Monitor,* pp. 36-37.

Fitzgerald, L.F., & Nutt, R. (1986). The Division 17 principles concerning the counseling/psychotherapy of women: Rationale and implementation. *The Counseling Psychologist, 14,* 180-216.

Foreman, M.E. (1977). The changing scene in higher education and the identity of counseling psychology. *Counseling Psychologist, 7,* 45-48.

Foster, T.V. (1982). Merger 1980: The organizational integration of college mental health services. *Journal of the American College Health Association, 30,* 171-174.

Fretz, B.R., & Mills, D.H. (1980). *Licensing and certification of psychologists and counselors: A guide to current policies, procedures, and legislation.* San Francisco: Jossey-Bass.

Gallagher, R.P. (1986). Urban/non-urban interest group. *Proceedings of 35th Annual Conference of the Association of University and College Counseling Center Directors* (pp. 17-19). San Diego, CA.

Garni, K.F., Gelwick, B.P., Lamb, D.H., McKinley, D.L., Schoenberg, B.M., Simono, R.B., Smith, J.E., Wierson, P.W., & Wrenn, R.L. (1982). Accreditation guidelines for university and college counseling services. *Personnel and Guidance Journal, 61,* 116-121.

Gelso, C.J., Birk, J.M., Utz, P.W., & Silver, A.E. (1977). A multigroup evaluation of the models and functions of university counseling centers. *Journal of Counseling Psychology, 24,* 338-348.

Gibson, R.L., Mitchell, M.H., & Higgins, R.E. (1983). *Development and management of counseling programs and guidance services.* New York: MacMillan.

Giddan, N.S., & Austin, M. (Eds.). (1982). *Peer counseling and self-help groups on campus.* Springfield, IL: Charles C Thomas.

Goodman, L.H., & Beard, R.L. (1976). An analysis of reported counseling services in selected public community colleges in the Southeastern United States. *Community/Junior College Research Quarterly, 1,* 81-90.

Hanfmann, E. (1978). *Effective therapy for college students: Alternatives to traditional counseling.* San Francisco: Jossey-Bass.

Harmon, F.M., & Baron, A. (1982). A student-focused model for the development of counseling services. *Personnel and Guidance Journal, 60,* 290-293.

Hedahl, B.M. (1978). The professionalization of change agents: Growth and development of counseling centers as institutions. In B.M. Schoenberg (Ed.), *A handbook and guide for the college and university counseling center* (pp. 24-39). Westport, CT: Greenwood.

Heppner, M.J., & Johnston, J.A. (1985). Computerized career guidance and information systems: Guidelines for selection. *Journal of College Student Personnel, 26,* 156-163.

Heppner, P.P., & Neal, G.W. (1983). Holding up the mirror: Research on the roles and functions of counseling centers in higher education. *Counseling Psychologist, 11,* 81-98.

Holloway, E.L., & Roehlke, H.J. (1987). Internship: The applied training of a counseling psychologist. *The Counseling Psychologist, 15,* 205-260.

Higgins, E.B. (1981). Community college counseling centers: Structure and focus. *Community College Review, 9,* 18-23.

Iwai, S.I., Churchill, W.D., & Cummings, L.T. (1983). The physical characteristics of college and university counseling services. *Journal of College Student Personnel, 24,* 55-60.

Jenks, S. (1986). Services for learning disabled students. Report to the Accountability Task Force. *Proceedings of 35th Annual Conference of the Association of University and College Counseling Center Directors,* (pp. 3-5). San Diego, CA.

Kirk, B.A., Johnson, A.P., Redfield, J.E., Free, J.E., Michel, J., Roston, R.A., & Warman, R.E. (1971). Guidelines for university and college counseling services. *American Psychologist, 26,* 585-589.

Lamb, D.H., Garni, K.F., & Gelwick, B.P. (1983). A historical overview of university counseling centers: Changing functions and emerging trends. Unpublished manuscript.

Lewing, R.L., & Cowger, E.L. (1982). Time spent on college counselor functions. *Journal of College Student Personnel, 23,* 41-48.

Magoon, T.M. (1984). College and university counseling centers data bank: Analysis by enrollment. Unpublished manuscript. University of Maryland, College Park.

Magoon, T.M. (1985). College and university counseling centers data bank. Unpublished manuscript, University of Maryland, College Park.

Magoon, T. (1987, October). *Future trends in counseling centers.* Paper presented at the 36th Annual Conference of University and College Counseling Center Directors, Rockport, ME.

Magoon, T., Cook, T., Jones, B., & Jenks, S. (1987, October). *Future trends in counseling centers.* Paper presented at the 36th Annual Conference of University and College Counseling Center Directors, Rockport, ME.

McKinley, D. (1980). Counseling. In W.H. Morrill, J.C. Hurst, with E.R. Oetting and Others, *Dimensions of intervention for student development*. New York: Wiley.

Morrill, W.H., Oetting, E.R., & Hurst, J.C. (1974). Dimensions of counselor functioning. *Personnel and Guidance Journal, 52,* 354-359.

Oetting, E.R., Ivey, A.E., & Weigel, R.G. (1970). The college and university counseling center. *Student Personnel Series No. 11.* Washington, D.C.: American College Personnel Association.

Paradise, L.V., & Long, T.J. (1981). *Counseling in the community college.* New York: Praeger.

Pascale, J., Hattauer, E., Sommers, L., Wilson, W., & Evans, M. (1987, October). *Mandatory counseling.* Paper presented at the 36th Annual Conference of University and College Counseling Center Directors, Rockport, ME.

Pavela, G. (1982-83). Therapeutic paternalism and the misuse of mandatory psychiatric withdrawals on campus. *The Journal of College and University Law, 9,* 101-147.

Pavela, G. (1985). *The dismissal of students with mental disorders: Legal issues, policy considerations and alternative responses.* The Higher Education Administration Series. College Administration Publications, Inc., P.O. Box 8492, Asheville, NC 28814.

Preston, C.F. (1978). The place of counseling in the university organization. In B.M. Schoenberg (Ed.). *A handbook and guide for the college and university counseling center.* Westport, CT: Greenwood.

Quintana, J.G. (1974). Counseling center receptionist: Where client contact begins. *Journal of College Student Personnel, 15,* 439-441.

Rademacher, B.G., May, R.J., & Throckmorton, R. Consultation as a change strategy in student personnel divisions. *NASPA Journal, 17,* 46-51.

Richardson, B.K., Seim, D., Eddy, J.P., & Brindley, M. (1985). Delivery of counseling and psychological services in small colleges: A national study. *Journal of College Student Personnel, 26,* 508-512.

Roark, M.L. (1987). Preventing violence on college campuses. *Journal of counseling and development, 65,* 367-371.

Robbins, S.B., May, T.M., & Corazzini, J.G. (1985). Perceptions of client needs and counseling center staff roles and functions. *Journal of Counseling Psychology, 32,* 641-644.

Schneider, L.D. (1977). Counseling. In W.T. Packwood (Ed.), *College student personnel services* (pp. 340-367). Springfield, IL: Charles C Thomas.

Stimpson, R. (Ed.). (1986, Summer). CAS standards and guidelines for student services/development programs (Special Edition). *ACPA Developments.*

Talley, J.E., & Rockwell, W.J.K. (Eds.). (1985). Counseling and psychotherapy services for university students. Springfield, IL: Charles C Thomas.

The counseling center: Its role and function in higher education. (1984, October). *Commission VII Newsletter,* p. 3.

Thurman, C.W., Baron, A., & Klein, R.L. (1979). Self-help tapes in a telephone counseling service: A three-year analysis. *Journal of College Student Personnel, 20,* 546-550.

Tryon, G.S. (1980). A review of the literature concerning perceptions of and preferences for counseling center services. *Journal of College Student Personnel, 21,* 304-311.

Tyler, L.E. (1969). *The work of the counselor* (3rd ed.). Englewood Cliffs, NJ: Prentice-Hall, Inc.

Wagman, M., & Kerber, K.W. (1980). PLATO DCS, an interactive computer system for personal counseling: Further development and evaluation. *Journal of Counseling Psychology, 27,* 31-39.

Warnath, C.F. (1971). *New myths and old realities: College counseling in transition.* London: Jossey-Bass.

Warnath, C.F. (1973). *New directions for college counselors: A handbook for redesigning professional roles.* San Francisco: Jossey-Bass.

Weissberg, M. (1987). Testing services in college and university counseling centers. *Journal of Counseling and Development, 65,* 253-256.

Western Interstate Commission for Higher Education. (1973). *The ecosystem model: Designing campus environments.* Boulder, CO: Author.

Whiteley, J.M. (1980). *The history of counseling psychology.* Monterey, CA: Brooks/Cole.

Whiteley, J.M. (Ed.). (1984). Counseling psychology: A historical perspective (Special issue). *The Counseling Psychologist, 12*(1).

Wolf, J.C., & Aguren, C.T. (1978). The counseling center in the community/junior college. In B.M. Schoenberg (Ed.) *A handbook and guide for the college and university counseling center.* Westport, CT: Greenwood Press.

CHAPTER 6

DISCIPLINE

MICHAEL DANNELLS

HISTORY

STUDENT DISCIPLINE is as old as higher education itself, dating back to the nascent University of Paris almost 800 years ago (Ardaiolo, 1983). In the early colonial colleges, the president and the faculty exerted total behavior control over their students as part of the strict moral, ethical, and religious training that, along with the classical curriculum, was the accepted role and mission of the institution. To keep the young, most were in their early to mid-teens, colonial college students under control, extensively detailed codes of behavior and harsh penalties, including public confessions and ridicule, fines, and corporal punishment were employed. The handling of more serious disciplinary matters was shared with the trustees, while the president often delegated less serious offenses to the faculty (Leonard, 1956; Schetlin, 1967; Smith & Kirk, 1971).

The paternalistic and behavior control approach to discipline changed during the Federal period and into the nineteenth century with the rise of the public university, the broadening of the university's aims and objectives, the increasing secularization and pluralism of higher education in general, and increasing enrollments. Punishments became milder with corporal punishment almost disappearing; trustee participation in conduct matters declined; and counseling of student offenders emerged. Later, in the nineteenth century, as the president became more and more occupied with an expanding curriculum, fiscal and administrative matters, and external relations, specialists were chosen from amongst the faculty to deal with non-academic conduct of the students (Leonard, 1956; Schetlin, 1967).

127

In the mid to late 1800s, the introduction of the German university model, with its disregard for all but the intellectual growth of students, coupled with the demands of the Industrial Revolution on the faculty for development of their academic disciplines resulted in a major shift away from rigid behavior control to greater emphasis on self-discipline and self-governance (Brubacher & Rudy, 1968; Durst, 1969; Schetlin, 1967). More humanitarian and individualized methods of discipline were used, and more democratic systems involving student participation developed concurrently with student governments and honor systems. As faculty became increasingly less inclined to monitor the behavior of students, discipline was left more and more to the president, who, in turn, increasingly delegated it to a faculty member chosen for his or her rapport with students (Smith & Kirk, 1971).

By the turn of the century, the first deans of men and women had been appointed, and during the early 1900s such positions were established on most college campuses. These early deans expanded both the philosophy and the programs of discipline in higher education. They were idealistic and optimistic about the kinds of students they could develop. They approached discipline with the ultimate goal of student self-control or self-discipline, and they used more individualized, humanistic, and preventative methods. The concept of the student as a whole began to develop (Durst, 1969), and counseling as a form of corrective action became popular (Fley, 1964).

It is interesting that within our professional history discipline became an unfortunate point of separation between the early deans and the emerging student personnel specialists (Appleton, Briggs, & Rhatigan, 1978; Knock, 1985). While they had many purposes and approaches in common, the "personnel workers tended to view the deans' disciplining of students as antithetical to their developmental efforts" because they regarded the dean's role as a disciplinarian only in the sense of punishment. This view separated the 'punishing' dean from the 'promoting' personnel worker" (Knock, 1985, pp. 32-33). As higher education expanded under the philosophies of meritocracy and egalitarianism, the campus student body became larger and more heterogeneous, resulting in increased disciplinary (as punishment) work for the dean, while the personnel worker "became the specialist in human development" (Knock, p. 33). Thus, the unfortunate schism widened as the dean was perceived as the "bad guy," interested more in control and punishment, while the student personnel worker was viewed more positively as the true promoter of student interests and growth (Appleton et al., 1978).

With the end of World War II and the influx of veterans into colleges and universities, both campus facilities and regulations were tested by the large number of older and more worldly students. Veterans "could not digest the traditional palliatives served up by the dean to justify student conduct regulation and discipline" (Smith & Kirk, 1971, p. 277). A crisis was avoided because the veterans' overriding vocational orientation kept them preoccupied with academics.

Throughout the 1950s and 1960s, disciplinary affairs became less punishment and control oriented, less autocratic and more democratic, and more aimed toward education and rehabilitation. Professionally trained counselors were delegated more responsibility and disciplinary hearing boards composed of both staff and students were established (Sims, 1971). The 1960s and 1970s were characterized by increased student input into disciplinary codes and processes, broadened legal and educational conceptions of students' rights and responsibilities, and the introduction of due process safeguards in the hearing of misconduct cases. These developments may be attributed to several factors: older students, the lowered age of majority, an increasingly permissive society, the civil rights movement, the realization of the power of student activism and disruption on many campuses (in the 1960s and early 1970s), and court intervention in the disciplinary process (Dannells, 1977).

It was this court intervention coupled with genuine concern for students' constitutional rights which led many colleges and universities in the 1960s to establish formal, legalistic "judicial systems" for the adjudication of misconduct and the determination of appropriate sanctions. This movement brought with it the challenge and concern that such adversarial systems, borrowed from our system of criminal justice, focused primarily on the mechanism of the disciplinary process to the detriment of the educative purpose (Dannells, 1978). Recent trends in the literature and in the practice of disciplinary affairs suggest a renewed and continuing interest in the reintegration of the concept and goals of student development within the framework of campus judicial systems designed to protect the legal rights of students and to educate all students involved in the process (Greenleaf, 1978; Ardaiolo, 1983; and see in general Caruso & Travelstead, 1987). The fear of litigation and the overzealous adoption of criminal-like proceedings seems to be fading in favor of a balanced approach designed to ensure fairness *and* learning.

ISSUES IN DISCIPLINE

This section could easily be titled "The Issue *of* Discipline," for probably no other area in student services has engendered so much debate, disagreement, and dissension (Fley, 1964). As Appleton et al. (1978) put it, "the subject of discipline has been one of the most pervasive and painful topics in the history of student personnel administration" (p. 21).

Discipline raises fundamental questions about the purposes of higher education, the role of student personnel work within it, and our view of students. The pain associated with this process may result from the inevitable discomfort of facing such basic philosophical and educational issues as the nature of people, their moral and legal rights and responsibilities, and our personal and professional assumptions and beliefs about these issues. These issues deserve mention, if only to recognize their underlying importance and to suggest that perhaps the subject of discipline should be problematic and controversial.

The Definition and Purpose of Discipline

Underlying much of the controversy and disagreement about discipline is the matter of its several meanings and purposes. Within the context of student personnel work, discipline may be variously defined as: (1) *self-discipline,* or that virtue which may be regarded as the essence of education (Appleton et al., 1978; Hawkes, 1930; Mueller, 1961; Seward, 1961; Wrenn, 1949); (2) the *process of reeducation* or rehabilitation (Appleton et al., 1978); or (3) *punishment* as a means of external control of behavior (Appleton et al., 1978; Seward, 1961; Wrenn, 1949).

Discipline defined as self-discipline has a firm grounding in educational philosophy and has received wide acceptance in the professional literature (Dannells, 1977). Discipline as the process of reeducation may be thought of as having the former definition as its intended outcome. Likewise, it, too, is generally accepted within the field. The third definition which, while being generally rejected by today's student personnel workers, tends to conjure up images of their predecessors as "snooping, petty battle-axes who made it their business to ferret out wickedness and punish all offenders promptly" (Fley, 1963; as quoted in Appleton et al., 1978, p. 22). According to Fley, this image led to the denial of the disciplinary function in the field. However, judging from the growing body of literature and research on the moral and ethical development of college students today and its relationship to student discipline, it would appear that it is the discipline-as-punishment model which has been rejected in favor of discipline-as-student-development (Ardaiolo, 1983; Boots, 1987; Caruso, 1978; Greenleaf, 1978; Ostroth & Hill, 1987; Pavela, 1985).

Student Misconduct: Sources and Responses

Certainly what a college or university considers misconduct is a function of the number and nature of its rules and regulations (Foley, 1949; Seward, 1961; Williamson, 1956, 1961; Williamson & Foley, 1949; Wrenn, 1949) and, more fundamentally, of its purpose for student disciplinary affairs. Other institutional factors which influence the frequency and nature of student misconduct include the full array of campus environmental conditions, particularly the residential and social environment.

Intrapersonal sources of student misconduct may be categorized as pathological or nonpathological (Dannells, 1977). Nonpathological misbehavior may be viewed as stemming from lack of information or understanding or from inadequate or incomplete development, once referred to as immaturity or adolescent mischievousness and excess energy (Williamson, 1956).

One's view of the origin of student misconduct and one's philosophy of discipline are the primary determinants in forming the corrective action to be taken in any given disciplinary situation. Corrective actions may be categorized as punitive; rehabilitative, educational, or developmental are more popular terms today; and environmental; i.e., actions aimed at external sources of misconduct. The extent to which a given sanction is best categorized as punitive, as opposed to developmental, is a matter of philosophy and purpose. Today's student development educator would likely reject any action which had as its sole purpose punishment for punishment's sake.

Sanctions commonly employed, for whatever purpose, include various forms of "informative disciplinary communications such as oral and written warnings or admonitions, often accompanied by a reference to more severe sanctions to follow if the proscribed behavior continues; disciplinary probation; denial of relevant privileges or liberties, such as restrictions on social hours or the use of facilities, often used as a condition of probation; restitution, or monetary compensation for damage or injury; fines; denial of financial assistance (now thought to be rare); and actions which affect the student's status, such as suspension, the temporary dismissal of the student for either a finite period or indefinitely, and expulsion (permanent dismissal), the "capital punishment of student discipline" (Dannells, 1977, p. 238).

One special type of dismissal should be mentioned: the dismissal of students with mental disorders. Students who pose a danger to self, others, or if their behaviors "directly and substantially" impede the lawful activities of others on the campus: (Pavela, 1985, p. 11) may be withdrawn on an emergency or interim basis pending a hearing. Mandatory psychological or psychiatric withdrawal should be viewed as a means of last resort and should focus on the student's behavior, rather than their mental state, since persons suffering from mental disorders are protected from discrimination by Section 504 of the Federal Rehabilitation Act of 1973 (Pavela, 1985).

Institutional responses to student misconduct involving rehabilitation or intentional human development include counseling; referral, for medical or psychiatric care, and the assignment of a civic or public service project designed to enhance appreciation or awareness of personal responsibility. Disciplinary counseling may involve a professionally trained counselor; other professionals within the institution, such as an administrator or faculty member associated with the campus judicial system or with the residence hall program; or extra-institutional assistance from parents, clergy, social workers, or other helping professionals from the community.

Actions aimed at sources of misbehavior external to the student include changing living arrangements and finding financial assistance or employment. Other possible responses are academic assistance, such as tutoring or learning skills development, and policy revision, where the "misconduct" is more a function of outmoded or unnecessarily restrictive rules.

The choice of response in a disciplinary situation is affected by a number of considerations: one's philosophical beliefs about human nature; one's views on teaching, learning, and changing human behavior; the institution's educational mission as reflected in the nature and extent of its behavioral standards; the degree of divergence between those standards and those of its students; and the behavior itself. Important issues to be addressed include: Should the "punishment" (treatment) fit the "crime" (behavior) or the individual or both? What should be the role of punishment in changing behavior in general and higher education in particular? What is the basic purpose of our disciplinary and judicial systems?

Authority to Discipline

Closely related to the issue of the purpose of student discipline is the matter of the institution's authority to administer discipline. Seven different theories defining the source of the institution's power to discipline its students and describing to some degree the nature of the student-institutional relationship have been identified (Dannells, 1977).

In loco parentis, literally "in place of a parent; instead of a parent" (Black, 1968, p. 896), is a common law doctrine which views the institution as taking the role of the parent with respect to all student conduct. In this view the college is presumed to know best the needs of the student and is vested with great latitude in the disciplinary process (see *Gott v. Berea College,* 1913). As such, this doctrine was once used as the justification for paternalistic, informal, and sometimes arbitrary use of the power to discipline (Ratliff, 1972), even though, according to Appleton et al. (1978) "its formalization into the law occurred long after the original relationship was abandoned in practice" (p. 25). Ever since its application to the college disciplinary situation, this doctrine has been problematic; and it has been criticized as impractical, erroneous, and misleading as a viable educational concept (Penney, 1967; Ratliff, 1972; Strickland, 1965). Today, while vestiges of paternalism may still exist in the reaffirmation of concern for the whole student as reflected in the theory and practice of "student development" (Gregory & Ballou, 1986; Parr & Buchanan, 1979; Pitts, 1980), the doctrine of *in loco parentis* as a legal description of the student-institutional relationship is generally considered to be untenable, intolerable, or simply dead (Dannells, 1977).

The *contract theory* defines the relationship of the student and the institution as a contractual one, the terms of which are set forth in the college's catalogue, other publications, and oral addenda. The student enters the contract by signing the registration document and paying fees, and thereby accepts the conduct rules and academic regulations. Violations of the rules may then be met with those measures enumerated as sanctions in the contract. This theory was once restricted largely to private institutions and to academic affairs; but now, with the lowered age of majority, older students, increasing consumerism, and the general litigiousness in our society, it is seeing increasing acceptance and application to all student-institutional relationships (Hammond, 1978; Shur, 1983).

The *statutory theory* holds that the institution's power to discipline derives from a specific statutory grant or state law to the state governing board or directly to the institution (Dannells, 1977; Ratliff, 1972; Snoxell, 1965).

Ratliff (1972) notes two theories which have been proposed but which have received little legal support. In the *fiduciary theory* the institution assumes the fiduciary function, acting for the benefit of the student in "all matters relevant to the relation between them" (Seavey, 1957, p. 1407, n. 3). The *status theory* holds that "the rights and duties of students and colleges are inherent in the status of the parties . . . [as] they have developed through custom, tradition, and usage" (Ratliff, 1972, p. 48).

The *constitutional theory* of the relationship is actually no more than a legal limitation on the institution's power to discipline. As Fisher (1970) notes, it does not define the relationship *per se*, except that it prohibits a public institution from unreasonably proscribing, or requiring the forfeit of, constitutionally protected rights" (pp. 5-6). This limitation, established in *Dixon v. Alabama State Board of Higher Education* (1961) and reaffirmed and developed in several subsequent cases, will be considered in greater detail in the "Due Process" section.

Lastly, the *educational purpose theory* views the student-institutional relationship as an educational one, thereby limiting disciplinary control to student behavior that adversely affects the institution's pursuit of its educational mission. Given that the institution's *raison d'etre* is education and that this is the reason for its relationship with students, this view is considered by many to be the only realistic and justifiable basis for student discipline (Callis, 1967, 1969; Carnegie Commission, 1971; Dannells, 1977, 1978; National Education Association, 1971; Penney, 1967; Van Alstyne, 1966). It allows the institution to discipline students for the purpose of maintenance of order or in furtherance of its educational objectives vis-a-vis an individual student or group of students. Furthermore, it protects the institution from unwanted court intrusion by recognizing that the courts have historically adopted a policy of nonintervention or judicial restraint in the matters which are legitimately part of the educational enterprise (Ardaiolo, 1983; Travelstead, 1987).

Extent of Institutional Jurisdiction

Two basic issues arise with respect to the extent of the institution's jurisdiction. First, should it apply internal sanctions, seek external (i.e., criminal) sanctions, or both where institutional rules and criminal law both apply (Stein, 1972)? Second, should the institution concern itself with student's off-campus behavior? With respect to both questions, the trend of thought in recent years, which is in keeping with the educational purpose theory of discipline, makes internal actions appropriate in all cases, whether on- or off-campus behavior is involved. The question of the application of criminal law is essentially a separate matter, especially in dealing with students who are legal adults and when the criminal act is of a serious nature (Dannells, 1977; Sims, 1971; Stein, 1972).

An issue related to jurisdiction is the matter of double jeopardy. On occasion, students have argued that to be disciplined by their college and tried for a criminal offense for the same act constitutes double jeopardy. However, it is well established that the concept of double jeopardy applies only to criminal proceedings and does not apply to college disciplinary actions (Fisher, 1970; Dannells, 1977). Nonetheless, it is recommended that the institution avoid the mere duplication of criminal punishments by emphasizing the educational approach to its proceedings and subsequent response (Ardaiolo & Walker, 1987; Fisher, 1970).

Constitutional Limitations on Jurisdiction

Another general jurisdictional issue is the extent to which the institution can prescribe students' behavior. In the area of students' constitutional rights, four principles are well established: (1) The college cannot put a blanket restraint on student's First Amendment rights of freedom of assembly and expression, but it may restrain assembly and expression which will interfere with its educational and administrative duties (Mager, 1978; Pavela, 1985; Sherry, 1966; Young, 1970); (2) The institution cannot restrict, prohibit, or censor the content of speech, except for extraordinarily compelling reasons, such as someone's safety (Mager, 1978; Pavela, 1985; Sherry, 1966); (3) The college cannot apply its rules in a discriminatory manner (Sherry, 1966); and (4) Students are protected by the Fourth Amendment from unreasonable searches and seizures. For example, the institution may not enter and examine a residence hall room unless it does so in furtherance of its educational aims which include protection of its facilities (Bracewell, 1978; Fisher, 1970; Young, 1970).

Due Process

Due process, while a flexible concept related to time and circumstances (Ardaiolo, 1983), may be defined as "an *appropriate protection* of the rights of an individual while determining his [her] liability for wrongdoing and the applicability of punishment" (Fisher, 1970, p. 1). It is a Constitutional right granted by the Fifth Amendment with respect to action by the federal government and by the Fourteenth Amendment with respect to state action. The well-established standard used by the courts when questions of due process have arisen in the context of student discipline is that of *fundamental fairness* (Ardaiolo, 1983; Bakken, 1968; Buchanan, 1978; Fisher, 1970; Young, 1972).

Procedural due process refers to the individual's rights in the adjudication of an offense. That which is "due," or owing, to ensure fairness in any given circumstance will vary with the seriousness of the alleged offense and with the severity of the possible sanction. Substantive due process relates to the nature, purpose, or application of a rule or law. Again, applying the standard of fairness, rules must be clear and not overly broad, they must have a fair and reasonable purpose, and they must be applied in fairness and good faith (Young, 1972).

Since 1960 there have been a considerable number of court cases on due process in disciplinary proceedings, especially dismissal hearings. Prior to that time, under a combination of contract and *in loco parentis* theories, the courts generally assumed the college to be acting fairly and in the best educational interests of all concerned. But the civil rights movement, during which some students were summarily dismissed from college because of their participation in civil rights demonstrations, prompted significant legal and philosophical changes (Ardaiolo, 1983; Bakken, 1968; Dannells, 1977). In the landmark case *Dixon v. Alabama State Board of Education* (1961) the court, on the basis of an analogy of education as property, thus bringing dismissal from a state college under the due process clause of the Fourteenth Amendment, ruled that a student has almost a constitutional right to notice and a hearing. The *Dixon* court went on to recommend several procedural safeguards to ensure fairness in such cases: the notice should give specific charges; the hearing should consider both sides of the case; the accused should be informed about witnesses against them and the nature of their testimony; the student should have a chance to present a defense; the findings of the hearing should be reported to the student; and the "requirements of due process are met in dismissal hearings where the rudiments of fair play are followed" (Dannells, 1977, p. 249).

Numerous court decisions since *Dixon* established it as precedent and further specified the procedural due process safeguards for dismissal and other serious conduct hearings from public institutions (*Due v. Florida*

A & M University, 1963; *Esteban v. Central Missouri State College,* 1969; *Knight v. State Board of Education,* 1963; *Morale v. Grigel,* 1976; *Moresco v. Clark,* 1984; *Sohmer v. Kinnard,* 1982; and see also General Order, 1968). A thorough reiteration of all of the procedural due process safeguards which have and have not been accorded students in disciplinary proceedings is beyond the scope of this chapter. Pavela (1985; see pp. 41-45) provides a recent and detailed summary of relevant court cases. At this point it should be noted, however, that all of the procedural safeguards required in criminal proceedings are not required in student conduct hearings (Dannells, 1977; Shur, 1983) and that no one particular model of procedural due process is required (Buchanan, 1978; Travelstead, 1987).

In the area of substantive due process, several principles are well established (Arndt, 1971; Buchanan, 1978): (1) Colleges have the authority to make and enforce rules of student conduct to maintain discipline and order; (2) Behavioral standards, including rules applied to off-campus behavior, must be consistent with the institution's lawful purpose and function; (3) Rules must be constitutionally fair, reasonable, and not capricious or arbitrary; (4) The code of conduct should be written and available for all to see; (5) The constitutionally guaranteed rights of students can be limited to enable the institution to function, but blanket prohibitions are not permitted; and (6) A rule must be specific enough to give adequate notice of expected behavior and to allow the student to prepare a defense against a charge under it. Vague or overly broad rules, such as general proscriptions against "misconduct" or "conduct unbecoming a Siwash College student," have not been upheld.

Private institutions have not been required by the courts to meet these due process standards because they are not engaged in state action and so do not fall under the Fourteenth Amendment (Buchanan, 1978; Dannells, 1977; Shur, 1983). The analogy of education as a property right has not been extended to private schools, and their relationship with their students is still considered largely contractual. Thus, despite many projections in the 1970s that the courts would abolish the public-private distinction in disciplinary matters, the private institution still legally has considerably more latitude in defining and adjudicating student misconduct (Shur, 1983). But procedural reforms tend to become normative in higher education and many private colleges, as a matter of sound administrative and educational policy (Buchanan, 1978), now contract with their students to provide the basic due process protections expected in public institutions (Shur, 1983). Having done so, they are contractually required to follow their own rules and procedures (Pavela, 1985; Shur, 1983).

The Academic Evaluation/Student Conduct Dichotomy

The courts have generally distinguished between academic dismissal and dismissal for misconduct (Rhode, 1983), although the dichotomy "may be very difficult to apply in fact" (Ardaiolo, 1983, pp. 17-18). In the landmark case of *Board of Curators of the University of Missouri v. Horowitz* (1978), the U.S. Supreme Court placed limitations on the due process procedures required in academic dismissal situations. Instead of a hearing, the student need only be informed of the particular academic deficiencies and of the consequences of those shortcomings, e.g., dismissal, should they not be remedied. Once this warning has occurred, the decision-making person or body must then make a "careful and deliberate" decision based on "expert evaluation of cumulative information" (p. 79). The court noted that this process is "not readily adapted to the procedural tools of judicial or administrative decision making" (p. 79) and declined to enter this academic domain. It should be emphasized that this case involved the academic *evaluation* of a student, and was not a matter of academic *misconduct,* such as cheating or plagiarism, where an allegation of wrong-doing is made and fact-finding is central to the disciplinary process. That distinction may be blurred and problematic in cases where it is difficult to distinguish misconduct, e.g., plagiarism, from poor scholarship (Travelstead, 1987) or where standards of dress and interpersonal conduct are the focus of the evaluation in a professional/clinical training setting.

"Creeping Legalism" or Proceduralism

Following the *Dixon* case during the 1960s, many institutions, both public and private, rushed to establish disciplinary systems affording students their "due" protections. Some overreacted, went far beyond the court mandated due process requirements, and became "mired in legalistic disputes" (Lamont, 1979, p. 85). Critics of this "creeping legalism," or proceduralism, have argued that it has undermined the informal and uniquely educational aspect of the disciplinary process in higher education; it has resulted in unduly costly, complex, and time consuming processes; and it places the student and the institution in an unnecessarily adversarial relationship (Dannells, 1977; Pavela, 1985; Travelstead, 1987). Ironically, "[m]uch of the complaining about excessive proceduralism and legalism is hollow. The excessive proceduralism, where it exists, has been largely caused by the institutions themselves" (Travelstead, 1987, p. 15). Judging from the frequency of the reminders in the literature, it would appear student affairs administrators need to be periodically reminded that "due process" is, in fact, a flexible concept which allows for the less formal/legalistic disposition of most disciplinary cases, especially when the penalty or outcome is less than dismissal (Ardaiolo, 1983; Pavela, 1985; Travelstead, 1987).

Discipline and Student Development

Seemingly in reaction to this excessive proceduralism, in recent years the student personnel profession has shown increasing interest in the educational nature of discipline and the application of human development concepts and theories to the conduct of disciplinary affairs. Not only is there concern for protection of the individual's rights and of the institution itself, but there appears to be a growing realization, or perhaps a return, of the primacy of the educational value in the disciplinary function. This is not to suggest that meeting students' legal rights and fostering their development are or were incompatible, which they are not (Greenleaf, 1978), but rather that the increasingly adversarial nature of the process became a significant drain on and distraction to those student personnel workers charged with administering their campus' disciplinary system. It became more difficult to find that proper balance necessary to the survival of the Student Personnel Point of View (Caruso, 1978). But with the growing body of research and literature on cognitive, moral, and ethical development, there appears to be increasing interest in its application to the disciplinary setting (Saddlemire, 1980).

Student discipline is, and always has been, an excellent opportunity for developmental efforts. The traditional Dean of Students knew this, of course, but operated without the benefit of formal, developmental theories; it would be unfair and inaccurate to say that the earlier deans worked without ideas of how students grow and mature, especially those which emphasize moral and ethical growth and so lend themselves to the disciplinary process. Much of discipline involves teaching (Ardaiolo, 1983; Ostroth & Hill, 1978; Travelstead, 1987) and counseling (Foley, 1947; Gometz & Parker, 1968; Ostroth & Hill, 1978; Williamson, 1963; Williamson & Foley, 1949). Through the application of developmental theory, the individual may be better understood and counseling/developmental interventions may be more scientifically and accurately fashioned (Boots, 1987).

Various developmental theories have been applied to the disciplinary process and its impact on the individual student (e.g., see Boots, 1987; Greenleaf, 1978; Ostroth & Hill, 1978; Smith, 1978). While space limitation prevents a thorough treatment of the subject, certain common elements and objectives of the different views and approaches should be noted. First, insight is a commonly stated objective and a means to further growth in the individual "offender" (Dannells, 1977). Second, self-understanding or clarification of personal identity, attitudes and values, especially in relation to authority, for both the student whose behavior is in question and also for students who sit on judicial boards, is often described (Boots, 1987; Greenleaf, 1978). Third, the goals of self-control, responsibility, and accountability are often mentioned (Caruso, 1978; Pavela, 1985; Travelstead, 1987). Fourth, the use of ethical dialogue in confronting the impact of the individual's behavior and its moral implications and in examining the fairness of rules is receiving increasing attention (Pavela, 1985; Smith, 1978). Lastly, there appears to have been an extension of the scope and goals of student discipline beyond that of simple adjudication and control/rehabilitation to a broader objective of moral and ethical development as it relates to contemporary social issues such as prejudice, health and wellness, sexism, racism, and human sexuality (Dalton & Healy, 1984).

ADMINISTRATION OF DISCIPLINARY AFFAIRS

The administration of student discipline, or campus judicial affairs/systems/programs, as it has become known in recent years, may be divided into three key dimensions: (1) the roles and functions of student affairs professionals in discipline; (2) the nature and scope of campus judicial systems; and (3) the handling of disciplinary records. Research findings in this area have been consistent in one important respect—from campus to campus there is substantial variety, or heterogeneity, in approaches to student discipline (Dannells, 1978; Durst, 1969; Dutton, Smith, & Zarle, 1969; Ostroth & Hill, 1978; Steele, Johnson, & Rickard, 1984). Institutional factors which influence the nature of a campus' system include its educational philosophy, i.e., its mission; its size, type of control, public or private, and residential character; the needs of the community; and the extent to which governance is shared with students (Ardaiolo & Walker, 1987).

Roles and Functions of
Student Affairs Professionals in Discipline

Student affairs professionals may be charged with a broad range of roles and functions related to the disciplinary process. At one end of the spectrum, they may function in the role of ombudsman or mediator, independently and informally resolving conflicts and handling minor complaints. This approach has the advantage of brevity, keeping the problem at the lowest possible level of resolution, and it provides an educational, nonadversarial alternative for settling differences in certain situations (Serr & Taber, 1987). At the other end of the spectrum there may be a specialist, often called a hearing officer or judicial affairs officer, charged with the responsibility of the total disciplinary system, including orchestrating the workings of one or more tribunals or boards, handling all disciplinary records, and investigating and preparing cases in more serious matters. The main advantages of this model are expertise and the freeing of other student affairs staff from the disciplinary function. Continuity, equity, and improved management of the process are also arguments for the specialist (Steele et al., 1984). Specialized judicial affairs officers are rare in smaller colleges, whereas Steele et al. found that of the 18 schools (12% of their respondents) which reported judicial affairs officers, ten were large (10,000 + students) institutions.

The most common model is that of a middle-level student affairs professional, most often associated with the dean of students office or the office of residence life, who informally handles relatively minor violations and who presents serious cases to a hearing board for final disposition. At smaller and private institutions, the dean of students for many years has had and continued to retain the major responsibility for adjudicating student misconduct (Dannells, 1978; Ostroth, Armstrong, & Campbell, 1978; Steele et al., 1984).

Dutton, Smith, and Zarle (1969) identify four levels of involvement for those responsible for discipline: (1) non-involvement, which frees the student personnel worker to concentrate on other matters; (2) involvement limited to case investigation and preparation; (3) involvement limited to case investigation, preparation, and adjudication in minor cases, and (4) full involvement, with action in all minor cases and referral of major cases to a judicial body on which the administrator sits as chairperson and final authority. In choosing a level of involvement, they suggest consideration of several factors: (1) What are the student personnel worker's most essential functions? (2) What is the purpose of discipline?

(3) What role should students and faculty have in the process? (4) Should student conduct be more of an administrative or community concern? (5) What approach best protects the student and the institution?

The student affairs professional involved in disciplinary programs may function in an educational role in several regards. As a coordinator, advisor, and trainer of tribunals, policy boards, and their members, the student affairs professional has many opportunities to encourage the development of students along moral, ethical, and legal lines (Boots, 1987; Cordner & Brooks, 1987). In working with the student whose behavior is in question, the student affairs professional may, through a combination of teaching and counseling techniques, help the individual gain insight and understanding about his/her behavior and responsibilities. Furthermore, discipline officers can contribute to the intellectual climate of the institution not only by helping to preserve a safe and educationally conducive atmosphere (Boots, 1987), but also by leading the entire campus community in the process of defining and disseminating a behavioral code which represents a set of shared beliefs and values about the educational environment and the student's responsibilities within it (Pavela, 1985).

Caruso (1978) defines the important roles of the student discipline specialist in terms of the basic student personnel functions outlined by Miller and Prince (1976). Goal setting is important for keeping the discipline system in accord with the broader institutional goals; for working developmentally with the individuals; and for designing outcomes-oriented training programs for student judicial boards. Assessing student growth can provide important, yet frequently lacking, evaluative information about the efficacy of the disciplinary process, both for the miscreant as well as for tribunal members. Instruction may take the form of teaching credit or noncredit courses on the legal aspects of the profession, may involve student leadership training and judicial board member education, or may take the form of offering "mainstream" coursework, in a collaborative or team-teaching approach with another academic unit in subjects like moral development, legal aspects of higher education, parliamentary procedure, or one of various life skills such as parent effectiveness. Consultation in disciplinary affairs includes working with the campus disciplinary policy/rules committee, judicial boards, and paraprofessionals in the residence halls, and assisting the academic units with the administration of academic misconduct cases. Within the context of student discipline, environmental management involves any response to a behavior problem which is designed to reduce or eliminate conditions which contribute to that problem, such as the placement of residence hall fire protection equipment, campus lighting, and the sale and distribution of alcoholic beverages on the campus. Lastly, is the important function of program evaluation through which the discipline program may study itself for purposes of improvement and justification of resources.

Disciplinary counseling is another function basic to the educational approach to the disciplinary role. It has been defined as "sympathetic but firm counseling to aid the individual to gain insight and be willing to accept restrictions on his [her] individual autonomy and behavior" (Williamson, 1963, p. 13). Frequently cited objectives of disciplinary counseling include rehabilitation and behavior change, insight, maturation, emotional stability, moral judgment, self-reliance, self-control, understanding and accepting responsibility for and consequences of personal behavior (Dannells, 1977). The counseling techniques of information-giving, i.e., teaching, and confrontation are central to the "helping encounter in discipline" and may be employed throughout the disciplinary process (Ostroth & Hill, 1978).

The Nature and Scope of Campus Judicial Systems

Like the roles and functions of the student affairs professional in discipline, campus judicial systems vary greatly depending on those key institutional factors, e.g., philosophy, size, etc., cited previously. Smaller and private institutions tend to have more informal, centralized systems, while larger and public universities tend toward the more formal, legalistic, and decentralized/specialized model (Dannells, 1978; Steele et al., 1984). More particularly, campus judicial systems differ on the extent of their authority and responsibility; the extent of differentiation between criminal and campus codes and procedures, and between academic and non-academic misconduct; how specifically behavior is defined and proscribed; the due process rights accorded the student at both the prehearing and the hearing phases of the adjudicatory process; the availability and application of sanctions, conditions, appeals, and rehabilitative actions; the nature and extent of student input into the code of conduct, the level of student involvement in the process of adjudication; and the availability of alternative adjudicative mechanisms (Ardaiolo & Walker, 1987).

On the basis of the research conducted over the past 25 years on the administration of student discipline, including studies by Van Alstyne

(1963), Durst (1968), Dutton et al. (1969), Leslie and Satryb (1974), Ostroth et al. (1978), Dannells (1978), and, most recently, Steele et al. (1984), the following trends may be noted: (1) In the 1960s there was a dramatic increase in student input into conduct rules and procedures and the adjudication of misconduct. That trend has leveled and student involvement remains high on most campuses. (2) There has been a similar trend in the provision of both procedural and substantive due process mechanisms, starting with a major shift toward more legalistic processes and leveling in more recent years. Today, on almost all campuses, students can be expected to be afforded fair notice and application of conduct rules and fair procedures in the process of adjudicating an offense. More involved, legalistic procedures can be expected for cases which may result in dismissal, while more informal processes are used with more minor cases. As Travelstead (1987) points out, there have been very few court decisions on student discipline in the last ten years. (3) Milder sanctions are more often employed than stiffer penalties. Warnings, both oral and written, and disciplinary probation have been and continue to be the most common responses to student misconduct. (4) Disciplinary counseling continues to be the most common rehabilitative action, but over the years it is increasingly more likely to take place in either a disciplinary specialist's office or in the counseling center, especially in larger institutions. At smaller colleges, the disciplinary function, including post-hearing counseling, continues to be performed in the dean of student's office. (5) The concern for overly legalistic judicial processes has resulted in some moderating, and while most institutions do not anticipate changes in their programs, those which do indicate a need for change suggest that it should be in the direction of streamlining and simplifying their processes and making their hearing less legalistic. (6) Diversity continues to characterize the administration of disciplinary affairs.

The Handling of Disciplinary Records

The greatest changes in disciplinary affairs over the past 15 years have occurred in the areas of confidentiality of records and notification of parents. Prior to the enactment of the Family Educational Rights and Privacy Act of 1974, often called the Buckley Amendment, and the lowering of the age of majority, college students' parents were routinely notified of disciplinary actions involving their sons or daughters. Such notification was expected by most parents and by the greater society and was, in and of itself, an established disciplinary sanction and often an effective point of leverage for future behavior change. "This time I won't call your folks, but . . ." was probably one of the more impactful statements the dean could make. Prior to the Buckley Amendment, student records, including disciplinary files, were also available to other agencies and prospective employers.

In a national survey conducted in 1977, Dannells (1978) found that the great majority of the respondent institutions were in keeping with the law and with then-current philosophical trends in the administration of student records. Four-fifths of the respondents kept their disciplinary records separate from other student records. Further, disciplinary records were highly confidential, with very few institutions making them available to outside agencies or prospective employers without the student's consent; and only eight percent reported releasing records to parents. Parents were notified of their student's involvement in the disciplinary process by 37 percent of the respondents if the student was a minor, but 30 percent indicated they did not notify parents regardless of the student's age.

The widespread inclusion of students on disciplinary hearing boards raises an interesting question under the Buckley Amendment. That law permits access to student records by faculty and staff for educational or administrative purposes, but it does not allow students, other than the student for whom the record exists, to have access. Is it a violation of the law for student members of judicial panels to review prior conduct records in the determination of sanctions or rehabilitative actions? What of their role in the creation of new disciplinary records? Pavela (1985) notes that not only do students not have a constitutional right to an open hearing, but the Buckley Amendment "would preclude holding an 'open' hearing without the consent of the accused student" (p. 43). Since it is arguable that the presence of other students on the hearing board constitutes an "open" hearing, it may be advisable to obtain a signed release from the accused.

THE FUTURE OF DISCIPLINARY AFFAIRS

The future of the disciplinary function in student affairs is inextricably tied to the future of student affairs and to the future of higher education. Innumerable influences will come to bear on those institutions, rendering futurism a risky and perhaps foolish enterprise. Nonetheless, in this section, a forecast of the future of student discipline will be attempted.

Resolution of the Legal-Developmental Dichotomy

If the first 50 years of student discipline can be characterized, perhaps unfairly, as "paternalistic," then the 1960s and 1970s can be described as "legalistic." The marked increase in due process protections instituted ostensibly for the protection of the student took on the proportions of an over-reaction and seemingly were intended more for the protection of the institution from court intervention. Processes became the dominant focus, and on many campuses the developmental value of student discipline was often overshadowed by criminalistic judicial systems and the mechanistic application of due process requirements. In recent years there has been growing recognition that that trend was both unnecessary and unfortunate. Today there is considerable discussion about making disciplinary processes simpler while maintaining the fundamental fairness the courts and the Constitution require. As fears of court intervention subside with the reaffirmation of the principle of nonintervention in that which is truly educational, we should see simpler disciplinary/judicial systems and a return to a more relaxed, cooperative approach. This should enable us to concentrate on the "liaison between student discipline and student development described by many of the original leaders in the student personnel field [which] still stands as the key to the future of this area of professional endeavor" (Caruso, 1978, p. 127).

Continuation of the Academic-Nonacademic Dichotomy

For the foreseeable future, the distinction on most campuses between misconduct which is "academic," primarily cheating on tests and plagiarism, and that which is "social," or nonacademic, will continue. Although a good disciplinary affairs program/specialist can bring impartiality and procedural expertise to the adjudication of academic misconduct, this has historically been and will remain the domain of the faculty and the academic administrative hierarchy. Despite its unpleasantness, faculty have a strong sense of duty in this area and do possess more expertise, and perhaps leniency, when poor scholarship blurs the problem. This approach also has the advantage of handling the problem at the lowest/ closest possible level; however, alternative appeal routes outside of the academic hierarchy are becoming common. Steele et al. (1984) report that the highest level judicial body at 52 percent of their sample, heard cases, presumably on appeal, of academic dishonesty. Thus, cases involving cheating or plagiarism by a student will, in general, continue to be initially handled by the faculty, with some mechanism for appeal or grievance to a judicial body outside the academic hierarchy.

Continuing Scrutiny of Psychiatric Withdrawal Policies

Involuntary withdrawal of students on psychiatric grounds will continue to be carefully scrutinized by the courts because of the protection afforded those with mental disorders by Section 504 of the Rehabilitation Act of 1973. Many colleges either do not have a clear policy for such cases or their policies give too much discretionary authority (Pavela, 1985; Steele et al., 1984). Students may not be removed because they are perceived and labeled "mentally ill," but the behavioral manifestations of such a condition may be dealt with appropriately through normal disciplinary channels. But according to Steele et al. (1984), after noting that 93 students were withdrawn from only seven schools in two years and one institution alone removed 21 during that same period, "some schools might be resorting to psychiatric withdrawals as an alternative to the traditional disciplinary process . . . by employing them to remove students who are simply perceived as troublesome or eccentric" (pp. 340-341). It is expected that, with continuing judicial review and simplification of disciplinary processes, such misuses of psychiatric withdrawal policies will decrease in frequency.

Rising Consumerism and the Contract Model

With the growing recognition and acceptance that the academy is a part of the "real world" and a microcosm of the greater society, the student-institutional relationship has become increasingly viewed as a consumer-business one subject to many of the same contractual expectations and contraints as any other seller-buyer relationship. Society, students, and even some of the students' parents no longer expect institutions of higher education to act on a vague set of social or parental rules in disciplinary matters. In particularly, older students have little tolerance for paternalistic policies and processes. Instead, they wish to know exactly what is expected of them as adult learners. This has undoubtedly influenced many colleges to take a careful look at their catalogues and other official documents, including codes of conduct, which may be considered part of the enrollment contract. This trend will continue, and it will benefit those who administer their campus' disciplinary system by requiring them to closely review their rules and methods to ensure they are treating students like the adults they legally are.

Related to this subject is the fact that in addition to the increasing average age of future students, more will be part-time and more will be attending commuter institutions in urban settings (Hodgkinson, 1985). Since most student misconduct involves traditional-aged students in residential settings, this would suggest that the relative incidence of student misconduct should decrease over time. Alternatively, increasing pressure to get good grades may lead to higher rates of academic dishonesty. Both hypotheses are ripe for future research.

The Continuing Need for Program Evaluation

Like any other student affairs program, disciplinary programs should be periodically and systematically evaluated to ensure that they are effectively meeting their established objectives (Council for the Advancement of Standards, 1986). Those objectives should be defined in terms of measurable outcomes statements and evaluated on the basis of pre-established criteria and processes. The various components of the programs, such as its publications, training program for judicial board members, consistency of sanctions, and procedures and practices, as well as the personnel involved in the execution of the program, should be included in a comprehensive review (Emmanuel & Miser, 1987). Methods of evaluation will certainly vary according to the nature and needs of the individual program, but may include interviews, direct observation, written reports, surveys, community feedback, task force review, and questionnaires (Emmanuel & Miser, 1987). It must be acknowledged, however, that scientific research in the area of student discipline has been and will continue to be problematic because of difficulties in identifying and controlling variables and in gathering data from recalcitrant program participants.

The Profession and Discipline

As noted at the outset of this chapter, student discipline has been, and perhaps should continue to be, a topic of professional concern and debate because it is such a dramatic reflection of our attitudes and assumptions about the nature of our students, our relationship to them, and our role in their development. There was a period in the history of our profession when the subject was all but ignored, a source of embarrassment to be apologetically dispatched and forgotten in favor of more glamorous and "positive" functions. But some recent developments suggest that we may be approaching this central function with increasing professionalism and acceptance:

1. the publication of the CAS Standards, which include a section on "Judicial Programs and Services"
2. the publication of a new Jossey-Bass sourcebook, *Enhancing Campus Judicial Systems* (Caruso & Travelstead, 1987)
3. ongoing efforts to integrate human development theories which focus on moral and ethical growth of students with the practice of disciplinary/judicial affairs
4. widespread efforts in higher education to develop an integrated core curriculum which reaffirms the traditional principles of a liberal education and which may help create a climate on campuses where the development of the whole person, including the moral aspect, is once again paramount.

This last point, in particular, suggests exciting possibilities for student affairs professionals engaged in student discipline on their campuses to "return to the academy." Many colleges are considering team-taught, interdisciplinary subject matter which will challenge an increasingly materialistic, aphilosophic, and career-oriented student body. Might there not be a place for a course entitled "Student Rights and Responsibilities in the College and the Community"? Such a course could be approached from a myriad of combinations of the different disciplines of law, political science, sociology, psychology, education, and philosophy and could include the campus' chief disciplinary/judicial officer. In this way the subject of student conduct and moral/ethical development could be considered within the broader context of civic responsibility and community involvement. Thus, the moral dialogue inherent in a developmental approach to discipline (Pavela, 1985) could be brought to the classroom with the student affairs professional as an integral part of the teaching partnership and process.

REFERENCES

Appleton, J.R., Briggs, C.M., & Rhatigan, J.J. (1978). *Pieces of eight.* Portland, OR: National Association of Student Personnel Administrators.

Ardaiolo, F.P. (1983). What process is due? In M.J. Barr (Ed.), *Student affairs and the law*. New directions for student services, no. 39 (pp. 13-25). San Francisco: Jossey-Bass.

Ardaiolo, F.P., & Walker, S.J. (1987). Models of practice. In R. Caruso & W.W. Travelstead (Eds.), *Enhancing campus judicial systems*. New directions for student services, no. 39 (pp. 43-61). San Francisco: Jossey-Bass.

Arndt, J.R. (1971). Substantive due process in public higher education: 1959-1969. *Journal of College Student Personnel, 12,* 83-94.

Bakken, C.J. (1968). *The legal basis of college student personnel work* (Student Personnel Monograph Series No. 2). Washington, D.C.: American Personnel and Guidance Association.

Black, H.C. (1968). *Black's law dictionary.* St. Paul, MN: West. *Board of Curators of the University of Missouri v. Horowitz,* 90 S. Ct. 948 (1978).

Boots, C.C. (1987). Human development theory applied to judicial affairs work. In R. Caruso & W.W. Travelstead (Eds.), *Enhancing campus judicial systems*. New directions for student services, no. 39 (pp. 63-72). San Francisco: Jossey-Bass.

Bracewell, W.R. (1978). An application of the privacy concept to student life. In E.H. Hammond & R.H. Shaffer (Eds.), *The legal foundations of student personnel services in higher education* (pp. 24-33). Washington, D.C.: American College Personnel Association.

Brubacher, J.S., & Rudy, W. (1968). *Higher education in transition.* New York: Harper & Row.

Buchanan, E.T., III. (1978). Student disciplinary proceedings in collegiate institutions—Substantive and procedural due proces requirements. In E.H. Hammond & R.H. Shaffer (Eds.), *The legal foundation of student personnel services in hgiher education* (pp. 94-115). Washington, D.C.: American College Personnel Association.

Callis, R. (1967). Educational aspects of *in loco parentis. Journal of College Student Personnel, 8,* 231-233.

Callis, R. (1969). The courts and the colleges: 1968. *Journal of College Student Personnel, 10,* 75-86.

Carnegie Commission on Higher Education. (1971). *Dissent and disruption.* New York: McGraw-Hill.

Caruso, R. (1987). Organizing for judicial affairs work. In R. Caruso & W.W. Travelstead (Eds.), *Enhancing campus judicial systems,* New directions for student services, no. 39 (pp. 17-29). San Francisco: Jossey-Bass.

Caruso, R.G. (1978). The professional approach to student discipline in the years ahead. In E.H. Hammond & R.H. Shaffer (Eds.), *The legal foundations of student personnel services in higher education* (pp. 116-127). Washington, D.C.: American College Personnel Association.

Caruso, R., & Travelstead, W.W. (Eds.). (1987). *Enhancing campus judicial systems.* New directions for student services, no. 39. San Francisco: Jossey-Bass.

Cordner, P., & Brooks, T.F. (1987). Training techniques for judicial systems. In R. Caruso & W.W. Travelstead (Eds.), *Enhancing campus judicial systems*. New directions for student services, no. 39 (pp. 31-42). San Francisco: Jossey-Bass.

Council for the Advancement of Standards for Student Services/Development Programs. (1986). *CAS standards and guidelines for student services/development programs.* Washington, D.C.: Consortium of Student Affairs Professional Organizations.

Dalton, J.C., & Healy, M.A. (1984). Using values education activities to confront student conduct issues. *NASPA Journal, 22*(2), 19-25.

Dannells, M. (1977). Discipline. In W.T. Packwood (Ed.), *College student personnel services* (pp. 232-278). Springfield, IL: Charles C Thomas.

Dannells, M. (1978). *Disciplinary practices and procedures in baccalaureate-granting institutions of higher education in the United States.* Unpublished doctoral dissertation, University of Iowa, Iowa City, IA.

Dixon v. Alabama State Board of Education, 294 F.2d 150 (1961).

Due v. Florida A & M University, 233 F.Supp. 396 (1963).

Durst, R.H. (1969). The impact of court decisions rendered in the Dixon and Knight cases on student disciplinary procedures in public institutions of higher education in the United States. (Doctoral dissertation, Purdue University, 1968). *Dissertation Abstracts, 29,* 2473A-2474A. (University Microfilms No. 69-2910).

Dutton, T.B., Smith, F.W., & Zarle, T. (1969). *Institutional approaches to the adjudication of student misconduct.* Buffalo: National Association of Student Personnel Administrators.

Emmanuel, N.R., & Miser, K.M. (1987). Evaluating judicial program effectiveness. In R. Caruso & W.W. Travelstead (Eds.), *Enhancing campus judicial systems.* New directions for student services, no. 39 (pp. 85-94). San Francisco: Jossey-Bass.

Esteban v. Central Missouri State College, 290 F.Supp. 622 (1969).

Fisher, T.C. (1970). *Due process in the student-institutional relationship.* Washington, D.C.: American Association of State Colleges and Universities.

Fley, J. (1963). *Discipline in student personnel work: The changing views of deans and personnel workers.* Unpublished doctoral dissertation, University of Illinois, Champaign, IL.

Fley, J. (1964). Changing approaches to discipline in student personnel work. *NAWDAC Journal, 27,* 105-113.

Foley, J.D. (1947). Discipline. A student counseling approach. *Educational and Psychological Measurement, 7,* 569-582.

General order on judicial standards of procedure and substance in review of student discipline in tax supported institutions of higher education, 45 F.R.D. 133 (W.D. Mo. 1968).

Gometz, L., & Parker, C.A. (1968). Disciplinary counseling: A contradiction? *Personnel and Guidance Journal, 46,* 437-443.

Gott v. Berea College, 156 Ky 376 (1913).

Greenleaf, E.A. (1978). The relationship of legal issues and procedures to student development. In E.H. Hammond & R.H. Shaffer (Eds.), *The legal foundations of student personnel services in higher education* (pp. 34-46). Washington, D.C.: American College Personnel Association.

Gregory, D.E., & Ballou, R.A. (1986). Point of view: In loco parentis *reinventis:* Is there still a parenting function in higher education? *NASPA Journal, 24*(2), 28-31.

Hammond, E.H. (1978). The consumer-institutional relationshp. In E.H. Hammond & R.H. Shaffer (Eds.), *The legal foundations of student personnel services in higher education* (pp. 1-11). Washington, D.C.: American College Personnel Association.

Hawkes, H.E. (1930). College administration. *Journal of Higher Education, 1,* 245-253.

Hodgkinson, H.L. (1985). *All one system: Demographics of education — kindergarten through graduate school.* Washington, D.C.: Institute for Educational Leadership.

Knight v. State Board of Education, 200 F.Supp. 174 (1963).

Knock, G.H. (1985). Development of student services in higher education. In M.J. Barr, L.A. Keating & Associates, *Developing effective student services programs* (pp. 15-42). San Francisco: Jossey-Bass.

Lamont, L. (1979). *Campus shock.* New York: Dutton.

Leonard, E.A. (1956). *Origins of personnel services in American higher education.* Minneapolis: University of Minnesota Press.

Leslie, D.W., & Satryb, R.P. (1974). Due process on due process? Some observations. *Journal of College Student Personnel, 15,* 340-345.

Mager, T.R. (1978). A new perspective for the first amendment in higher education. In E.H. Hammond & R.H. Shaffer (Eds.), *The legal foundations of student personnel services in higher education* (pp. 12-23). Washington, D.C.: American College Personnel Association.

Miller, T.K., & Prince, J.S. (1976). *The future of student affairs.* San Francisco: Jossey-Bass.

Morale v. Grigel, 422 F.Supp. 988 (1976).

Moresco v. Clark, #45523 Supreme Court of New York, Appellate Division, (1984).

Muller, K.H. (1961). *Student personnel work in higher education.* Boston: Houghton-Mifflin.

National Education Association Task Force on Student Involvement. (1971). *Code of student rights and responsibilities.* Washington, D.C.: National Education Association Publications.

Ostroth, D.D., Armstrong, M.R., & Campbell, T.J., III (1978). A nationwide survey of judicial systems in large institutions of higher education. *Journal of College Student Personnel, 19,* 21-27.

Ostroth, D.D., & Hill, D.E. (1978). The helping relationship in student discipline. *NASPA Journal, 16*(2), 33-39.

Parr, P., & Buchanan, E.T. (1979). Responses to the law: A word of caution. *NASPA Journal, 17*(2), 12-15.

Pavela, G. (1985). *The dismissal of students with mental disorders.* Asheville, NC: College Administration Publications.

Penney, J.F. (1967). Variations on a theme: *In loco parentis. Journal of College Student Personnel, 8,* 22-25.

Pitts, J.H. (1980). In loco parentis indulgentis? *NASPA Journal, 17*(4), 20-25.

Ratliff, R.C. (1972). *Constitutional rights of college students: A study in case law.* Metuchen, NJ: Scarecrow.

Rhode, S. (1983). Use of legal counsel: Avoiding problems. In M.J. Barr (Ed.), *Student affairs and the law.* New directions for student services, no. 22 (pp. 67-80). San Francisco: Jossey-Bass.

Saddlemire, G.L. (1980). Professional developments. In U. Delworth, G.R. Hanson & Associates, *Student services* (pp. 25-44). San Francisco: Jossey-Bass.

Schetlin, E.M. (1967). Disorders, deans, and discipline: A record of change. *NAWDAC Journal, 30,* 169-173.

Seavey, W.A. (1957). Dismissal of Students: "Due process." *Harvard Law Review, 70,* 1406-1410.

Serr, R.L., & Taber, R.S. (1987). Mediation: A judicial affairs alternative. In R. Caruso & W.W. Travelstead (Eds.), *Enhancing Campus Judicial Systems,* New directions for student services, no. 39 (pp. 73-84). San Francisco: Jossey-Bass.

Seward, D.M. (1961). Educational discipline. *NAWDAC Journal, 24,* 192-197.

Sherry, A.H. (1966). Governance of the university: Rules, rights, and responsibilities. *California Law Review, 54,* 23-29.

Shur, G.M. (1983). Contractual relationships. In M.J. Barr (Ed.), *Student affairs and the law.* New directions for student services, no. 22 (pp. 27-38). San Francisco: Jossey-Bass.

Sims, O.H. (1971). Student conduct and campus law enforcement: A proposal. In O.S. Sims (Ed.), *New directions in campus law enforcement.* Athens: University of Georgia, Center for Continuing Education.

Smith, A.F. (1978). Lawrence Kohlberg's cognitive stage theory of the development of moral judgment. In L. Knefelkamp, C. Widick, & C.A. Parker (Eds.), *Applying new developmental findings.* New directions for student services, no. 4 (pp. 53-67). San Francisco: Jossey-Bass.

Snoxell, L.F. (1960). Counseling reluctant and recalcitrant students. *Journal of College Student Personnel, 2,* 16-20.

Snoxell, L.F. (1965). Due process and discipline. In T.A. Brady & L.F. Snoxell, *Student discipline in higher education.* Student personnel monograph series, no. 5 (pp. 27-35). Washington, D.C.: American Personnel and Guidance Association.

Sohmer v. Kinnard, 535 F.Supp. 50 (1982).

Steele, B.H., Johnson, D.H., & Rickard, S.T. (1984). Managing the judicial function in student affairs. *Journal of College Student Personnel, 25,* 337-342.

Stein, R.H. (1972). Discipline: On campus, downtown, or both, a need for a standard. *NASPA Journal, 10,* 41-47.

Strickland, D.A. (1965). *In loco parentis* — legal mots and student morals. *Journal of College Student Personnel, 6,* 335-340.

Travelstead, W.W. (1987). Introduction and historical context. In R. Caruso & W.W. Travelstead (Eds.), *Enhancing campus judicial systems.* New directions for student services, no. 39 (pp. 3-16). San Francisco: Jossey-Bass.

Van Alstyne, W.W. (1963). Procedural due process and state university students. *UCLA Law Review, 10,* 368-389.

Van Alstyne, W.W. (1966). The prerogatives of students, the powers of universities, and the due process of law. *NAWDAC Journal, 30,* 11-16.

Williamson, E.G. (1956). Preventative aspects of disciplinary counseling. *Educational and Psychological Measurement, 16,* 68-81.

Williamson, E.G. (1961). *Student personnel services in college and universities.* New York: McGraw-Hill.

Williamson, E.G. (1963). A new look at discipline. *Journal of Secondary Education, 38,* 10-14.

Williamson, E.G., & Foley, J.D. (1949). *Counseling and discipline.* New York: McGraw-Hill.

Wrenn, C.G. (1949). Student discipline in college. *Educational and Psychological*

Measurement, 9, 625-633.

Young, D.P. (1970). *The legal aspects of student dissent and discipline in higher education.* Athens: University of Georgia, Institute of Higher Education.

Young, D.P. (1972). The colleges and the courts. In L.J. Peterson & L.O. Garber (Eds.), *The yearbook of school law 1972* (pp. 201-260). Topeka: National Organization on Legal Problems of Education.

CHAPTER 7

STUDENT FINANCIAL AID

MICHAEL D. COOMES

AN HISTORICAL PERSPECTIVE

Early Initiatives

EFFORTS to aid American college students are generally traced to a bequest of £100 from Lady Ann Radcliffe Mowlson to Harvard College in 1643 for the "yea(rly) maintenance of some poor scholler . . . till such time as such poore scholler doth attain the degree of Master of Arts and no longer" (Scholarship & beneficiary aid, in Godzicki, p. 15). Scholarships funded through the gifts of alumni and other generous benefactors coupled with employment opportunities for needy students, constituted the student aid programs prior to the Civil War. The other major source of student aid instituted during this period was the tuition remission grant "probably the greatest discovery in the development of student aid" (Moon, 1975, p. 4). This discovery allowed colleges to give needy students scholarships without the benefit of endowments or gifts. By raising tuition charges to an amount above their actual costs, institutions were able to subsidize the education of poorer students (Fenske, 1983). These programs of funded grants, tuition remission, and student employment established a number of trends, e.g., providing aid to the needy, multiple sources and types of aid, and institutional commitments of student assistance, that would influence the development of student aid programs sponsored by the states and the federal government.

Federal Involvement

Comprehensive far-reaching federal involvement in higher education is primarily a modern phenomenon (Babbidge & Rosenzweig, 1962;

Fenske, 1983). The first major program of federal aid to students was implemented by the National Youth Administration (NYA). From 1935 to 1943, the federal government expended over $93 million and employed 620,000 students in the NYA. Like much of the higher education legislation that would follow, the NYA program was prompted by a noneducational policy issue, the need to provide work during the Depression, rather than the desire to provide aid to institutions or students (Brubacher & Rudy, 1976).

The Serviceman's Readjustment Act, more commonly known as the G.I. Bill, was passed by Congress in 1944 and was also enacted for noneducational reasons: to reward the veterans of the Second World War for their service and to ease the burden on a fragile economy that a substantial increase in the number of employable men would represent (Rivlin, 1961). By providing support to countless returning servicemen of both the Second World War and the Korean War, the G.I. Bill became the first broad-based student aid legislation enacted by the federal government.

In 1958, prompted by the launching of the Sputnik satellite in 1957 and by a number of national reports outlining the nation's need for improved scientific and technical education, Congress passed the National Defense Education Act (P.L. 85-864). This Act authorized funds for colleges to improve the teaching of modern foreign languages and for conducting research on innovative teaching techniques, created a graduate fellowship program, and authorized funds for the National Science Foundation for the dissemination of scientific information. The cornerstone of the act was a student loan program for students planning teaching careers or pursuing programs in science, mathematics, or modern foreign languages (Conlan, 1981). In addition to creating the first program of generally available federal student aid, NDEA reemphasized a national interest in the quality of education at the state and local level (King, 1975), moved the federal government toward guaranteed opportunity for education (Conlan, 1981), and established the precedent for making students and not institutions the primary beneficiary of federal education funds.

The next major piece of student aid legislation, the Higher Education Act of 1965 (P.L. 89-329), was to be an outgrowth of a growing national concern for the welfare of the underprivileged and a belief that the federal government had a responsibility to provide for its "neediest" citizens. That legislation created the Supplemental Educational Opportunity Grant and Guaranteed Student Loan programs and transferred the

College Work-Study program from the Office of Economic Opportunity to the Office of Education (Moore, 1983). Enacted in a watershed year for federal domestic legislation, Medicare, the Voting Rights Act, and the Elementary and Secondary School Act were also passed in 1965; HEA "embodied for the first time an explicit commitment to equalizing college opportunities for needy students through grants and through such programs as Talent Search designed to facilitate access for the college-able poor" (Gladieux, 1983, p. 410).

The final pieces of the federal student aid puzzle were set in place when the Education Amendments of 1972 (P.L. 92-318) created the Basic Educational Opportunity Grant (BEOG) and the State Student Incentive Grant programs. The creation of BEOG, a program intended to serve as the foundation for a students financial aid package, firmly established that "students, not institutions, are the first priority in federal support" for postsecondary education (Gladieux & Wolanin, 1976, p. 225). Furthermore, as its title implies, BEOG was a reaffirmation of the federal government's commitment to provide access to postsecondary opportunities for all students (Gladieux & Wolanin, 1976).

The passage of the Middle Income Student Assistance Act (P.L. 95-566) in 1978 extended participation in the federal student aid programs to the children of middle class families. According to Finn (1985), that expanded participation added a third goal to access and choice, that of comfort. Not only would the traditional recipients of student aid, the needy and financially disadvantaged, be able to attend their choice of postsecondary institution, but now middle income students would be able to as well (Finn, 1985). The Education Amendments of 1980 (P.L. 96-374) further expanded the federal student aid programs and created a new loan program, the Parents Loan for Undergraduate Study (PLUS).

Subsequent legislation, most specifically the Omnibus Budget Reconciliation Act of 1981 (P.L. 97-35) and the Balanced Budget and Emergency Deficit Control Act of 1985 (P.L. 99-177), has focused attention on the rising costs of federal student aid and has attempted to modify the existing programs in an effort to reduce costs. In addition, the primary outcome of Education Amendments of 1986 was fine tuning the existing system and not the creation of major new initiatives.

State Student Aid

In addition to the significant efforts on the part of the federal government to assist students in meeting postsecondary costs, the states have been involved in the creation and implementation of student aid programs. Many of the early state aid programs were created to assist high ability students. The creation of state aid programs based on financial need with the intention of equalizing opportunity occurred concurrently with the development of the federal role in student aid (Carnegie Council, 1979; Marmaduke, 1983). Nineteen state aid programs existed prior to the 1969-1970 academic year. Since then, the remaining 31 states and seven territories have instituted programs (Marmaduke, 1983).

While state scholarship programs are the oldest form of direct state assistance, state governments also fund loans and student employment programs. The most significant trend in state aid in the past ten years has been the growth of state participation in the Guaranteed Student Loan/PLUS program. State participation in the program takes three forms: (1) states that function as the guarantor through existing state agencies or state chartered corporations; (2) states that assign all operational responsibility to a non-profit corporation like United Student Aid Funds of New York City (USAF); or (3) states that establish their own guarantee agency but contract with non-profit organizations for loan servicing (Johnson, 1981).

The Growth of Student Aid

The growth in the number of programs created to aid students in meeting college costs has been accompanied by significant increases in funding. During the 1965-1966 academic year, aid from all sources, i.e., institutions, states, and the federal government, totaled $546 million; by the 1986-1987 academic year that amount was estimated to be $20.5 billion, an increase of 3,655 percent (Gillespie & Carlson, 1983; Lewis & Merisotis, 1987).

The largest single source of student aid funds is the federal government which accounted for approximately 75 percent of the $20.5 billion awarded to students during the 1986-1987 academic year. State funds accounted for seven percent of that total and institutions accounted for 18 percent (Lewis & Merisotis, 1987).

As was the case with the federal student aid programs, the expansion of state aid programs was accompanied by significant growth in funding for state assistance programs. From 1970-1971 to 1984-1985, state grant aid increased from $236 million to $1.26 billion. During that same time period the number of students aided with state grant funds increased from 535,000 to 1.6 million (Gillespie & Quincy, 1984).

PHILOSOPHY AND PURPOSES

As would be expected from a system that developed incrementally over a period of nearly two hundred years and involved the efforts of postsecondary institutions, state and federal governments, and private industry, student financial aid lacks a clear, consistent philosophy (Conlan, 1981; Fenske, 1983; Gladieux & Wolanin, 1976). Although a consistent and clear student aid philosophy does not exist, Finn (1985) has identified the various purposes financial aid has served. Those purposes are:

1. To increase society's aggregate supply of well-educated and highly skilled manpower.
2. To meet specific manpower shortages and enlarge the supply of men and women with particular kinds of expertise, training, and credentials.
3. To nurture extraordinary individual talent, which otherwise might not be developed to its full potential, through such means as merit scholarships.
4. To encourage the study of particular subjects or disciplines by competent individuals who might not otherwise pursue them.
5. To increase social mobility, foster equality of opportunity, and diminish the importance of private wealth.
6. To advance interests of members of designated groups judged to be deprived in part by lack of access to or participation in higher education.
7. To offset the preexisting economic distortions in the higher education 'marketplace.'
8. To help individual colleges and universities (or particular subdivisions thereof) survive and prosper as institutions, with all that entails for those who cherish and depend on them.
9. To reward or compensate people for services rendered.
10. To carry out a near-infinity of idiosyncratic wishes of donors and benefactors (pp. 2-3).

TYPES OF AID

Student aid resources are also frequently differentiated on the basis of type: loans, grants, and student employment (Binder, 1983; Dannells, 1977; Mueller, 1961; Sharpe, Risty, Guthrie, & Pepinsky, 1946;

VanDusen & O'Hearne, 1973). This section will briefly examine those three general aid types; descriptions of specific aid programs will be presented in a subsequent section.

Grants

Grants are nonrepayable student aid resources or gift aid. Dannells (1977), classified five different types of gift aid:

1. Grants. Nonrepayable student aid based on financial need. Examples include the Pell Grant and state grant aid programs (e.g., Ohio Instructional Grants, Washington State Need Grants).
2. Merit/honors scholarships. Awards to students based on past performance, future promise, exceptional intellectual potential, or outstanding leadership abilities (Finn, 1985).
3. Graduate fellowships. Awards for graduate study and based upon the students high intellectual and academic capabilities (Dannells, 1977).
4. Tuition remission. Subsidized tuition. Frequently awarded to the spouses or children of university employees (Finn, 1985).
5. Service awards. Awards to students for services rendered (e.g., veterans benefits), or for future services (e.g., athletic scholarships, performing arts scholarships) (Finn, 1985, Mueller, 1961).

Although merit scholarships and service awards are highly popular with students and parents, and while much has been written on the need to recognize academic excellence through merit scholarships, the vast majority of grant funds are awarded on the basis of need.

Loans

Loan funds require repayment, either while the student is enrolled or after leaving the institution. While the majority of loan funds carry interest, this interest is frequently subsidized by a lender or by state or federal governments, and as such, student loan interest rates are often below market levels. Loan funds may be secured for short-term or emergency purposes, or they may be long-term in nature intended to cover some or all the expenses related to postsecondary attendance. Lenders include individual postsecondary institutions; commercial banks, savings and loan associations, or credit unions; state loan guarantee agencies; or a national loan marketing agency like the Student Loan Marketing Association (Sallie Mae).

Student Employment

Student employment funds may be either need-based or non-need-based. Although many students are employed while attending a post-secondary institution, only those jobs provided or arranged by the institutions are rightfully considered student aid (Dannells, 1977). Recipients of student employment funds may work in a variety of job settings ranging from the campus food service to off-campus positions in business and industry. Frequently, aid officers and student employment coordinators attempt to place students in jobs that complement their academic interests.

THE AID AWARDING PROCESS

Financial Needs Analysis

A fundamental assumption of the student aid profession is that "the primary responsibility for financing postsecondary education rests with the student and his/her family. Financial assistance from institutions and other sources is only intended as supplementary to the efforts of the family" (National Association of Student Financial Aid Administrators, 1986b, p. 6). To realize that goal, a system for assessing the family's ability to pay has been developed. That system evolved from attempts by a small group of Eastern colleges and universities to equitably distribute their institutional aid resources and reduce the use of student aid as a recruiting tool (Nelson, 1985). From those early attempts to build a rational model for determining a family's ability to pay, and through the efforts of the College Scholarship Service, and numerous student aid officers, a nationwide needs analysis system was developed. Major accomplishments of that system have been the creation of a common needs analysis application, which can be utilized for all federal student aid programs and most state and institutional aid programs, and the implementation of a uniform methodology for assessing financial need. The Higher Education Amendments of 1986 created a new needs analysis process, the Congressional Methodology, which is now the standard for calculating eligibility for all federal student aid programs with the exception of Pell Grants and State Student Incentive Grants (College Entrance Examination Board, 1987).

Stated most simply, financial need is the difference between the costs incurred by a student to attend a postsecondary institution and the resources the student has available to meet those costs. While that definition adequately captures the concept it does not adequately explain the nuances of that concept. Fife (1975) identified the following three criteria for establishing financial need: (1) a "measurement of the economic well-being of the student and/or parent family unit;" (2) a "measure of the family's ability to meet postsecondary expenses;" and (3) a "determination of the actual student educational expense budget" (p. 45). A fourth criterion, the establishment of the economic independence of the student, could be added to that list.

Measuring the Ability to Pay

Needs analysis systems are a type of progressive taxation plan (Carnegie Council, 1979). As such, they are an attempt to determine equitably how much a family can contribute from discretionary income to meet educational costs. The National Task Force on Student Aid Problems (1975) defined ability to pay as "a process which involves the measurement of the economic well being or financial strength of the candidate and/or his or her family and the subsequent determination of a contribution toward educational expenses through the application of some 'taxation rate' to the measure of family strength" (p. 13). It is easy to identify the necessary data to establish a student's or family's economic well-being. These data include, but are not limited to, the family's taxable and non-taxable income, medical expenses, savings and investments, home equity and business worth, other educational benefits, family size, and the number of family members attending postsecondary institutions. Difficulties arise, however, in the establishment of taxation rates. The percentage of the family/student's income and assets that will be taxed is determined by subjective conceptions of what is fair or equitable, and is, therefore, a debatable issue (Davis & VanDusen, 1978). The scope of that debate is beyond the purposes of this discussion. Readers wishing to explore the philosophical reasons for and policy implications of standardized needs-tests are recommended to Case (1983); Finn (1985); and Kramer (1985).

It is important to note that needs analysis systems attempt to calculate the family's ability to pay for postsecondary educational costs, not its willingness. No matter how liberal the needs analysis, some families will be unwilling to tap their discretionary income and use those resources for educational costs. "The most one can perhaps say is that a means test is about right if under it most families at each level of income could not provide, by practicing routine economies, much more financial support than is expected of them" (Carnegie Council, 1979, p. 80).

The Educational Expense Budget

To adequately assess a student's eligibility for need-based student aid it is necessary to establish the student's cost of education. For financial aid purposes, the concept of cost is more complex than tuition charges. To adequately establish the cost incurred by students, aid officers construct elaborate, and hopefully accurate student expense budgets. Typical student expense budgets include the cost of tuition and generally assessed fees, room and board costs, and allowances for books and supplies, transportation expenses, and personal expenses (Case, 1983; Clark, 1983). Certain special expenses, e.g., required medical costs, child care, special equipment fees, may also be included in the student's budget (Case, 1983; Clark, 1983).

Independent Student Criteria

A critical component of any needs analysis is the determination of the financial independence of students. Few financial aid related topics generate as many intense feelings among aid officers, public policy makers, students, and parents as the criteria that have been established for determining financial emancipation. While many students, and not a few parents, believe that students are financially independent upon reaching the age of majority, few aid officers see this as an adequate assessment of independence.

As of 1986, students are considered independent for purposes of establishing eligibility for the federal student aid programs if they meet one of the following conditions:

1. They are at least 24 years of age, or are armed service veterans, or they are orphans or wards of the court, or have dependents other than a spouse (Burns & Moore, 1984).
2. If they are single undergraduates, they must not have been claimed as exemptions on their parents income tax returns for the two years prior to the year for which they are applying for aid. In addition, they must demonstrate that they had at least $4,000 a year in non-parental resources for that same two-year period.
3. They must be married or graduate students who will not be claimed as exemptions on their parents income tax returns for the year in which they are applying for financial aid (Burns & Moore, 1984).

These criteria are arbitrary and may fail to adequately assess the independence of all students. To ensure that students with unique situations who are not covered by the above criteria are treated fairly, the Higher Education Amendments of 1986 allow aid officers to utilize their professional discretion in evaluating students' financial dependency status. Students who are classified as independent students are only required to report their own resources on financial needs analysis documents.

Financial Aid Packaging

Few students receive only one type of aid, rather, most students receive a combination of all three types of aid, grants, loans, and student employment funds, referred to as a financial aid package (Binder, 1983). The College Scholarship Service's (College Entrance Examination Board, 1987) Statement of Practices encourages financial aid offices to use "all forms of aid — grant, loan, employment — and consider other resources available to the student in order to provide the most equitable apportionment of limited funds to eligible students" and to meet "the full need of students to the extent possible within the institution's capabilities" (p. 1.2).

While most aid offices utilize some type of packaging formula to determine the mix of grant, loan, and student employment funds, the formulae used from institution to institution differ greatly. In an effort to bring some uniformity to the awarding process the National Association of Student Aid Administrators established a set of principles for awarding aid that included: (1) awarding sufficient resources to each eligible student, or as many students as possible, to meet his or her needs; (2) setting reasonable self-help (i.e., loan and employment opportunities) expectations; and (3) making awards in a fair and equitable manner (Burns & Moore, 1984).

A number of models have been established to facilitate those principles. Examples include: (1) individual circumstances models that treat each student separately and tailor his/her financial aid to the student's unique needs and circumstances; (2) models that awarded aid on a first come, first serve basis; and (3) ladder models that treat all students in the same manner and after establishing student need, meet that need by awarding Pell Grants, then grants and scholarships, and finally self-help (Binder, 1988).

Like the determination of the family/student's ability to pay and the establishment of realistic expense budgets, financial aid packaging is a complex process. Unlike those other processes, however, packaging can be highly idiosyncratic, and can be based as much on the personal preference and the particular needs of the institution as on concepts of equity and fairness. To assure equitable packaging, the National Association of Student Financial Aid Administrators (1983) suggests adherence to the principles and policies contained in their publication, *Standards for the Development of Policy Guidelines for Packaging Need-based Financial Aid.*

FEDERAL STUDENT ASSISTANCE

The National Task Force on Student Aid Problems (1975) identified four sources of student assistance funds: (1) the federal government; (2) states; (3) institutions; (4) private industry and donors (Binder, 1983). As noted earlier, the largest single source of student aid funds is the federal government. Since there is significant variability in private, institutional, and state aid programs, this section will be devoted to a discussion of the major federal student aid programs covered by Title IV of the Higher Education Act of 1965 and its amendments.

General Student Eligibility Requirements

The federal Title IV aid programs share a number of general eligibility requirements which applicants must meet prior to receiving assistance. To receive federal aid, students must be United States citizens or eligible non-citizens and must be enrolled in or admitted to a program of study that leads to a degree or certificate. Students must also be eligible for aid based on financial need, not be in default on a federal student loan or owe refund on any Title IV grant, state that they will use their aid solely to meet educational expenses, certify that they are either registered with the Selective Service or are not required to be registered, and maintain satisfactory academic progress (Burns & Moore, 1984). Students receiving Pell Grant, GSL, and PLUS/Supplemental Loans must be enrolled at least half-time (Burns & Moore, 1984). Postsecondary institutions participating in the Perkins Loan, Supplemental Educational Opportunity Grant, and College Work-Study programs may use a portion of their allocation for those programs to fund less than half-time students (Burns & Moore, 1984).

Pell Grants

Created by the Higher Education Amendments of 1972, the Pell Grant program (originally the Basic Educational Opportunity Grant program) represented the following new concepts for the federal student aid system: (1) Pell grants were entitlements to individual students based on a formula that established the family's ability to pay for a post-secondary education (Moore, 1983); (2) "Congress established certain controls over the eligibility criteria to be used in the program and therefore made certain that the selection system was to a large extent insulated from change by successive administrations" (Moore, 1983, p. 37); (3) The grant was a direct transaction between the Commissioner of Education (now the Secretary of Education) and the student (Moore, 1983). Because the student receives the Grant from the Department of Education, Pell Grants are completely portable and can be used at any eligible institution (Burns & Moore, 1984). The institution's sole responsibility is to calculate the amount of the grant from a pre-established payment schedule based upon the cost of education at that institution.

Since the Pell Grant is intended to meet a basic level of assistance, it is limited to a specified percentage of a students educational expenses or a specific dollar amount, whichever is lower (Burns & Moore, 1984). For the 1987-1988 academic year those amounts were $2,100 or 60 percent of cost of attendance (Burns & Moore, 1984).

Supplemental Educational Opportunity Grants

The Supplemental Educational Opportunity Grant (SEOG) program was created by Higher Education Amendments of 1972 as a supplement to the Basic Educational Opportunity Grant program which was also created that year (Burns & Moore, 1984). While it was technically a new program, it traced its lineage from the Educational Opportunity Grant (EOG) which was created by the Higher Education Act of 1965 and was the first generally available federal grant aid program (Gladieux & Wolanin, 1976).

The purpose of the EOG/SEOG program has been modified since 1965. It was originally intended as a program of assistance for the exceptionally needy student (Burns & Moore, 1984). The condition that SEOG funds be limited to students with exceptional financial need was eliminated with the passage of the Higher Education Amendments of 1980 but was reinstated with passage of the 1986 Amendments. That law required that SEOG funds be awarded to students with the lowest expected family contribution at the institution and that priority for SEOG funds be given to Pell Grant recipients.

Like Perkins Loans and the College Work-Study program, SEOG funds are allocated directly to institutions to be awarded to students per program requirements and institutional awarding policy (Moore, 1983). The minimum annual SEOG award is $100; the maximum is $4,000 (Burns & Moore, 1984).

State Student Incentive Grants

Created by the Higher Education Amendments of 1972, State Student Incentive Grants (SSIG) were intended to serve as a federal incentive to states to begin or expand their own need-based grant programs (Carnegie Council, 1979). "States apply to the Department of Education for their allotment, up to the amount they can match with qualified state funds . . . State Student Incentive Grant funds must be administered by a single state agency" (Marmaduke, 1983, p. 69). Although the program was originally intended to provide funds solely to undergraduate students, the Higher Education Amendments of 1980 extended eligibility to graduate students (Marmaduke, 1983).

The SSIG program has been extremely successful in encouraging states to begin grant programs. In 1974-1975, the first year of SSIG funding, 28 states sponsored need-based undergraduate grant programs (Marmaduke, 1983). By the 1977-1978 academic year, all 50 states and the District of Columbia had sponsored programs. Since the program has accomplished its major goal, the establishment of state funded grant programs, the Department of Education has recommended the elimination of SSIG funds in each of its annual budgets since Fiscal Year 1982 (Moore, 1983).

Perkins Loan Program

Created originally as the National Defense Student Loan program by the National Defense Education Act of 1958, Perkins Loans are the oldest generally available student aid program sponsored by the federal government, and the first to require that financial need be a criteria for establishing eligibility (Moore, 1983). NDSL was created as a long-term, low-interest loan intended to ensure educational opportunity (Burns & Moore, 1984). The program's name was changed in 1972 to the National Direct Student Loan Program, and again, in 1986 to honor Congressman Carl D. Perkins.

Students may receive a maximum of $4,500 in Perkins Loans if they have not completed the first two years of their program of study. Students who have completed the first two years of study may receive a maximum of $9,000, while students studying for a graduate or professional degree are eligible for a maximum of $18,000 (this amount includes any Perkins, Direct, or Defense loans the student may have received as an undergraduate) (Burns & Moore, 1984). As of October 1, 1981, the annual interest rate for a Perkins Loan was five percent (Moore, 1983).

Although each of the three incarnations of the Perkins Loan program carries different repayment provisions, repayment is generally limited to ten years with minimum payment of $30 per month (Burns & Moore, 1984). Students may defer loan payments for a variety of reasons (e.g., enrollment as at least a half-time student in a postsecondary institution, service in the Armed Forces or the Peace Corps, temporary total disability, parental leave) and they may have all or a portion of their loan cancelled for certain purposes including permanent total disability, and teaching in areas that the Secretary of Education has designated as teacher shortage areas (Burns & Moore, 1984).

Guaranteed Student Loans

Of all the Title IV programs, the Guaranteed Student Loan (GSL) program has "accounted for the largest provision of support for students, and, consequently revenue for colleges and universities" (Moore, 1983). The GSL program which was created in 1965, was intended to encourage states and nonprofit organizations to establish programs of adequate loan insurance for students, to pay a portion of the interest on loans made to students, and guarantee the proceeds of loans insured by states or nonprofit organizations (Burns & Moore, 1984). Unlike other Title IV programs, federal funds for the GSL program do not accrue directly to students but are appropriated for payments to lenders (banks, savings and loans, credit unions) in the form of interest subsidies and guarantee payments. It is the lender who actually makes the loan to the student. Burns and Moore (1984) noted that the "ultimate purpose of the program is to make long-term, deferred payback, educational loans available to all eligible students, and since students are generally without either loan collateral or a credit history, it is necessary to include loan guarantes to the lender against loss through borrower default, bankruptcy, death, or permanent disability" (p. 6.3-1).

Since 1965, the program has gone through a number of modifications. As policy goals have changed, the program has been changed from a need-based loan program to a program available to all students regardless of family or student income and back again to a need-based program. As of 1986, all students must establish financial need to qualify for a GSL.

The Higher Education Amendments of 1986 set maximum loan limits at $2,625 a year for students who have not completed the first two years of their program of study and $4,000 annually for students who have completed their first two years of study. Students enrolled in graduate or professional programs of study are eligible to receive, assuming their financial need warrants it, up to $7,500 annually (Burns & Moore, 1984). The maximum cumulative amount a student may borrow for undergraduate study is $17,250; for undergraduate and graduate/professional study, $54,750. Depending on the size of the loan, students will have from five to ten years to repay their GSL. Like the Perkins Loan program, GSL receipients may have their loan payments deferred for qualified reasons (Burns & Moore, 1984).

PLUS/Supplemental Loans

Authorized by the Higher Education Amendments of 1980, the PLUS program was created as a program of guaranteed, non-subsidized loans for the parents of undergraduate students (Burns & Moore, 1984). The program was divided into two programs in 1986 with the first program, PLUS, intended to serve parents and the second program, Supplemental Loans, intended for independent, graduate and professional students.

With the exception of differences in repayment provisions, interest rates, deferment provisions, and the lack of a needs test to establish eligibility, PLUS/Supplemental Loans are similar to Guaranteed Student Loans. As of 1986, the interest rate on PLUS/Supplemental Loans was capped at 12 percent. If borrowers are not eligible for a deferment, repayment of principal and interest on the loan begins 60 days after the loan is disbursed.

College Work-Study

Originally authorized by the Economic Opportunity Act of 1964, College Work-Study (CWS) was transferred to the Office of Education by the Higher Education Act of 1965 (Moore, 1983). "The purpose of the College Work-Study Program is to stimulate and promote the part-time employment of students who are enrolled as undergraduate, graduate, or professional students who are in need of earnings from employment to pursue courses of study at eligible institutions" (Burns & Moore, 1984, p. 4.1-1). To meet those ends, students may be employed by: (1) their institution; (2) federal, state, or local public agencies; (3) private nonprofit organizations; or (4) the private sector. In order to place students in private, for profit organizations, the institution must demonstrate the academic relevancy of the student's job (Burns & Moore, 1984). Students may be employed during the academic term and during periods (holidays, summer vacation) when they are not enrolled.

While most institutions limit the number of hours a student employee may work, no hourly limitations are placed on the program by statute or regulation (Burns & Moore, 1984). All CWS students must be paid the minimum wage rate.

Specialized Federal Aid Programs

In addition to the Title IV student aid programs, the federal government also funds programs of assistance for unique student populations. Probably the most well known of these are the benefits programs operated by the Veterans Administration (VA). The Veterans Administration currently operates three benefit programs: (1) the GI Bill, the successor World War II and Korean War GI Bill; (2) the Dependents' Educational Assistance Program; and (3) the Veterans Administration Contributory Benefits Program (VEAP). Other aid programs funded by the federal government include Bureau of Indian Affairs (BIA) funding for native Americans, and the Nursing Student Loan program. Unlike BIA and VA benefits, Nursing Student Loans are awarded by participating post-secondary institutions from allocations received from the Department of Health and Human Services and from funds repaid by former borrowers.

THE ADMINISTRATION OF STUDENT AID

Organizational Structure

The establishment of a single office to manage financial aid is a relatively recent phenomena (Johnstone & Huff, 1983; Lange, 1983; North, 1975). Prior to the emergence of large federal and state student aid programs, institutions generally managed their limited scholarship funds through the Admissions Office. If the institution operated a loan program, that program was generally administered by the business or fiscal office (Lange, 1983). With the advent of the National Direct Student Loan program in 1958, and the subsequent growth of federal and state student aid, most institutions saw the need to centralize their student aid operation in one office. This process was given additional impetus by federal requirements to designate a single individual as responsible for the coordination of all the institution's aid programs (Lange, 1983).

The student financial aid office may be a part of any of the three main administrative units of the institution: (1) business and finance, (2) student affairs, or (3) academic affairs (Johnstone & Huff, 1983). A 1981 survey of financial aid administrators disclosed that 63 percent of the respondents worked within the student affairs division, 20 percent worked within the division of business and finance, seven percent were housed in academic affairs, and four percent reported directly to the chief executive officer of the institution (Davis, Ross, Blanchard, & Bennett, 1983).

While North (1975) supported organizational structures that establish a direct line of authority to the institution's chief executive officer, it is most frequently suggested that the aid office be part of the student affairs division (DeJarnett, 1975; Lange, 1985). Johnstone and Huff (1983) provide an eloquent rationale for this type of organizational relationship:

> The office of financial aid reports to the dean of students or vice president for student affairs not merely because it is manifestly a 'helping' service but because it must have extensive communication with all the offices that deal closely with the out-of-class-room problems of students; also, it must share the basic 'helping' orientation traditionally associated with student affairs. (p. 249).

It is for this reason, that student aid is seen as a "helping" service, that it was included as one of the 23 services recognized as student personnel services by *Student Personnel Point of View* (American Council on Education, 1937).

While strong philosophical arguments can be made for considering the student aid office a "student service," the actual disposition of the aid office within the institution's organizational structure is most likely a result of institutional mission (DeJarnett, 1975), the personal preference and expertise of the aid administrator (Adams, 1975), historical accident, or institutional politics.

Functional Roles and Relationships

The purpose of the financial aid office is relatively straightforward: Providing financial assistance to students who, without such aid, would be unable to attain a postsecondary education (Davis & VanDusen, 1978). The roles played by the financial aid office to fulfill that purpose and the relationships the aid office must maintain are numerous. These roles include: (1) enrollment planning, (2) budgeting, (3) serving students, (4) financial stewardship, and (5) governmental relations (Johnstone & Huff, 1983). Three of those roles, enrollment planning, financial stewardship, and serving students, require specialized skills and necessitate close interaction with other functional areas and thus warrant further discussion.

Enrollment Planning

The effects that financial aid can have on the matriculation of students necessitate that the student aid office maintain a good working relationship with the office of admissions, the registrar and the institution's orientation program. While stories of loosely-coupled relationships between admissions and financial aid offices abound (Kuh, 1983), few postsecondary institutions can afford to support such a relationship (Boyd & Henning, 1983). Both functional areas must rely on the information collected and maintained by the other if they wish to positively influence the enrollment trends of the institution (Boyd & Henning, 1983; Phillips & Lewis, 1981).

A recent development has been the establishment of the enrollment management divisions headed by a cabinet level vice-president (Hossler, 1986a). With the goal of keeping "qualified students moving into or through the institutions" (Hossler, 1986b, p. 13), these divisions frequently include the functional areas of admissions, financial aid, marketing, and registration, orientation, institutional research, and academic advising (Graff, 1986; Johnstone & Huff, 1983).

Financial Stewardship

The resources provided an institution through federal, state, and private financial aid allocations and gifts represent a substantial part of the institution's budget (Fenske & Huff, 1983). Since the financial aid office is charged with the efficient management of those resources, it is extremely important that the office maintain effective relationships with the institution's business office (McCormick, 1978). The seminal work on aid office organization (VanDusen & O'Hearne, 1973) stated:

> Because it deals with money, the aid office is perceived as a business function. There is a strong need for a harmonious relationship in the reporting and recording of both incoming money to be added to student aid funds and of the commitments against and actual disbursements from those accounts made by the business office to students upon approval of the aid office. The reporting and the research activities of the student aid office necessarily concern both students and money; therefore, coordination between the business office and the aid office is a virtual necessity if reports are to be prepared accurately and on schedule. (p. 41)

The requirement to responsibly fulfill its stewardship role has been reinforced by regulations that require institutions participating in the federal student aid programs to conduct regular program reviews and audits to ensure that they are meeting their fiduciary responsibilities (Ryan, 1983). Extensive recommendations for ensuring the good stewardship of student aid resources and for establishing efficient disbursement and accounting systems are provided in *The Institutional Guide for Financial Aid Self-evaluation* (National Association of Student Financial Aid Administrators, 1986a), *Management of Student Aid* (National Association of College and University Business Officers, 1979), and Ryan (1983).

Serving Students

A traditional role within the student aid office has been counseling (Lange, 1983). McDougal (1983) emphasized that:

> Using proper and effective counseling techniques with students is a must if financial aid officers are to be responsive to their clientele. It should be stressed that proving scant information, misinformation, or poor service, and failing to attend to the individual student can create formidable obstacles to a student's admission or continuous enrollment at an educational institution. (p. 32)

McDougal (1983) described three primary functions of the counseling role in the financial aid office: (1) providing accurate and complete information to the students; (2) assisting students in integrating financial concerns with other personal and academic concerns and (3) making referrals to other university functional areas (e.g., academic advising, the counseling center, career planning and placement) "when aid officers recognize the situation is beyond their capabilities or scope of responsibility" (p. 32).

Counseling is a labor-intensive function. As will be noted elsewhere, most financial aid offices are small and fulfill a number of functions. As such, they are often unable to adequately meet the counseling needs of students. A frequently proposed solution to resolve this problem is the implementation of a peer-counselor or para-professional program (Cunningham, 1981; Gómez & Treviño-Martínez, 1980). Student peer counselors can be used in a number of roles ranging from intake specialist dealing with common questions proffered by aid recipients to in-house financial aid authorities in residence halls and other living units. While issues of training, responsibility, and staff turnover are of concern when implementing a peer-counseling program, the advantages of using students who understand the needs of their fellow aid recipients outweigh the disadvantages.

In addition to counseling individual students, a common counseling function performed by aid offices is community outreach. Outreach activities include financial aid application workshops, newsletters, workshops for special interest groups at the institution and in the community, and training workshops for high school counselors (Johnson & Frambs, 1979). Trutko (1981), and Burt, Calvert, and Peterson (1985) offer extensive models for establishing local and statewide outreach programs for providing financial aid information to families and students.

Office Organization

Student aid offices tend to be small. Fifty-eight percent of the respondents to the National Association of Student Financial Aid Administrators survey (Davis, Ross, Blanchard, & Bennett, 1983) reported that their offices were staffed by one or two professional staff members. In addition, nearly 67 percent of the respondents reported having three or fewer clerical staff members. Office size was directly related to institutional size however, with offices serving large numbers of aid recipients utilizing much larger student, clerical, and professional staffs.

A number of models has been suggested for organizing larger student aid office staffs. The most common organizes the operation of the staff around programmatic responsibility (Adams, 1975; Lange, 1983; Van-Dusen & O'Hearne, 1973). Such an organization would assign staff to manage each of the three general categories of aid, grants, loans, and student employment. In some larger institutions, with large aid recipient populations, it is not uncommon to see a further subdivision of these areas, with staff teams or administrative units handling the processing of aid applications and documentation for the two largest federal aid programs, Guaranteed Student Loans and Pell Grants. Similarly, it is not uncommon to find large aid offices containing a validation section. These staff sections have as their sole responsibility the validation and verification of the information that students supply on their aid applications.

An alternative approach to the programmatic structure is to organize the aid office around function, i.e., administration and policy development, application intake and document processing, needs analysis and aid packaging, student aid counseling (Lange, 1983). Some large aid offices have used a matrix approach that combines features of the programmatic and functional models.

As was the case with the location of the student aid office within the institution, the structure of the office will be determined by institutional size, administrator preference, work load and staff size. Furthermore, it is likely that most aid offices will experiment with different organizational structures as clientele and demands change.

Regardless of size, many aid offices have found that computerizing their operation has greatly improved services to students and has assisted in meeting regulatory requirements for program management. The operation of the finanical aid office is particularly well suited to computerization. Tasks such as fund accounting, needs analysis, aid packaging, award letter printing, document tracking, and student data validation are highly quantifiable and labor intensive, and as such, they lend themselves readily to the application of computerized technology.

TRENDS

Deficit Reduction

Continued concern for a federal budget deficit poses the potential for reductions in student aid. Although the Balanced Budget and Emergency Deficit Control Act of 1985, commonly known as Gramm-Rudman-Hollings, has not imposed significant reductions on the federal student aid programs, it has served to reinforce a concern for costs within the federal government. Student aid is a "big ticket" item in the federal government, accounting for well over half of all federal support for higher education. Should the nation's economy fail to stay strong, and should the federal deficit fail to shrink, Congressional supporters of financial aid may find it impossible to protect the student aid programs from legislated budget cuts. Should such cuts materialize, the effects on students could be devastating. As Dallas Maratin, president of the National Association of Student Finanical Aid Administrators noted: "I think . . . [a] number one concern should be the availability of financial aid. Considering the deficit, it's obvious that student aid, like other non-defense programs, is likely to experience some reductions. If that actuality occurs, I think its going to have a dramatic impact on the availability of student aid on campuses" ("Dallas Martin," p. 4).

Growing Need Gap

Even though legislation has not significantly reduced student aid appropriations, a continued concern for costs and a concerted effort by the Reagan Administration to reduce the size of the federal commitment to student aid has resulted in a real dollar loss in student aid funding. From the 1980-1981 academic year to the 1986-1987 academic year, total student aid resources, when adjusted for inflation, declined by six percent (Lewis & Merisotis, 1987).

While student aid resources were declining, the cost of attending all types of postsecondary institutions was outpacing inflation (Lewis & Merisotis, 1987). From 1980 to 1987, the increase in tuition and room and board costs ranged from 22 percent at public two-year institutions to 41 percent at independent colleges and universities (Lewis & Merisotis, 1987). This disparity between rising costs and falling student aid resources is resulting in an expanding need-gap which is the difference between the student's calculated financial need and the student aid resources he/she receives to meet that need. That need-gap, which is affecting a growing number of students, holds the potential to prevent significant numbers of students from attending any postsecondary institution.

Limited Access

As noted elsewhere, postsecondary education costs have risen most significantly at the nation's independent colleges and universities (Gillespie & Quincy, 1984). Without state aid to offset increasing expenses, these institutions will experience the most significant cost increases during the remainder of the decade. Federal student aid funding has not kept pace with rising costs, and state and institutional sources of funding have been unable to make up the difference. Students who rely on financial aid to meet college costs may find themselves precluded from attending the nation's independent colleges and universities. While they will still find it possible to attend lower-cost institutions, the goal of using student aid to assure choice of educational opportunities may be seriously threatened.

Student Debt Burden

Perhaps the most significant trend in financial aid in the past decade has been the increasing emphasis on self-help in financing educational costs. During the 1975-1976 academic year, loans and work-study funds accounted for 19 percent of the total aid awarded to students (Hansen, 1987). For the 1985-1986 academic year that amount increased to an estimated 52 percent. The largest increase was in the Guaranteed Student Loan program. From 1975-1976 to 1985-1986, total loan volume grew from $1.27 billion a year, to an estimated $8.3 billion a year (Hansen, 1987). As of 1987, average debt levels (GSL/PLUS and Perkins Loans) for students attending public four-year colleges and universities was $6,665; for students attending four-year independent colleges and universities the average was $8,950 (Hansen, 1987). Furthermore, student loans are no longer simply the financing vehicle of choice for the middle-class and traditional students but are becoming a necessity for a growing number of low-income students, women, and blacks (Hansen, 1987). These facts prompted Hansen (1987) to note:

> It is clear that whether or not traditionally-disadvantaged students are discouraged from participating in higher education because of a swing toward loans as a major form of available assistance, they will find the burden of loan repayment heavier than their white male counterparts because of disparities in income. (p. 23)

Whether these increased debt levels translate into a reduction in the number of minority, low-income, and/or women matriculants remains to be seen. What is known, however, is that those debt levels do increase the cost of attending a postsecondary institution and that low income students are highly sensitive to increased college costs (Hossler, 1984). The effects that large debt levels will have on both students and on the nation's financial health warrant close scrutiny and further research.

Changing Student Populations

Through the early 1990's, the number of full-time, traditional aged, and non-minority students will decline. The number of part-time, older, and minority students will increase (Hodgkinson, 1985). A significant number of minority students come from lower socio-economic backgrounds and qualify for substantial student aid awards. If student aid resources continue to shrink and if college costs rise, these students may be the most directly affected by a growing need-gap. In reporting on the problems of unmet need, Hearn, Fenske, and Curry (1985) noted that for students in the state of Washington in 1983-1984, unmet need was greater for: (1) students at independent four-year colleges and universities than public ones; (2) non-traditional (over age 24) students than traditional students; (3) independent than dependent students; and (4) women than men (with the exception of women under the age of 22 and over the age of 39).

As they are currently eligible for very limited assistance, part-time students may be in an equally difficult position. In the past, when resources have been scarce, these limited resources have been targeted for full-time students. Part-time students may find themselves facing higher costs with less help from limited federal and state aid programs.

Postsecondary education is counting on minority and part-time students to make up for the decline in traditional, non-minority enrollments. If aid for part-time and minority students is limited, however, the postsecondary education system may find itself in a double bind, a declining pool of traditional students to draw from, and a pool of part-time and minority students who are locked out of education for reasons of cost.

Overregulation

The student financial aid office is one of, if not the, most heavily regulated offices on campus. Efforts to curb fraud and abuse and ensure comprehensive and efficient program management, coupled with non-educational policy goals for student aid, e.g., selective service registration verification, have resulted in burdensome administrative responsibilities that are rapidly becoming unbearable. A survey of student aid professionals conducted in 1981 disclosed that 71 percent of the respondents felt that student aid programs were overregulated and 79 percent felt they were becoming overregulated (National Association of Student Financial Aid Administrators, 1983). Since that survey was conducted, the demands placed on student aid offices have increased significantly. In addition to their traditional responsibilities to establish eligibility for aid, determine student need, package awards, account for fund expenditures, and counsel students and parents, student aid officers are now required to verify applicant information, monitor satisfactory academic progress, certify selective service registration status, record student employment earnings to avoid over-awards, and provide increasingly detailed and yet understandable consumer information to students. This type of additional workload has prompted concerns for the effective fulfillment of the counseling role in the student aid office ("Dallas Maratin," 1988).

New Financing Plans

In an effort to offset the declining value of the federal student aid dollar and to provide new financing options for parents and students, a number of alternative aid programs and financing plans have been created. Foose and Meyerson (1986) identified the following categories of alternative approaches to tuition financing: (1) accelerated payment plans, e.g., prepayment plans, tuition stabilization plans, tuition futures plans; (2) delayed payment plans, e.g., installment plans, loan programs, commercial financing plans; (3) pricing and discounted payment plans, e.g., differential pricing, volume discounts, lotteries, tuition matching, employee discounts; and (4) other techniques, e.g., credit card payment, electronic funds transfer, work programs. While all of these programs cannot accurately be classified under the rubric of financial aid, they all serve the same purpose which is to make the payment of tuition and other direct educational expenses easier to bear for students and families.

Accelerated payment plans which "allow the consumer to trade off the use of cash and its potential earnings for the opportunity to avoid some or all future tuition increases" have become increasingly popular with institutions and some states (Foose & Meyerson, 1986, p. 2). These plans are advantageous to institutions because they provide a stable source of income for investment and encourage students to commit to an institution early and maintain that commitment through graduation (Foose & Meyerson, 1986). Families and students find these plans attractive because they serve as a hedge against inflationary increases in tuition and because they allow families to spread the cost of a postsecondary education over a longer period of time. One type of accelerated payment plan, tuition futures, has been adopted by a number of states (California, Florida, Indiana, Michigan, Tennessee, and Wyoming) (Grotrian, 1987; ("Prepaid tuition plans," 1987). These plans allow "families or students [to] purchase today, for fixed discounted amount, future college education" by guaranteeing tuition at a participating institution in the state (Foose & Meyerson, 1986, p. 10).

While accelerated or prepayment plans have become very popular with institutions, families, and public policy makers, they are not without their detractors. As noted in the *NASPA Forum* ("Prepaid Tuition," 1987) prepayment plans may limit students' choice of institutions or discourage them from attending out of state institutions. Hart (1987) also questioned the intended market of such plans, noting that they will be most attractive to middle- and upper-class families. As such they will not serve as a substitute for the existing need-based student aid programs sponsored by states and the federal government.

While accelerated payment plans are gaining wider acceptance, new forms of delayed tuition payment are also being considered. Deferring the payment of educational costs is not new. The Perkins Loan program has been in existence for 30 years. Certain "new" loan programs, such as the Income Contingent Loan program created by the Higher Education Amendments of 1986, can trace their origins to programs like "PAYE" (pay-as-you-earn) and the Zacharias Plan of the late 1960s and early 1970s (Dannells, 1977). As of the 1987-1988 academic year, the program was being pilot-tested in ten postsecondary institutions. The feature that sets this program apart is its graduated repayment schedule, a schedule that is based on the student's post-enrollment income. Proponents of the program argue that it will make repayment easier for students in low paying jobs and thus will make certain public service occupations more appealing to students. Opponents argue that the program favors students who secure well paying positions and can repay their loans more quickly thus avoiding protracted interest charges. Results of the pilot testing of the program should resolve some of these issues.

While all of the alternative financing options present opportuntiies for students and parents, Grotrian (1987) raises a fundamental concern with the proliferation of schemes, plans, and programs;

> New financing strategies sponsored by colleges and states will remain a *confusing patchwork* [author's emphasis] of assistance for planning purposes, for at least the near future . . .
>
> Perhaps what is needed more than the current wave of new financing arrangements and plans is a fundamental revamping of student aid policy at the federal level. The creation of individualized financing plans by institutions and states is not the long-term, broad solution to the growing problem of paying for higher education. Hopefully, a more lasting strategy will come out of the current intense struggle over na-

tional priorities and the role of the federal government in helping finance educational opportunities. (p. 48)

REFERENCES

Adams, F.C. (1975). Administering the office of student work and financial assistance. In R. Keene, F.C. Adams & J.E. King (Eds.), *Money, marbles, or chalk: Student financial support in higher education* (pp. 214-228). Carbondale, IL: Southern Illinois University Press.

American Council on Education. (1937). *The student personnel point of view.* Washington, D.C.: American Council on Education.

Babbidge, J.D., & Rosenzweig, R.M. (1962). *The federal interest in higher education.* New York: McGraw-Hill.

Binder, S.F. (1983). Meeting student needs with different types of financial aid awards. In R.H. Fenske, R.P. Huff & Associates, *Handbook of student financial aid: Programs, procedures and policies* (pp. 149-168). San Francisco: Jossey-Bass.

Boyd, J.D., & Henning, G.E. (1983). Using student aid in recruiting and admissions. In R.H. Fenske, R.P. Huff & Associates, *Handbook of student financial aid: Programs, procedures and policies* (pp. 307-329). San Francisco: Jossey-Bass.

Brubacher, J.S., & Rudy, W. (1976). *Higher education in transition: A history of American colleges and universities, 1963-1976.* New York: Harper & Row.

Burns, R.K. & Moore, J.W. (1984). *NASFAA encyclopedia of student financial aid.* Washington, D.C.: National Association of Student Financial Aid Administrators.

Burt, B., Calvert, J., & Peterson, L. (1985). Coordinated financial aid outreach: A working mode. *The Journal of Student Financial Aid, 15*(2), 38-43.

Carnegie Council on Policy Studies in Higher Education. (1979). *Next steps for the 1980s in student financial aid.* San Francisco: Jossey-Bass.

Case, J.P. (1983). Determining financial need. In R.H. Fenske, R.P. Huff & Associates, *Handbook of student financial aid: Programs, procedures and policies* (pp. 124-148). San Francisco: Jossey-Bass.

Clark, R.B. (1983). *A handbook for use in preparation of student expense budgets. (Rev. Ed.).* Washington, D.C.: National Association of Student Financial Aid Administrators.

College Entrance Examination Board. (1987). *Manual for student aid administrators: 1988-89 policies and procedures.* New York: College Entrance Examination Board.

Conlan, T.J. (1981). *The federal role in the federal system: The dynamics of growth. The evolution of a problematic partnership: The Feds and higher ed.* Washington, D.C.: Advisory Commission on Intergovernmental Relations.

Cunningham, O.J. (1981). The peer counselor: A possible solution to two problems in financial aid administration. *The Journal of Student Financial Aid 11* (1), 22-24.

Dallas Maratin: At the helm. (1987-1988, December-Jaunary). *NASPA Forum, 8,* 1, 4-5.

Dannells, M. (1977). Financial aid. In W.T. Packwood (Ed.), *College student personnel services* (pp. 51-91). Springfield, IL: Charles C Thomas.

Davis, J.S., Ross, J., Blanchard, S.G., & Bennett, R. (1983). *A profession in transition:*

Characteristics and attitudes of the financial aid administrator Fall, 1981. Washington, D.C.: National Association of Student Financial Aid Administrators.

Davis, J.S., & VanDusen, W.D. (1978). *Guide to the literature of student financial aid.* New York: College Entrance Examination Board.

DeJarnett, R.P. (1975). The organization of student support programs in institutions of higher learning. In R. Keene, F.C. Adams, & J.E. King (Eds.), *Money, marbles, or chalk: Student financial support in higher education* (pp. 206-213). Carbondale, IL: Southern Illinois University Press.

Fenske, R.H. (1983). Student aid past and present. In R.H. Fenske, R.P. Huff, & Associates, *Handbook of student financial aid: Programs, procedures and policies* (pp. 5-26). San Francisco: Jossey-Bass.

Fenske, R.H., & Huff, R.P. (1983). Overview, synthesis, and additional perspectives. In R.H. Fenske, R.P. Huff & Associates, *Handbook of student financial aid: Programs, procedures and policies* (pp. 371-398). San Francisco: Jossey-Bass.

Fife, J.D. (1975). *Applying the goals of student financial aid.* AAHE-ERIC/Higher Education Research Report No. 10. Washington, D.C.: American Association for Higher Education.

Finn, C.E., Jr. (1978). *Scholars, dollars and bureaucrats.* Washington, D.C.: Brookings Institute.

Finn, C.E., Jr. (1985). Why do we need financial aid? or, Desanctifying student assistance. In College Entrance Examination Board, *An agenda for the year 2000: Thirtieth anniversary colloquia proceeding* (pp. 1-23). New York: College Entrance Examination Board.

Foose, R.A., & Meyerson, J.W. (1986). *Alternative approaches to tuition financing: Making tuition more affordable.* Washington, D.C.: National Association of College and University Business Officers.

Gillespie, D.A., & Carlson, N. (1983). *Trends in student aid: 1963 to 1983.* New York: The College Board.

Gillespie, D.A., & Quincy, L. (1984). *Trends in student aid: 1980 to 1984.* New York: The College Board.

Gladieux, L.E., & Wolanin, T.R. (1976). *Congress and the colleges: The national politics of higher education.* Lexington, MA: Lexington Books.

Gladieux, L.E. (1983). Future directions of student aid. In R.H. Fenske, R.P. Huff & Associates, *Handbook of student financial aid: Programs, procedures and policies* (pp. 399-433). San Francisco: Jossey-Bass.

Godzicki, R.J. (1975). A history of financial aids in the United States. In R. Keene, F.C. Adams, & J.E. King (Eds.), *Money, marbles, or chalk: Student financial support in higher education* (pp. 14-21). Carbondale, IL: Southern Illinois University Press.

Gómez, J., & Treviño-Martinez, R. (1980). Peer counseling: Can it save financial aid recipients on scholastic probation? In S.F. Binder (Ed.), *Responding to changes in financial aid programs.* New directions for student services, no. 12 (pp. 49-67). San Francisco: Jossey-Bass.

Graff, A.S. (1986). Organizing the resources that can be effective. In D. Hossler (Ed.), *Managing college enrollments.* New directions for higher education, no. 53 (pp. 89-101). San Francisco: Jossey-Bass.

Grotrian, H.P. (1987). New strategies for financing a college education: What are they and will they work? *The Journal of Student Financial Aid, 17* (2), 45-48.

Hansen, J.S. (1987, January 7). *Student loans: Are they overburdening a generation?* In *The Chronicle of Higher Education, 33,* 17, pp. 18-25.

Hart, L. (1987). Financing tuition: Are prepayment plans the right answer. In R.E. Anderson & J.W. Meyerson (Eds.), *Financing higher education: Strategies after tax reform. New Directions for Higher Education, No. 58.* San Francisco: Jossey-Bass.

Hearn, J.C., Fenske, R.H., & Curry, D.J. (1985). Unmet financial need among postsecondary students: A statewide study. *The Journal of Student Financial Aid, 15* (3), 31-44.

Hodgkinson, H. (1985). *All one system: Demographics of education, kindergarten through graduate school.* Washington, D.C.: Institute for Educational Leadership.

Hossler, D. (1984). *Enrollment management: An integrated approach.* New York: College Entrance Examination Board.

Hossler, D. (1986a). *Creating effective enrollment management systems.* New York: College Entrance Examination Board.

Hossler, D. (1986b). Enrollment management and its context. In. Hossler, D. (Ed.). *Managing college enrollments: New Directions for Higher Education, No. 53* (pp. 5-14). San Francisco: Jossey-Bass.

Johnson, J.L. (1981). The Guaranteed Student Loan Program: A survey of state-level administration. *The Journal of Student Financial Aid, 11* (3), 9-15.

Johnson, R.W., & Frambs, G. (1979). Financial aid office: Counseling and outreach. *The Journal of Student Financial Aid, 9* (3), 28-34.

Johnstone, D.B., & Huff, R.P. (1983). Relationship of student aid to other college programs and services. In R.H. Fenske, R.P. Huff & Associates, *Handbook of student financial aid: Programs, procedures and policies* (pp. 237-257). San Francisco: Jossey-Bass.

Kramer, M.A. (1985). The costs of higher education: Who pays and who should pay? In College Entrance Examination Board, *An agenda for the year 2000: Thirtieth anniversary colloquia proceeding* (pp. 55-68). New York: College Entrance Examination Board.

King, L. (1975). *The Washington lobbyists for higher education.* Lexington, MA: Lexington Books.

Kuh, G.D. (1983). Guiding assumptions about student affairs organizations. In G.D. Kuh (Ed.), *Understanding student affairs organizations: New Directions for Student Services, No. 23* (pp. 15-26). San Francisco: Jossey-Bass.

Lange, M.L. (1983). Factors in organizing an effective student aid office. In R.H. Fenske, R.P. Huff & Associates, *Handbook of student financial aid: Programs, procedures, and policies* (221-236). San Francisco: Jossey-Bass.

Lewis, G., & Merisotis, J.P. (1987). *Trends in student aid: 1980 to 1987.* New York: The College Board.

Marmaduke, A.S. (1983). State student aid programs. In R.H. Fenske, R.P. Huff & Associates, *Handbook of student financial aid: Programs, procedures and policies* (pp. 55-76). San Francisco: Jossey-Bass.

McCormick, J.L. (1978). The student financial aid administrator and the business officer: A management team? *The Journal of Student Financial Aid, 8* (2), 19-27.

McDougal, J. (1983). The role of counseling in student financial aid—The most sensitive function that takes place in a financial aid office.

Moon, R.G. (1975). History of institutional aid in the United States. In College Entrance Examination Board, *Perspectives on financial aid.* New York: College Entrance Examination Board.

Moore, J.W. (1983). Purposes and provisions of federal programs. In R.H. Fenske, R.P. Huff & Associates, *Handbook of student financial aid: Programs, procedures and policies* (pp. 27-54). San Francisco: Jossey-Bass.

Mueller, K.H. (1961). *Student personnel work in higher education.* Boston: Houghton-Mifflin.

National Association of College and University Business Officers. (1979). *Management of student aid.* Washington, D.C. National Association of College and University Business Officers.

National Association of Student Financial Aid Administrators. (1983). *Standards for the development of policy guidelines for packaging need-based financial aid.* Washington, D.C.: National Association of Student Financial Aid Administrators.

National Association of Student Financial Aid Administrators. (1986a). *Institutional guide for financial aid self-evaluation* (7th ed.). Washington, D.C.: National Association of Student Financial Aid Administrators.

National Association of Student Financial Aid Administrators. (1986b). *National membership directory, 1986.* Washington, D.C.: National Association of Student Financial Aid Administrators.

National Task Force on Student Aid Problems. (1975). *Final report,* Brookdale, CA: National Task Force on Student Aid Problems.

Nelson, J.E. (1985). The role of the College Scholarship Service in the year 2000. In College Entrance Examination Board, *An agenda for the year 2000: Thirtieth anniversary colloquia proceedings, The College Scholarship Service* (pp. 151-170). New York: College Entrance Examination Board.

North, W.M. (1975). The role of the aid officer in the institution. In R. Keene, F.C. Adams, & J.E. King (Eds.), *Money, marbles, or chalk: Student financial support in higher education* (pp. 259-275). Carbondale, IL: Southern Illinois University Press.

Phillips, P., & Lewis, J.A. (1981, March 26). Will the odd couple find happiness? *College Board Review,* 13-15.

Prepaid tuition plans: A help or a hindrance? (1987, November). *NASPA Forum, 8* (3), p. 3.

Rivlin, A. (1961). *The role of the federal government in financing higher education.* Washington, D.C.: Brookings Institute.

Ryan, D.R. (1983). Disbursing and controlling aid funds. In R.H. Fenske, R.P. Huff & Associates, *Handbook of student financial aid: Programs, procedures and policies* (pp. 169-193). San Francisco: Jossey-Bass.

Sharpe, R.T., Risty, G.B., Guthrie, W.S., & Pepinsky, H.B. (1946). *Financial assistance for college students.* Series VI—Student personnel work—Number 7. Washington, D.C.: American Council on Education.

Trutko, H.M. (1981). Reducing the counseling load: Better use of professional associations, the media, and paraprofessionals. *The Journal of Student Financial Aid, 11* (1), 25-30.

VanDusen, W.D., & O'Hearne, J.J. (1973). *A design for a model college financial aid office* (Rev. Ed.). Washington, D.C.: College Entrance Examination Board.

CHAPTER 8

HEALTH SERVICES

GERALD L. SADDLEMIRE

HISTORY

FOR THE FIRST two hundred years of higher education in the United States, the health of students was considered to be a personal matter rather than a responsibility of the institution. The well-to-do student could seek out medical resources in the community while the poorer student was at the mercy of any charitable citizen who might be moved to offer assistance (Farnsworth, 1965).

Early developments of health work among college students started with the gymnastic period in 1825 when German and Scandinavian methods of physical exercise were introduced into the United States (Packwood, 1977). Later, in 1859, Edward Hitchcock, M.D. was employed at Amherst College as the first professor of hygiene to provide student health services. Boynton (1962) in her history of college health called Hitchcock the father of college health. He promoted the concept that the body and mind should work together harmoniously and offered health education lectures on such topics as tobacco use, skin care, and venereal disease (VD).

In the latter part of the nineteenth century, the concern about off campus living conditions, control of communicable diseases, sanitation, and mental health led to the establishment of infirmaries to care for students too ill to remain in their room but not sick enough to warrant hospitalization. Late in the nineteenth century, the growth of athletic programs brought "team doctors" to the campus where they often found themselves taking care of students who were not participating in intercollegiate athletics.

Early in the 1900s, some colleges initiated programs that broadened the health services available to the students by placing greater attention on treatment, prevention and health education. After World War I, the federal government provided funds to colleges and universities for research in VD education and prevention and to provide more extensive health services for army units on campus.

> Additional impetus for the development of the college health movement came from increased interest in prevention and public health in education, the development of medical schools, the principle of *in loco parentis,* the fact that many colleges were built away from communities which could provide health care, and the notion that college work endangers health with its accompanying stereotype of the college student being an anemic, frail, bespectacled anthropoid (American Medical Association, 1936). (Packwood, 1977, p. 299).

The American Student Health Association, founded in 1920, soon became the American College Health Association, a major force in promoting health education, medical services, and environmental concerns. Quality program development was encouraged through professional associations, conferences, and publications, *Recommended Standards and Practices for a College Health Program* (ACHA, 1977, 1984).

College health programs developed very slowly for the first few decades after World War I. Even as community health education became acceptable during the 1930s, college health professionals retained a narrow vision of their educational responsibilities. As late as 1953, the Moore and Summerskill survey of health programs in higher education found that health education was defined as a course in hygiene and health. Boynton, Director of Health Services at the University of Minnesota, was the first to add a health educator to her college health staff in 1954, opening a new era in college health history that emphasized preventive health techniques. However, during the 1960s, many campus health services and affiliated private practitioners were still not addressing such problems as VD, contraception, drug use, and mental health. Students turned to other resources such as the free clinics that began to appear in the late 1960s. Students and health service professionals realized that new health needs and rights had developed. As a result, substantial changes were made in college health services to make them more comprehensive. The latest revision of ACHA standards recommended programming in the following areas: (1) outpatient and inpatient services, (2) mental health, (3) athletic medicine, (4) dental services, (5) rehabilitation/physical medicine, (6) preventive medicine, (7) health education and promotion, (8) environmental health and safety, and (9) occupational health.

College health services are placing greater importance on the role of preventive medicine and health education. In preparing the nation's health objectives for the 1990s, the Surgeon General designated one of the priority areas as "improving the health and health habits of adolescents and young adults" (Public Health Service, 1979). Emphasis has shifted from infectious diseases, the primary concern in the early twentieth century, to preventable illnesses, self care issues, and health promotion concepts for a healthier lifestyle (D.C. Sloane & B.C. Sloane, 1986).

Since the central goal of higher education is to develop expertise in problem solving, this cognitive process can and should be applied to health matters. The need to involve students in decisions related to their health habits and behavior is now widely accepted as a responsibility of all who have some influence on health care in higher education institutions (Zapka & Love, 1986).

ADMINISTRATION

In 1965, Dana Farnsworth wrote in the monograph *College Health Services in the United States* that health service directors prefer to report to the president, or in a large organization, to the vice president for student affairs. The chief student affairs officer must appreciate the functions of the health service and provide the necessary freedom and support for the practice of the best possible medicine.

The director should have a full time appointment. In some institutions the director of the health service is a nurse. A nurse-director should have a masters level education with clinical and administrative experience. All nurse-directors must have a qualified physician consultant to provide direction for medical treatment according to ACHA (1984) *Recommended Standards and Practices for a College Health Program.*

When a new health service is to be developed, standards and procedures are available from the American College Health Association. Burnett (1987) described a successful creation of a health service for an urban campus that followed very closely the ecosystem design process originally described by Banning (1974). The successful health service is appropriately designed for its environment, is well organized and responsive to student needs, and is adequately staffed.

The method of financing a college health program depends on the amount of support from one or more of the following sources: health fees, allocation from general funds, generated income by direct fees to students, faculty and/or staff health insurance program, endowment gifts and grants.

The financing of health care services changes with new demands, shifting priorities and escalating costs forcing colleges and universities to seek alternative arrangements and creative mechanisms for both providing and financing student health programs. A study of the New England (excluding the greater Boston area) campuses examined the similarities and differences in financing health services among 11 institutions (Hiller, Patterson, & Kaufman, 1985). They concluded that on the basis of the data collected, there was little question concerning the most feasible approach to financing a student health program in institutions under 12,000 students. Clearly, the evidence demonstrated that some form of combined general fund and student prepaid health fee held the most equitable and feasible means of supporting a successful student program. Furthermore, it was concluded that the size of the student population was one of the critically important variables in determining whether the health fee paid by students should be voluntary or involuntary.

The stronger and more comprehensive programs were supported by a significant level (minimum of 50%) of general funds augmented by either a mandatory health fee (in schools of less than 10,000 students) or voluntary health fee. Thus, the authors suggest that, in institutions with a student population in excess of about 10,000, the use of a voluntary fee approach might sustain the necessary enrollment to provide an adequate supplementary source of revenue. However, in smaller institutions using a combined financing approach, it appears that mandatory fees must be imposed to assure the collection of necessary supplementary funds to facilitate sound planning, staffing, and the operation of a well-rounded program.

> In the opinion of the authors, however, even many of the larger and more comprehensive-looking programs described in this study exhibited areas in which major improvements could be made. Thus, for purposes of providing optimum health and medical care, particularly in an environment in which inflation is forcing cutbacks in most university-supported budgets, implementation of mandatory health fees to supplement general fund support is recommended over the voluntary approach to assure more adequate funding. It should be firmly stated, however, that implementing a mandated student fee should *not* serve to replace existing university commitments to student health. In that

regard, analysis of the available data suggested that regardless of the voluntary or involuntary nature of the fee, general university support should not fall below the level necessary to maintain a moderately comprehensive, accessible program providing continuity of quality care. (Hiller, Patterson, & Kaufman, 1985, pp. 117-118)

Health education programs may also be funded or co-sponsored by residence life or student activities because of campus wide concern about alcohol abuse or drug dependency. Federal funding and even the alcohol industry are a resource for developing and implementing alcohol education programs (Heiling, 1977; Kraft, 1978; Engs, 1978).

MISSION

The *Recommended Standards and Practices for a College Health Program* (1984) issued by the American College Health Association state that the main areas of responsibility should include: (1) personal health services including medical, dental and surgical care, encompassing preventive, diagnostic, therapeutic and rehabilitative services for both physical and emotional problems; (2) environmental surveillance and control; and (3) education for health through educational programs.

The delivery system needed to provide these systems varies because of the diversity of the institutions in which health services are located. The size of the institution, philosophy of the administration, the number of resident students, the size of the community and extent of community hospital facilities are variables that cause the differences among campus health services (DeYoung, 1977).

In 1985, ACHA formed the Task Force on Achieving the Health Objectives for the Nation in Higher Education to address the national health objectives for students in colleges and universities. This task force has the responsibility of monitoring the progress made by college and university populations toward meeting those objectives that refer to adolescents and young adults. An example of one of the broad national goals established by the Department of Health and Human Services is to improve the health and health habits of adolescents and young adults, and, by 1990, to reduce deaths among people ages 15 to 24 by at least 20 per cent to fewer than 93 per 100,000.

The Task Force, in examining the national objectives, identified areas in preventative health services requiring immediate attention: AIDS, cancer screening, self health care, pregnancy and sexuality.

Health promotion objectives that need careful attention are (1) the interrelationship of alcohol, injury, and violent behavior; as well as (2) the interrelationship of exercise, fitness, nutrition, and stress. Other issues that need to be addressed include: (1) depression, (2) suicide, (3) sexual assault and harassment, (4) sexual identity (need and concerns of homosexual and bisexual students), and (5) child and spouse abuse according to the task force.

In the area of health protection, objectives that must be emphasized are the predisposing factors for injury and risk taking behavior. In 15 to 24 year olds, 79 percent of all deaths are the result of injury involving a combination of alcohol and vehicles. Factors associated with preventing injury include the maintenance of proper lighting at night, escort services, hotlines, disaster plans, and monitoring the risks of organized sports and personal recreational exercise (Chervin, Sloane, Gordon, & Gold, 1986).

EMERGING ISSUES

The executive director of the American College Health Association (Blom, 1987) identified the five areas that will require continuing attention in the future. They are: (1) student health, (2) insurance plans, (3) seeking grant money for AIDS education, (4) collaboration with national student affairs associations (such as ACUHO-I, NASFA, ACPA, NASPA), and (5) sharing with the higher education community the reports of task forces on alcohol and substance abuse, drug testing, health objectives for the nation, minority and student involvement and insurance.

After reviewing the health status of the age group of greatest concern to college health programs, McGinnis (1987) predicted two general trends for college health. One is that preventive services are going to play a larger role in college health.

> . . . But as science yields ever more sophisticated screening techniques to identify populations at special risk for certain conditions, conditions that will shape the rest of the lives of these people, screening techniques will play a larger part in college health programs . . . You will be offering not only screening but intervention services as well. Of course, more immunizations will be offered as recombinant DNA technology makes more multiple antigens available for respiratory diseases, for sexually transmissible diseases, for AIDS and so on. You will have better and more effective contraceptives to draw upon in your preventive

services, better blood pressure medications, and more definitive dietary and exercise intervention packages. A host of new preventive services will be available and assimilated into your armamentarium. (p. 169).

McGinnis' second prediction is that psychological support services will become an increasingly important component of college health.

. . . Such services will grow in response to demands created by drug and alcohol dependence, sexual assault and violence, competition for employment, population and urbanization pressures, intergenerational dependence, and the like — the host of pressures emerging as prominent issues on our national scene. And, with the advent of tools derivative of better risk-factor identification, of motivational research, and developments in the basic neuro-sciences, it seems clear to me that the future holds a growing emphasis on the need for college health to provide services that address the pressures and stresses that increasingly intrude upon the youth of today and can only be expected to expand in the future. (p. 169).

Speculation on the future for college and university health services must take into consideration two dynamic arenas: higher education and health care. Recent national studies that examine higher education have put a spotlight on such areas as: curriculum, accountability, student involvement, cost effective programs, and competency achievement. At the same time, the health care field is being affected by skyrocketing costs, increased consumer participation in medical care and its demystification, increasing government regulation, competition among health-service providers and demands for quality and cost effectiveness (Zapka & Love, 1986).

The ability of the health service to compete for resources with other campus services can be met best by managing and documenting health programs that earn strong student support and convincing skeptics of the legitimacy of the health-promotion role of health services. Health promotion programs that support an active, healthy campus image can strengthen the marketing strategy for the recruitment of students. As colleges give more attention to the overall quality of campus life, a health services staff skilled in outreach-promotion programs becomes an increasingly valued campus resource for recruitment and retention of students.

The number of students in colleges and universities makes them an attractive potential market for health service providers outside the campus. This challenge can best be met by making a case for the unique product required by the college market where student characteristics and the campus environment must be well understood for implementing programs on sexuality and responsible drinking.

A strategic planning process should be in place to explore programs that anticipate new developments. Faculty, staff, and community friends are increasingly interested in exercise, stress management, and wellness type programs (Parsons, 1987; Love, Morphis, & Page, 1981). As the student body becomes more diverse, constituency support can be increased by giving more attention to older students, community, handicapped students, and international students.

Zapka and Love (1986) describe the need and difficulty in evaluating college health services. Additional empirical data are needed describing the long term health benefits achieved from health promotion programs. Rigorous evaluation is needed to help determine whether benefits are worth the cost. While the issue of cost effectiveness will continue, there needs to be a better way to argue for supporting the cost of health promotion programs. Better arguments for support may be found in contributing to a positive campus image, enhancing student health that improves retention and class attendance, and describing benefits that can be marketed by the admissions officers.

AIDS/ARC/HIV

The American College Health Association, through its task forces and publications, has taken the lead in providing the college and university community with useful information about Acquired Immune Deficiency Syndrome (AIDS); Human Immunodeficiency Virus (HIV) and AIDS Related Complex (ARC). A special report,, *AIDS on the College Campus*, edited by Richard Keiling and produced by the ACHA Task Force on AIDS assists campuses with their educational programs and policy development. A general statement on institutional response to AIDS is followed by a chapter that discusses the development of institutional policies and administrative liaisons. The statement on housing policies sets guidelines to protect the healthy resident student from possible infection and to protect the rights of the student with AIDS. The housing policy was approved and recommended by the Association of College and University Housing Officers — International. Another chapter identifies resources for AIDS education and an outline of programs that answers such questions as What is AIDS? What are the symptoms? How is AIDS transmitted? Who is at risk for getting AIDS? How can people reduce risks? What if you have AIDS, ARC, or a positive antibody test? What if someone you know has AIDS, ARC, or a positive antibody test?

INTERNATIONAL STUDENTS

The nearly 400,000 students from foreign countries, particularly Asia, are placing increasing responsibility on health services to provide appropriate assistance. In a study of the delivery of health care to international students, Williamson (1982) identified four features of the international student which may influence diagnosis and treatment. They are (1) a health background which may include practices and beliefs that differ greatly from those of the typical domestic student; (2) an illness not commonly seen in the area surrounding the health center, i.e., parasites; (3) a language barrier that may present difficulty in describing the student's condition and related the inability to discuss concepts such as stress or depression; (4) culture shock, described feelings of helplessness, discomfort, and a state of disorientation.

Ebbin and Blankenship (1986) reviewed 96,804 diagnoses from student visits to the University of Southern California Student Health Center over a three year period. They compared the frequency of diagnoses between international and domestic students and identified the diagnoses that may be stress related. They found that the international students use the health center more frequently than domestic students. International students are not familiar with health care systems off campus and are often lonely and respond well to special programs to orient international students. Cough and inflammation of the trachea were the most frequent causes of visits to the health service. Recommendations were made to conduct special orientation with particular reference to the differences and similarities between the United States systems of care and those seen in other countries. Written materials about health services in a number of languages will help. Peer helpers may assist the student in dealing with emotional stress. Interpreters should be used when a language barrier exists. Ebbin and Blankenship (1986) recommend further that the student should be asked specifically, "What would you do, and how would you be treated if you had these symptoms in your home setting?"

At the Seminar on International Students, jointly sponsored by the American College Health Association and the National Association for Foreign Student Affairs held in Washington in 1985, many campus and federal government representatives indicated that medical problems are the single most important reason for termination of study by international students (Blom, 1986). These two associations created a joint task force responsible for developing guidelines and programs for college campuses regarding the provision of health care services to international students.

Increasingly, international scholars and graduate students bring their families with them to United States campuses. Vogel (1986) describes what happens when people from one country try to live and function within a very different society. She discusses the nature of communication problems, the pervasive anxiety of living overseas, and social isolation as adjustment areas that are inevitable and normal in the international family setting.

MENTAL HEALTH

There is some general agreement that 10 to 15 percent of college students need some professional assistance each year because of emotional difficulties (Farnsworth, 1965; American College Health Association, 1984). The response to this need depends on the resources available on the campus and in the nearby community. The mental health service must establish a close working relationship with many off campus individuals and offices concerned with the problems of mental health, and with other members of the health service staff. The counseling office, chaplain, residence life staff, faculty, and coaches, as well as off campus professionals such as clergymen, mental health personnel and social service workers, should be a part of a working relationship with the health service that helps resolve the emotional problems of students.

The behavior of disruptive students attending colleges and universities interferes with the academic and administrative activities on many campuses. Predictably, a disproportionally large number of disruptive students are seriously emotionally disturbed; their emotional disturbance being either a cause or effect of their disruptive behavior. Amada (1986) argued that in order to deal effectively and humanely with such students, schools must establish a systematic and legally acceptable set of procedures for dealing with disruptive behavior. The campus mental health program can be an invaluable asset in assisting the college staff in developing and implementing such procedures. Deinstitutionalization and revolving door hospital admissions policies have meant that campuses may have their own equivalent of "street people" and must cope responsibly with them while at the same time protecting the rights of the other students on campus (Babineau, 1986).

Offer and Spiro (1987) undertook epidemiological study of mental health and mental illness among high school students who continued on to college, their help seeking behavior and the implications for the campus mental health professional. It is apparent that students come to college with a variety of "psychological baggage," and some may benefit from professional assistance in "unpacking." In discussing the transition from high school to college, Offer and Spiro stated that

> The day a college opens its doors to the incoming freshmen and freshwomen, 20% of those students will be emotionally disturbed or have significant psychic distress. They might or might not have been disturbed in high school. We believe that approximately 50% of the disturbed college students were disturbed in high school—in other words, their disturbance is stable across at least one developmental stage. The other half (10% of the freshman student body) are transiently disturbed, possibly due to an immediate crisis (i.e., leaving home, an unhappy love affair, poor choice of college, etc.). Put another way, one out of every five students entering college that first week is disturbed. (p. 213)

While mental health services to college students has increased, the need to bring mental health services to the "quietly disturbed" student remains (Ostrov, 1986). A study of the psychiatric emergencies among college students (Perlmutter, Schwartz, & Reifler, 1984) showed the need to consider the role played by the students "campus family," the roommates, eating companions, teammates and classmates so that their needs are also addressed. Many people can be keenly affected by one student's emergency. A suicide attempt or an episode of bizarre behavior can create a ripple effect that is far reaching. Accordingly, those who intervene in an emotional crisis must extend their attention beyond the student to others who are likely to be affected.

The college mental health professional must follow carefully established procedures in order to respond properly to the student, the student's family and the rest of the college community including fellow students, faculty, and administrators. Moorman, Urbach, and Ross (1984) developed guidelines for notifying or consulting with university officials when a student has a psychiatric problem. The issues to be considered are the confidential nature of the psychiatrist/patient relationship, the limitations on that confidentiality when the safety of the patient or others is threatened, and the perceived but amorphous obligation of the university to permit limited disclosure to appropriate campus personnel in some cases.

Perlmutter, Schwartz, and Reifler (1984) studied the diagnosis and disposition of 1,156 visits to a hospital psychiatric emergency department made by 933 students over an eight year period. Only about 30 percent of the visits resulted in admission to the hospital. Seventy percent of psychiatric emergencies returned to campus environment can be a source of anxiety to persons associated with many areas of campus life. The campus authorities want the disturbed student removed and protected and prefer to have someone else treat suicidal and/or bizarre behavior. On the other hand, the psychiatric emergency staff is expected to use the least restrictive treatment possible. This staff may also see a student who has already recovered from an acute upset so that in the absence of symptoms the staff is reluctant to use hospitalization because it could be counterproductive.

> The only chance of reconciliation of these two very different perspectives is for each side to try to understand the other's viewpoint. These observations also underscore the importance for colleges of gaining an accurate understanding of what an emergency evaluation can and cannot provide, and of establishing a working liaison with a local hospital facility as part of its overall program of mental health services. For instance, a college mental health professional could be designated as the liaison or contact person both in referral of students and in the negotiation process around disposition from the emergency service. A plan or policy about the level of campus responsiveness to students who return to the campus after either an emergency visit or hospitalization is particularly useful. Such plans and policies should include a clear statement about the level of service that can be provided by campus mental health facilities. (p. 157)

Peplau (1986) stated that the college health nurse with counseling training is in a key position to recognize that students, especially freshmen, often conceal their personal difficulties in vague complaints or by acting out their difficulties in other arenas. When college nurses are receptive to the broadest possible definition of health problems, then the problems presented will include test anxiety, fear of failure or of high places, loneliness, sexual harassment, rape attempts, unfair treatment by professors, impotence on a date, grief responses to death of family member or friend, fear of violence, etc.

The student mental health service at a small college campus, particularly one that is relatively isolated, has problems maintaining the same degree of confidentiality that is possible on the larger university setting.

Grayson (1986) identified four conditions that have implications for mental health confidentiality: (1) therapists are relatively visible on the small campus, (2) they are more inclined to form social ties with people on campus from outside the mental health and health services, (3) it is relatively common for patients who know one another to share the same therapist, and (4) the communications network on campus is highly efficient.

However, Grayson (1986) indicated that health services staff can earn a reputation for keeping patient confidence on the small college campus and in fact must take special precautions to use prudent and clear cut policies to assure an untarnished reputation for confidentiality.

WELLNESS

Wellness or healthy life style is a movement that is an integral part of the health education aspect of the student health services. A basic goal is to develop a favorable attitude in students toward the acquisition of knowledge and skills that will protect their health (Farnsworth, 1965). The wellness strategy calls for educating students about health risk factors such as obesity, smoking, poor nutrition, lack of exercise, alcohol and/or drug use, high stress levels. Students are helped to identify individual health risk factors through various assessment instruments. In an attempt to reach the entire student body, The Pennsylvania State University health service published a newsletter in 1987 that shows students how to take charge of their future health and includes a self-test to make the student aware of their basic life style habits in order to decide how to maintain or improve them in the future.

While wellness is of direct concern to the health services, many other parts of the campus are also involved and may, in fact, provide leadership for preventive health programming. Chandler (1979) described the need for college health services to be considered as a resource for student development. Health center, counseling center and residence hall staffs should function together to present health education material. In a study of wellness programs and trends in corporate America and in midwestern universities, Parsons (1986) concluded that university based wellness programs for students, faculty and staff—and actual research as to overall impact—lag far behind business and industry in the United States. This circumstance seems contradictory in view of the societal leadership role higher education should play; however, fortunately, preventive health care is becoming increasingly the concern of colleges and universities. Leadership in providing wellness information and consultation is available from the National Wellness Institute based at University of Wisconsin-Stevens Point. This institute sponsors an annual national conference, consultative services workshops and training seminars, and publishes a life style assessment instrument.

A source book, *Developing Campus Recreation and Wellness Programs,* edited by Leafgren (1986) discussed programs at a number of institutions that take a holistic view of wellness, a view consistent with the traditional college student personnel philosophy. In another discussion of wellness programs at six universities, Warner (1984) included illness prevention, history of wellness, the institutional context, and programming dimensions.

After reviewing extensive data from higher education institutions, Boyer (1986) was encouraged to find the emerging emphasis on wellness. Noting that peer counselors were used as "health promoters" who study everything from birth control and sexually transmitted diseases to nutrition and coping with stress, Boyer urged "that every college consider educating a core of senior students who, in turn, would educate their fellow students through informal seminars about health, nutrition and first aid" (p. 187). He concludes the discussion on wellness by suggesting that leaders of student health centers work directly with their counterparts in food service, intramural athletics, residence hall supervision, student government and even the academic administration, to assure that the institution's "wellness" program has the resources and endorsement of the whole campus.

ADDITIONAL SERVICES AND CONCERNS

The 1984 edition of *Recommended Standards and Practices for a College Health Program* is an authoritative source for details about services, activities and ethical relationships that are not included in this chapter (American College Health Association, 1984). These recommendations are the basis for the improvement of existing programs and a point of reference for many institutions developing new programs or program components. Areas that deserve consideration are:

Rights, Responsibilities and Relationships of Patients and Staff
Athletic Medicine—Intermural Sports, Intercollegiate Sports
Dental Services

Rehabilitation/Physical Medicine

Environmental Health and Safety
Occupational Health
Provisions for Emergency/Disasters
Professional Staff Working Conditions

Communication Between Health Service and Other Responsible Adults, With Public Health and Police, With Other Health Professionals

Another resource for learning about the breadth of concerns of college health personnel is the scientific programs of the American College Health Association at their annual conferences. At their 1987 conference, the following presentations were examples of topics under discussion:

AIDS Update
Administrative Connections: The Dynamics of Networking on a College Campus
Development of a Marketing Department in a University Health Service
Legal Aspects and Ethics of College Health Administration

Collegiate Drug and Alcohol Program Management Issues
Human Values and Cocaine Use
Nutrition Education for Women Intercollegiate Athletes
Psychological Intervention with the College Athlete
Chlamydia Trachomatis: An Overview of Its Prevalence, Detection, Management, and Prevention

New Ways to Attack the Common Cold
Evolution of a Dental Program at the University of Georgia
Protocol for the Education of Practitioners in Eating Disorder Diagnosis and Therapy
An Empirical Study of Student Health Care Needs and Attitudes
An Analysis of Utilization, Costs, Funding, and Preadmission Requirements of Small College Health Services

Meeting the Challenge Posed by Vaccine-Preventable Diseases on the College Campus
Mental Health Care of International Students: Some Issues to Consider
Multi-Level Approaches to the Evaluation of Psychological Services at University Settings
The National Health Objectives: Status and Prospects
The Counseling Role of the College Health Nurse

Health Aides: Using Trained Peers to Aid Students
Pharmacy Services for Small College Health Services
Sex in the 1980s for the College-Age Group
Sex Roles and Student Mental Health: An Interactional Perspective
Data on Student Suicides

(American College Health Association, 1987)

The wide ranging needs that are met by the college health services require a staff that has a unique combination of medical competencies and a genuine interest in students and their development. Program administrators must help the rest of the campus understand how the campus health service contributes to the quality of life of all those associated with the institution.

REFERENCES

Amada, G. (1986, April). Dealing with the disruptive college student: Some theoretical and practical considerations. *Journal of American College Health, 34*(5), 221-225.

American College Health Association. (1987, July). Abstracts of the scientific programs of the American College Health Association Sixty-Fifth Annual Meeting, May 28-30, 1987, Chicago. *Journal of American College Health, 36*(1), 7-26.

American College Health Association. (1984, February). Recommended standards and practices for a college health program, Fourth Edition. *Journal of American College Health, 32*(4), 135-182.

Babienau, R. (1986, April). Dealing with the disruptive student. *Journal of American College Health, 34*(5), 220.

Banning, J.H., & Kaiser, L. (1974). An ecological perspective and model for campus design. *Personnel and Guidance Journal, 52,* 370-375.

Blom, S. (1987, July, August). Executive director's letter. *ACHA Action, 25*(6), 6.

Boyer, E. (1984). *College, the undergraduate experience in America.* New York: Harper & Row.

Boynton, R.E. (1962). Historical development of college health services. *Student Medicine, 10,* 294-305.

Burnett, D. (1987, January). A student health center for the urban campus: A nontraditional primary health care model. *Journal of American College Health, 35*(4), 171-174.

Chandler, E. (1979). Student development: Where is the health service? *Journal of College Student Personnel, 17*(1), 34-38.

Chervin, D.D., Sloane, B.C., Gordon, K.A., & Gold, R.S. (1986, July). Achieving the health objectives for the nation in higher education. *Journal of American College Health, 35*(1), 15-20.

DeYoung, P.D. (1977). *The impact of proposed national health legislation in college student health programs.* Unpublished master's thesis. University of Oregon, Eugene, OR.

Ebbin, A., & Blankenship, E. (1986, February). A longitudinal health care study: International versus domestic students. *Journal of American College Health, 34*(4), 177-182.

Farnsworth, D.L. (1965). *College health services in the United States.* Washington, D.C.: American College Personnel Association (Student Personnel Monograph Series #4).

Grayson, P.A. (1986, February). Mental health confidentiality on the small campus. *Journal of American College Health, 34*(4), 187-191.

Forouzesh, M., & Ratzker, L. (1984/85 December, January). Health promotion and wellness programs: An insight into the fortune 500. *Health Education, 15*(7), 18-21.

Hettler, B. (1980). Wellness promotion on a university campus. *The Journal of Health Promotion and Maintenance, 3,* 77-95.

Hiller, M., Patterson, P., & Kaufman, R. (1985, December). Financing rural New England University health services: A pilot study. *Journal of American College Health, 34*(3), 117-118.

Keeling, R. (Ed.). (1986). *AIDS on the college campus.* Rockville, MD: American College Health Association.

Krivaski, J.F., & Piccolo, A. (1980). A high level wellness: The good life in higher education. *The Journal of College and University Student Housing, 10*(2), 19-22.

Leafgren, F. (Ed.). (1986, June). Developing campus recreation and wellness programs. *New Directions for Student Services: No. 34.* San Francisco: Jossey-Bass.

Love, M., Morphis, L., & Page, P. (1981, February). Model for an employee wellness project. *Journal of American College Health, 29*(4), 171-173.

McGinnis, J.M. (1987, January). A health campus—forecasting from the 1990 health objectives for the nation. *Journal of American College Health, 35*(4), 158-170.

Moore, N.S., & Summerskill, J. (1954). *Health services in American colleges and universities.* Ithaca, NY: Cornell University.

Moorman, J.C., Urbach, J.R., & Ross, D. (1984, October). Guidelines for consultation with university personnel in student psychiatric emergencies. *Journal of American College Health, 33*(2), 91-94.

Offer, D., & Spiro, R.P. (1987, March). The disturbed adolescent goes to college. *Journal of American College Health, 35*(5), 209-214.

Ostrov, E. (1986). Loneliness, shyness and withdrawal in adolescence. In R. Feldman & A.R. Stiffman (Eds.), *Advances in Adolescent Mental Health, I.* Greenwich, CT: Jai.

Packwood, W.T. (1977). Health. In W.T. Packwood (Ed.), *College student personnel services,* (pp. 298-339). Springfield, IL: Charles C Thomas.

Parsons, T. (1986). *Faculty/staff wellness programs and trends.* (Mimeographed report to Dr. Paul Olscamp). Bowling Green: Bowling Green State University.

Peplau, H. (1986, July). The nurse as counselor. *Journal of American College Health, 35*(1), p. 11-14.

Perlmutter, R.A., Schwartz, A.J., & Reifler, C.B. (1984, April). The college student psychiatric emergency: A descriptive study. *Journal of American College Health, 32*(5), 191-196.

Public Health Services, Office of the Assistant Secretary for Health and Surgeon

General, U.S. Department of Health, Education and Welfare. (1979). *Health people: The Surgeon General's report on health promotion and disease prevention* (p. 43). Washington, D.C.: U.S. Government Printing Office.

Sloane, D.C., & Sloane, B.C. (1986, June). Changing opportunities: An overview of the history of college health education. *Journal of American College Health, 34*(6), 271-273.

Vogel, S. (1986, June). Toward understanding the adjustment problems of foreign students in the college community: The case of Japanese wives at the Harvard University Health Services. *Journal of American College Health, 34*(6), 274-279.

Warner, M.J. (1984). Wellness promotion in higher education. *NASPA Journal, 21*(3), 32-38.

Zapka, J.G., & Love, M.B. (1986, September). College health services: Setting for community, organizational and individual change. *Journal of American College Health, 35*(2), 81-91.

CHAPTER 9

ORIENTATION

AUDREY L. RENTZ

The objectives of orientation week are the objectives of the whole personnel program in miniature . . . His (the student personnel worker) objective is to persuade the freshman to assume responsibility for himself as soon as possible; therefore his greatest problem is exactly how much help to give the freshman, neither too little nor too much. A second objective is to find out all he can about the student at the same time that the student is informing himself about the college.

K. H. Mueller (1961, p. 223-224)

INTRODUCTION

ORIENTATION programs have existed since young male students at Harvard (1636) were socialized into their new environment through the shared efforts of dons and fellow upperclassmen. Although orientation programs have always been designed to guide students in their transition to the collegiate community, the popularity of orientation activities rarely has remained constant. Periodically, both faculty and students have criticized orientation programs and goals because needs met were perceived to be institutional rather than student centered. However, during the 1980's, orientation's contributions and its acceptance as an important feature of higher education have reached an unparalleled high level. Recent research has documented the relationship of participation in orientation programs to student satisfaction and to student retention. Because of the increased emphasis on student retention, educators now recognize orientation professionals as one of the more significant groups of individuals on campus capable of influencing students' educational and personal development.

Throughout the history of formal orientation activities, beginning in 1888, the nature of the program content, its form and staffing patterns have changed dramatically. From one-day programs at the beginning of an academic year to structured courses offered for academic credit, the evolution of orientation practices has been dynamic. Often these programmatic modifications reflected changes in the perceived purpose of higher education, the value system of the sponsoring institution, and/or were reactions to major issues and events within American society. For example, during the 1960s changes in the perceived mission of higher education and student affairs professionals' views of students were significantly influenced by the civil rights and student activist movements. These changes altered the goals and program formats of orientation activities.

Educational outcomes associated with participation in orientation programs have been linked directly to student satisfaction with the institutional environment and thus also to student persistence. The declining numbers of college-age students and the increasing diversity in the student population have provided student affairs practitioners with opportunities and challenges never before encountered in higher education. As an example, today many college and university administrators consider their orientation directors as members of the institution's enrollment management team.

Regardless of these structural and perceptual changes, the mission of orientation professionals has remained constant. Program planners have always sought to design programs to assist entering students to adjust to their new academic surroundings and to derive maximum benefit from their new educational environment. To achieve these goals, students are introduced to and helped to feel comfortable with the array of human support and physical resources available on their campus. In addition, students have been helped to understand not only how their own institution functions, but the general purpose and role of higher education in American culture.

In its broadest sense, orientation was most recently defined as "any effort on the part of the institution to help entering students make the transition from their previous environment to the collegiate environment and to enhance success in college" (Upcraft & Farnsworth, 1984). Contemporary student affairs professionals, with practice grounded in the theoretical approaches of Chickering and others view human development as a series of tasks or goals toward which they seek to move students by involving them in structured activities. These activities are designed to provide experiences to facilitate the mastery of tasks such as developing autonomy, freeing interpersonal relationships, managing emotions and establishing a sexual identity (Chickering, 1972).

Just as orientation goals have changed, so have the students served by these programs. From the homogeneous student grouping found in the early 1920s, today's class of entering students includes individuals representing one or more of the following student groups: traditional college-age, ethnic and racial minorities, cross-cultural, disabled, transfer, displaced homemakers and returning adult learners. Because of this increased diversity and the value traditionally assigned to individual differences, to be effective orientation professionals can no longer assume that a general program will meet the needs of all new students. Today, the ambiguity associated with the labelling of orientation programs for transfers or new students has been resolved by the use of the generic term "entering student." Thus the future role of student is emphasized rather than a status associated with class standing or the accumulation of academic credits.

The evolution of contemporary orientation activities can be understood by examining changes in certain persistent themes and perspectives that have been associated with this student affairs specialty area. Historical development, changes in program goals, needs of students, types of programs offered, program development and the nature of students served constitute the major topics to be reviewed in subsequent parts of this chapter.

HISTORICAL DEVELOPMENT

Two distinct programmatic emphases have been identified within the history of orientation. The first began in 1888 when Boston University sponsored an orientation day for its entering students. For the next 28 years, the literature described various forms of orientation days all of similar duration. These programs focused on students' personal adjustment to college rather than on an orientation to specific academic disciplines or to higher education (Bennett, 1966; Butts, 1966). As orientation programs expanded in scope and their duration increased, many practitioners adopted the Orientation or Freshman Week model.

The second emphasis associated with orientation programs originated at Reed College in 1911, when the freshman course entitled "College Life" was offered for academic credit. Within several months, both the

University of Washington and the University of Michigan sponsored weekly meetings for entering students and rewarded attendance with academic credit (Butts, 1966). These courses, usually offered in a series of 25 sessions, were designed to teach students "how to use the library . . . how to study . . . the purposes and aims of college and . . . how to participate in campus activities" (Fitts & Swift, 1928). National acceptance of these structured experiences was quickly achieved. From six sponsoring institutions in 1915 to 1916, the trend spread to include 82 campuses a decade later (Wharton, 1942).

During the years following World War I, student personnel professionals adopted the orientation function as a specialized responsibility within their administrative domain. In the 1930s, under the direction of E. G. Williamson, the University of Minnesota sponsored an orientation program for entering students that addressed the following areas of perceived student concern: (1) personal living; (2) home life; (3) vocational orientation; and (4) socio-civic orientation (Bennett, 1946).

Although these two emphases have been crucial to the development of orientation programs, they have raised additional concerns. For example, the most effective length of an orientation program has been debated since the mid-1920s. Writers described programs with broader goals than the initial adjustment stage. ". . . some personnel workers have recommended that a really effective program will continue through the subsequent college years to help students avoid difficulties — scholastic, health, social, economic, vocational and emotional" (Doermann, 1926). Almost 30 years later in 1951, both Strang (1951) and Wrenn (1951), and later Mueller (1961) expressed their belief that the orientation program should not be planned for one or two days, but rather should be a continuous and dynamic process beginning in high school and ending after college graduation. According to this belief, orientation implies a developmental process which assists entering students with specific tasks associated with the transition to higher education and the subsequent goals of self-direction and interdependence. Many administrators view orientation activities as continuous elements of the total freshman experience. Even today, the issue concerning the length of orientation programs continues to be the subject of debate.

Various labels and stereotypes have been linked to freshmen and orientation programs since the early nineteenth century. Mention orientation to most individuals, and depending on their age, one or more images appear in their minds' eyes. Racoon fur coats, yellow pom-poms, football banners and the swallowing of goldfish in the 1920s and 1930s;

freshman "beanies" in the 1950s; and college blazers, t-shirts, and buttons in the 1960s helped entering students maintain a visible profile on many campuses. Such adornments differ dramatically from the distinguishing lengths of the black academic robes worn by faculty and students in the early days of Harvard to denote status in the academic community: ankle-length for faculty, knee-length for upperclassmen, and mid-thigh for freshmen. Throughout the years, specific wardrobe items, customs and rituals identified entering students to others on campus and provided a prescribed rite of passage. Regardless of the symbols, entering students must successfully complete the transition to their new educational surroundings. This socialization process has been and continues to be the domain of orientation professionals and their programs.

CHANGING PROGRAM GOALS

Although the mission of orientation has remained constant, support for orientation programs, discussions of goal statements and institutional commitment to programs for entering students have varied during the past hundred years.

In 1930, as interest in orientation programs spread, specific factors were identified as support for the need for orientation programs. These factors included: (1) heterogeneity of freshman social backgrounds; (2) enlarged enrollments; (3) increasing complexity of instructional fields; (4) conflict and confusion over educational objectives; and (5) growing independence of secondary school curricula from college domination (Drake, 1966a; Knode, 1930).

National recognition and support for orientation programs was achieved in 1943 when the Council of Guidance and Personnel Associations recommended that programs be sponsored by high schools as well as colleges and universities. The Council suggested three program goals that would increase understanding of occupational and social problems; personal adjustment, and awareness of the importance of physical fitness, including social hygiene (Council of Guidance and Personnel Associations, 1943). While reviewing responses from all 123 institutional members of the North Central Association of Colleges and Secondary Schools, researchers identified commitments to offer orientation programs that would include: general lectures, testing, social activities, campus tours, religious activities, counseling, details of registration, establishment of faculty-student relationships, and "enabling courses" (voice and reading improvement) (Bookman, 1948; Kamm & Wrenn, 1947). The relevance of these topics has not changed. Many of them continue to constitute the core of orientation programs offered in the 1980s.

Because of these differing approaches to orientation, and the need to share ideas and concerns, 24 orientation directors met in Columbus, Ohio, in 1948 to convene the "First Annual Conference" of these student affairs specialists. Their national professional organization, now called the National Orientation Directors Association (NODA), had begun. Although interest in the fledgling association remained high, official charter approval did not occur until 1974 (Dannells, 1986).

As the goals of higher education and student affairs professionals' perceptions of students were altered by major societal events, orientation personnel revised their program goals. Representative of these changes are the following goal statements gleaned from a 30 year review of the literature: (1) to gain perspective, a sense of purpose and balance between the demands and opportunities of college life (Strang, 1951); (2) to increase the student's receptivity to the total higher education experience (McCann, 1967); (3) to complete enrollment procedures in a humane manner (Butts, 1971); (4) to develop cognitive, behavioral and communication skills to facilitate assimilation into the campus environment and (5) to foster development of a peer group, creating an atmosphere of comfortableness and reduced anxiety (Krall, 1981).

As a reaction against the perceived increasing emphasis on students' social and personal needs that dominated orientation programs in the 1950s, subsequent writers argued for a return to a focus on academic disciplines and the mission of higher education (Drake, 1966a). Their approach would define orientation as "an induction into or at least consistent with, college intellectual life rather than" an attempt to "meet freshman and institutional needs" (Drake, 1966). In 1960 the American Council of Education in its annual conference proceedings defined an orientation program as the process of inducting students into the community of learning (Brown, 1961). Sanford provided a rationale for this new position: "the major forces that oppose us when we try to initiate the freshman into the intellectual life are the student peer culture which make relatively few or no intellectual demands, and an adult culture which accentuates grades and the practical aspects of the college experience" (Brown, 1961). These opposing forces were significant elements within the educational community.

A year later, Shaffer described the purpose of orientation as communicating to the new student "a concept of college as a self-directed, intellectually oriented experience. To achieve this purpose the subject matter should include a description of the demands to be placed on the student, problems he will face in securing the best possible education, standards by which his work will be judged, and personal qualities the institution expects him to develop" (Shaffer, 1962). Shaffer also believed that a commitment to orientation must be made by the entire institution. "This (orientation) is a function of the whole college, not just for the student personnel worker or the registrar" (Shaffer, 1962). Orientation programs had achieved an institutional status beyond the arena of student affairs.

With the advent of student activism in the 1960s and the new emphasis on accountability in higher education, orientation directors found their programs criticized once again. Freshman Week was labeled "disorientation week" (Riesman, 1961). Orientation courses would no longer be included in institutional curricula unless evidence could be provided to prove that these programs served a utilitarian and meaningful purpose on campus (Caple, 1964). There was a paucity of research data available to document specific educational outcomes associated with orientation activities and the direct relationship between participation in orientation programs and student retention. The lack of a theoretical foundation for orientation programs led to the criticism that these programs were " . . . made up of hopes, good will, educated guesses and what we fondly believe to be the needs of new students" (Grier, 1966). Nevertheless, orientation directors remained committed to the concept of orientation and continued to provide acitivites that permitted students to learn to act on their own and to assume self-responsibility (Black, 1974).

Publication of research findings in the 1970s (Astin, 1976; Feldman & Newcomb et al., 1970) signalled a new period of support and legitimacy for orientation programs. Relationships among student satisfaction, the need for congruence between student and institutional "fits," and the necessity of balancing competing forces of support and challenge and student retention were established. As research validated these previously assumed relationships, orientation programs achieved a more valued and respected role on college and university campuses.

During the late 1970s and early 1980s, a projected decline in the number of college enrollments helped create a new role for orientation programs. Recruiting and retaining students became issues of major importance to many administrators in higher education. Support for the interrelationship of participation in orientation programs, student satisfaction and student persistence appeared with greater frequency in the research literature (Beal & Noel, 1980; Lenning, Sauer, & Beal, 1980; Ramist, 1981). Orientation professionals were now considered essential members of an institution's enrollment management team.

Against the framework of evolving programs and recognizing differences in institutional mission statements, Upcraft and Farnsworth (1984) recommended four goals to orientation program planners. They suggested that programs should: (1) aid students in their academic adjustment; (2) provide assistance with personal adjustment; (3) help entering students' families understand the collegiate experience; and (4) assist the institution in gathering data about its entering students. These goal statements of the mid-1980s reflect the influence of earlier student personnel writers (e.g. Strang, 1951; Mueller, 1961).

DEFINITION

To unify the various goal statements suggested for orientation programs and to provide a common base for future planning, the Council for the Advancement of Standards published *Guidelines for Student Services/Development Programs* in 1986. Within this document, the Council defined orientation as the provision of ". . . continuing services and assistance that will: (1) aid new students in their transition to the institution; (2) expose new students to the broad educational opportunities of the institution; and (3) integrate new students into the life of the institution" (Council for the Advancement of Standards, 1986, p. 97).

In addition, the Council presented 18 goals to assist orientation professionals in the achievement of their mission. The comprehensive list implies a broad institutional role for orientation activities. These goals are to "(1) assist students in understanding the purpose of higher education; (2) assist students in understanding the mission of the specific institution; (3) assist students in determining their purpose in attending the institution and developing relationships with faculty, staff, peers and other individuals within the community; (4) help students understand the institution's expectations of themselves; (5) provide information about and opportunities for self-assessment; (6) identify costs in attending the institution, both in terms of dollars and personal commitment; (7) improve the retention rate of new students; (8) provide an atmosphere and sufficient information to enable students to make reasoned and well-informed choices; (9) provide information concerning academic policies, procedures, requirements, and programs; (10) promote an awareness of nonclassroom opportunities; (11) provide referrals to qualified counselors and advisors; (12) explain the processes for class scheduling and registration and provide trained supportive assistance to accomplish these tasks; (13) develop familiarity with physical surroundings; (14) provide information and exposure to available institutional services; (15) help students identify and evaluate housing and commuting options; (16) create an atmosphere that minimizes anxiety, promotes positive attitudes, and stimulates an excitement for learning; (17) provide appropriate information on personal safety and security; and (18) provide opportunities for new students to discuss expectations and perceptions of the campus with continuing students" (National Orientation Directors Association, 1986, p. 95). This list serves as the most complete definition available.

CHANGING NEEDS OF STUDENTS

For three decades after the 1920s, the perceived needs of entering students were described as those generally associated with the "typical" student: an 18 year old, middle-class, Caucasian. For these first generation students, the collegiate environment was usually their first experience living away from home.

Based on this profile, the literature available to earlier student personnel professionals described four major concerns believed to be characteristic of all entering college students. These concerns were: (1) breaking away from the family, (2) choosing a vocation, (3) establishing satisfactory relationships with members of the opposite sex, and (4) integrating the personality. Later Mueller (1961) redefined these concerns as three developmental tasks: (1) ego-integration (the process of achieving physical control, emotional development and integration of values); (2) identification of different roles for the self (sex roles, dating and new identities); and (3) practice in future roles (social responsibilities, occupational roles, civic competence and family life). These bear a striking resemblance to the developmental tasks that would appear in the professional literature a decade later.

Student affairs practitioners initiated formal assessments of students' needs in response to the demand for data to evaluate and support the continued existence of orientation programs during the 1950s. Among the fears reported by entering students were their ability to do college work, to select the right major, to make friends, and to find a desirable roommate. The friendliness or anticipated lack of friendliness of their college teachers was also an area of concern (Drake, 1955). Academic-related issues began to replace concerns about social and personal adjustment among entering students when students at Purdue ranked their orientation needs in the following order: (1) inform them of academic responsibilities; (2) assist them with academic program planning; and (3) familiarize them with the campus (Tautfest, 1961). During the next ten years, the role of personal and social orientation to the academic community continued to be less important to students than issues related to academic achievement (Keil, 1966).

Many issues supported by student activists during the 1960s reflected criticisms directed toward societal institutions such as the federal government and higher education. Students labeled these institutions "the Establishment" and believed that these bureaucratic organizations should be reorganized and restructured around a more human-centered philosophy. Among the changes demanded by the activists was a greater value assigned to the individual within bureaucracies and the role the individual could play in promoting change. Characteristic of their lack of acceptance of authority, student activists argued that anyone over 30 was not to be trusted. Their opposition to American involvement in the Vietnam war was expressed by the slogan, "Make love, not war." These attitudes significantly changed the roles performed by student affairs professionals and altered their relationships with students. The traditional role of surrogate parent was recast as that of advisor, facilitator, counselor and educator. Students were perceived as responsible adults and active learners who assumed responsibility for their own development rather than as passive adolescents. The value of *in loco parentis* diminished.

Students increasingly questioned the relevance of many college courses and the academic preparation provided to help resolve societal problems. As a result, general education or core curriculum requirements were altered to permit students to pursue a wider range of interdisciplinary and individually designed topic-oriented seminars.

With the advent of the 1970s, the pattern in student orientation needs surveys changed once again. Previous interest in academic issues was now matched by a new concern for vocational preparation. This was the beginning of the period of vocationalism described by Astin

(1972) and later by Levine (1979). Entering students perceived "orientation to the academic discipline, its purpose, and career related goals as primary objectives . . ." of an orientation program (Moore, Pappas, & Vinton, 1979).

According to the literature of the 1970s and early 1980s, the freshman year, particularly the initial months, was the critical time during which students' attitudes, values and adjustment to higher education were most influenced (Butts, 1971; Chickering & Havighurst, 1981; Feldman & Newcomb, 1969; Knott & Daher, 1978; Lange & Gentry, 1974; Lowe, 1980). This knowledge helped administrators become aware of the significance of the freshman year to student retention. Institutional administrators, concerned about predicted declines in enrollment and the probable need to reduce operating budgets and staff personnel, endorsed research that examined factors related to student persistence.

Attrition was found to be most severe during or at the end of the first undergraduate year (Sagaria, 1979). At four year institutions, factors related to attrition were identified from questionnaires: (1) coursework requiring study habits many students did not possess; (2) large classes; (3) an impersonal, uncomfortable campus environment; and (4) academic and social regulations (Beal & Noel, 1980; Hall, 1982). This information and the new role orientation could assume in the transition process and student persistence resulted in greater institutional support for orientation professionals. Retention became a goal of orientation programs.

Researchers also studied high school students to assess characteristics thought to be associated with a successful transition to higher education. Entering students who possessed a competent self-image, were motivated to pursue activities to stimulate growth and development, and were willing to take risks, completed their transition more effectively (Knott & Daher, 1978). Many orientation directors attempted to design activities to develop or enhance these attitudes and behaviors.

After studying retention and attrition, the American Testing Service identified a number of issues related to high rates of student withdrawal. Most important were (1) academic boredom; (2) academic underpreparation; (3) uncertainty regarding academic major or career choice; (4) transition and adjustment difficulties; (5) dissonance or incompatibility; and (6) irrelevancy of education (Dannells, 1986). The significance of these issues has not changed and they continue to be the agenda addressed by orientation professionals as they plan annual programs.

TYPES OF PROGRAMS

As mentioned earlier, orientation directors have created programs of different lengths and with different purposes, depending on prevailing trends described in the orientation literature, students' needs, and levels of institutional support. Three prototypes have emerged to form the base from which all orientation programs developed. They are (1) the Freshman Day or Freshman Week model (scheduled before the beginning of academic classes); (2) the credit course model (scheduled during the first semester or the entire year); and (3) the pre-orientation or pre-registration model (offered during the summer months) (Bergman, 1978; Harris, 1980; Herron, 1974; McCann, 1967; Strang, 1951).

The Freshman Day or Week Model

The University of Maine is credited with developing the first Freshman Week in 1923. Mass meetings dominated the schedule and emphasized information dissemination, testing, counseling, registration, campus tours, recreational activities and social events (Drake, 1966; Jones, 1927). The popularity of these models varied. In 1938, 83 percent of all higher education institutions sponsored these programs. Support for the model declined during the 1940s when it was replaced by the structured orientation course. However, by the mid 1960s, the Freshman Week model had regained its earlier popularity. Many student affairs practitioners continue to implement this model as an extension of a summer pre-registration or pre-orientation program.

The Freshman Course Model

Introducing entering students to available fields of study and assisting students with problems associated with freshman status were the primary goals of the traditional freshman course (Drake, 1966). By 1930, more than 50 percent of all campuses sponsored courses emphasizing freshman adjustment issues (Knode, 1930; Miller, 1930). By the middle of the student activism period, however, this model of orientation was viewed as obsolete (Drake, 1966). Faculty voiced strong opposition to the perceived emphasis placed on "fun and games," social events and personal adjustment. They argued for a return to an orientation program focusing on academic concerns and the mission of general education (Dannells & Kuh, 1977). A revival of interest in the academic course model resulted, and orientation directors designed programs to meet students' academic and personal/social needs (O'Banion, 1969; Snider, 1970).

The Preregistration Model

The Pre-College Clinic, initiated by Michigan State University in 1949, was a summer program that included two to four days of testing, counseling, general information and social events (Goodrich & Pierson, 1959). It became valued as a public relations technique, an aid to personalizing large university environments and a means of improving grades and students' initial adjustment. The Clinic and the Freshman Week concept became the two most frequently implemented program models during the mid-1960s (Dannells & Kuh, 1977; Forrest & Knapp, 1966; Wall & Ford, 1966).

Programmatic emphases were linked to the two philosophical viewpoints that undergirded all orientation programs in the mid-1960s. The first was termed "microcosmic" and emphasized testing, campus tours, informational meetings and pre-registration activities. The second, called "macrocosmic" emphasized issues associated with the intellectual challenges of academic life, cognitive development and the mission of higher education (Fitzgerald & Evans, 1963). Most orientation programs implemented since then have incorporated both viewpoints.

STAFFING

Staffing patterns of orientation programs also reflected changing times and perspectives. Traditionally, orientation activities were the sole responsibility of student affairs professionals. During the years when the value ascribed to academic concerns was high, faculty members shared in planning and staffing programs. In the 1960s, the academic community's perception of students changed and undergraduate students assumed new roles as co-participants and collaborators in the planning and staffing activities. Their service as peer facilitators helped introduce the concept of paraprofessionals to other student affairs specialty areas.

PROGRAM FORMATS

From 1966 to 1976 program formats also changed. Modifications included the establishment of two or three-day overnight programs for entering students and their parents. Some institutions developed mini-courses taught by faculty during the five to ten day period before classes began that provided a preview of academic life. Small group sessions were utilized to teach T-group and other human relations and sensitivity skills, and Friendship Days emerged with a focus on social needs (Cohen & Judy, 1978; Foxley, 1969; Hall, 1982; Klostermann & Merseal, 1978; Terenzini & Pascarella, 1980).

To categorize orientation programs in light of these changes in staffing and program formats, Sagaria (1979) suggested a conceptual framework for classifying orientation programs. Three distinct categories were proposed: interdisciplinary, offered through liberal arts or general education departments and focusing on the student as learner; developmental, affiliated with counseling services or general education areas and emphasizing the student as a person as well as his/her self-perceptions and relationships with others; and utilitarian, aligned with student affairs divisions emphasizing the mastery of a defined knowledge base and resources as basic skills.

PROGRAM ASSESSMENT

By the mid-1980s, studies assessing effective orientation programs were underway. Kramer and Washburn (1983), having reviewed successful programs, recommended that orientation programs should be characterized as follows: (1) there should be a concern for the student as an individual; (2) new students should be afforded the opportunity to establish relationships with faculty; (3) primary emphasis of the program should be academic; (4) small group meetings should be used to ease the adjustment of new students; and (5) there should be a recognition of the stressful transition experienced by entering students.

In a similar review of orientation programs, Upcraft and Farnsworth (1984) identified seven traits of successful programs. The program must "(1) be a sustained and coordinated effort . . .; (2) have the support and involvement of the entire campus community . . .; (3) be based on sound concepts of student development and on what is known about the influence of the collegiate environment" and "on all available information concerning entering students . . ." (p. 30). Other recommendations are that "(4) the program be subject to evaluation; (5) use a wide variety of interventions including media approaches, group programming, academic courses, and individual tutoring, advising and counseling . . .;

(6) be appropriately timed . . .; and (7) must be coordinated by a central office or person . . ." (p. 30).

PROGRAM DEVELOPMENT

Throughout its long history, orientation programs have been designed to meet the specific needs of students, faculty, and/or institutions. Program goals have been grounded in perceived needs or have been based on responses to formalized need assessments. For many of the early years, all entering students participated in the same general program of mass meetings that addressed registration information and descriptions of institutional expectations. Beginning in the mid-1970s a more formalized approach to program development evolved. Students were no longer viewed as having identical needs and program variations were designed to address specific student groups.

To promote effective programming, models of program development were applied by student affairs professionals. Several authors have suggested models that require goal setting, the identification of clientele, assessment of student needs and the selection of appropriate intervention strategies (Barr & Associates, 1983; Morrill, Oetting, & Hurst, 1974). Most models include variations of a basic five step process that requires the program planner to: (1) analyze philosophical program assumptions; (2) define institutional characteristics; (3) assess developmental needs of entering minority students; (4) consider selection of appropriate staff members; and (5) program activities to retention strategies (Wright, 1984). A more recent model is Dannell's grounded in strategic planning concepts and described in the *Orientation Director's Manual*, 1986 edition. The reader is advised to consult these references sources cited previously and to become familiar with a generic approach to program development.

The *CAS Standards and Guidelines for Student Services/Development Programs* (Council for the Advancement of Standards, 1986) provided orientation professionals with additional assistance for program planners. The Council recommended that all orientation programs be designed to achieve two major goals. Programs should provide "an introduction to both the academic and student life aspects of the institution; and structured opportunities for the interaction of new students, faculty, staff, and continuing students" (p. 97). These recommendations emphasize retention-based activities that may contribute to an institution's enrollment management plan.

CHANGING NATURE OF STUDENTS

As the diversity of the entering student population increases, orientation professionals must understand not only models of program development but also be knowledgeable about specific characteristics and needs of minority student groups. A minority grouping is defined by the characteristics of a particular institutional environment. The term is derived from the identification of the majority student population in a given environment. For instance, entering minority students may be Baptists at a Catholic college or women at a men's university. Other applications of the label may include handicapped students, adult learners, educationally disadvanaged students, transfer students or cross-cultural students. Descriptions of three minority student groups (ethnic and racial minorities, transfers, and returning adult learners) will be provided to illustrate the implications of diverse student needs for orientation programs.

Ethnic Minority Students

During the past several years, the term "minority students" has been used in connection with a wide range of ethnic minorities, such as Chicanos, Japanese, and Alaskan Aleuts. While cultural and ethnic factors and conditions underscore differences among minority students, students in these groups tend to share a common background that includes a heritage of oppression, experiences as first generation college students, an emphasis on family life, and an appreciation of community membership.

Recent literature describing ethnic minority students reinforces the need for the orientation planner's expertise. The ability to meet students' needs is closely related to the student development educator's familiarity and knowledge of the historical and societal context of the institutions attended by these students. Designing specialized programs whose content differs significantly may not be as valuable as altering the format and the scheduling of an orientation program (Wright, 1984).

Transfer Students

Despite the enormous growth of community colleges and two-year institutions during the 1960s, students transferring to four-year institutions were often left to their own resources during their period of transition. A national survey of NASPA member institutions revealed that less than half of all campuses responding offered special programs for transfer students (Knoell & Medsker, 1965; Sandeen & Goodale, 1972).

Harrison and Varcoe (1983) surveyed 425 four-year institutions with minimum enrollments of 3,000 students to determine orientation practices developed for transfer students. With a 40 percent return rate, they were able to conclude that the percentage of institutions having special student need-based programs increased only slightly from previous studies: 68 percent now responded affirmatively. Most institutional programs were designed to include transfer students in mass meetings with other first-time entering students. Transcript evaluations, academic advising and registration information were typical agenda items. Continuous orientation programs scheduled during the first semester appeared to hold the most potential for assisting transfer students; however only 16 percent of responding institutions sponsored such programs. Of all the developmental tasks, only academic and intellectual development and interpersonal relationships were perceived to be appropriate goals of orientation programs. Similar dissatisfaction with this same narrow emphasis was expressed decades earlier by Wrenn (1951). Despite the changes in orientation program goals and formats, other student development tasks have not been integrated into programs for transfer students.

Sometimes referred to as "educational middlemen" (Kintzer, 1973), transfer students possess unique characteristics. Generally, their test scores and high school grades are lower than native four year students; their grades decline during the first term and improve thereafter; and their retention rate is lower than first-time entering students. Other traits identified suggest that transfer students require more time to complete baccalaureate degree programs since many of them are employed while attending classes. In addition, fewer scholarships, grants, or fellowships are awarded to transfer students and their educational aspirations do not exceed study beyond the undergraduate degree (Harrison & Varcoe, 1984).

Based on these findings, orientation programs for transfer students need to be designed to address the issues of academic articulation, academic transition, living or transportation arrangements, financial considerations, environmental adjustments, and developmental needs (Harrison & Varcoe, 1984).

Returning Adult Learners

Students 25 years of age or older accounted for one-third of all college students in 1984. By 1990, students over the age of 35 are predicted to number 11 million (Greenfeig & Goldberg, 1984). The retention of this group of entering minority students is increasingly important to college and university administrators.

Factors motivating returning adult learners to pursue higher education reflect their particular needs. Some adult learners find themselves without employment due to layoffs. Others may be recently divorced or widowed and have a need to be financially independent. Some may wish to make a mid-life career change. Obviously, these people are experiencing significant transitions within their own lives as well as to their new educational environment. Researchers have suggested that adult learners are generally characterized by low self-esteem and a lack of self-confidence, not only concerning themselves, but also in their abilities to perform in an academic setting. By adopting the student role in addition to the other roles assumed in their lives, they are subjected to increased stress (Greenfeig & Goldberg, 1984).

Because of these students' special needs, orientation programs for adult students should begin at the time of admission, continue during the first few days on campus, and progress the entire year (Greenfeig & Goldberg, 1984). Orientation planners need to employ multiple approaches rather than a single program format. Peer counseling, workshops, social activities, academic courses, and individual counseling or advising may all be necessary. In addition, information dissemination and the provision of support remain essential elements. To compensate for many adult learners' feelings of isolation, opportunities should be provided that allow them to meet and interact with other returning adult learners (Apps, 1982).

CONCLUSION

As one of the initial student affairs functional areas encountered by students, an orientation program has the opportunity and the potential to significantly affect student adjustment and the entire freshman year. Participation in orientation activities has been linked to student satisfaction and persistence in higher education. In addition, it has been demonstrated that the entire four year undergraduate experience can be influenced by orientation professionals and their programs.

Generally, the Orientation Director reports to the Chief Student Affairs Officer and assumes a valuable leadership role as a member of the professional staff team. Committed to student development and assisted by paraprofessionals, members of the orientation team comprise one of the more influential groups on campus because of their ability to facilitate student growth and development. These professionals' knowledge of student development theories and program development models assist them in achieving program and institutional goals. Student affairs professionals specializing in orientation must therefore possess skills that permit purposeful intervention in students' lives and a sensitivity to the complex issues associated with students' growth and welfare.

REFERENCES

Apps, J. (1978). *Study skills for those adults returning to school.* New York: McGraw-Hill.

Baker, R.W., & Siryk, B. (1980). Alienation and freshman transition into college. *Journal of College Student Personnel, 21,* 437-442.

Beal, P.E., & Noel, L. (1980). *What works in student retention.* The American College Testing Program and the National Center for Higher Education Management Systems. Iowa City: ACT.

Bennett, M.E. (1938). *The orientation of students in educational institutions.* Thirty-seventh Yearbook (pp. 163-166). NSSE, Part I, Public-Sch.

Bergman, I.B. (1978). Freshman orientation in the college classroom. *Journal of College Student Personnel, 19*(5), 363-364.

Bookman, G. (1948). Freshmen orientation techniques in colleges and universities. *Occupations, 27,* 163-166.

Brinkerhoff, D.B., & Sullivan, P.E. (1982). Concerns of new students: A pre-test — post-test evaluation of orientation. *Journal of College Student Personnel, 23*(5), 384-390.

Brown, R. (1972). *Tomorrow's higher education: A return to the academy.* The American College Personnel Association.

Brubaker, J.S., & Rudy, W. (1958). *Education in transition.* New York: Harper.

Butts, T.H. (1971). *Personnel service review: New practices in student orientation.* Ann Arbor. (ERIC Document Reproduction Service No. ED 057 416).

Caple, R.B. (1964). A rationale for the orientation course. *Journal of College Student Personnel, 6,* 42-46.

Chandler, E.M. (1972). Freshman orientation — is it worthwhile? *NASPA Journal, 10,* 55-61.

Chickering, A., & Havighurst, R.J. (1981). The life cycle. In Chickering & Associates (Eds.), *The modern American college* (pp. 16-50). San Francisco: Jossey-Bass.

Cohen, R.D., & Jody, R. (1978). *Freshman seminar: A new orientation.* Boulder: Westview.

Council for the Advancement of Standards for Student Services/Development Programs. (1986). *CAS standards and guidelines for student services/development programs.* Iowa City: ACT.

Council of Guidance and Personnel Associations. (1943). Recommendations, *Occupations, 21,* 46-48.

Creamer, D.G., & Kramer, T. (1978). An in-class orientation method. *Journal of College Student Personnel, 19*(3), 287-288.

Cross, K. (1970). Occupationally oriented students. *Junior College Review, 5*(3).

Dannells, M. (1986). *Orientation director's manual,* NODA.

Dannells, M., & Kuh, G.D. (1977). Orientation. In W.T. Packwood (Ed.), *College student personnel services* (pp. 102-124). Springfield, IL: Charles C Thomas.

Doermann, H.J. (1926). *Orientation of college freshmen.* Williams & Williams, p. 162.

Doman, E.F., & Christensen, M.G. (1976). Effects of a group life seminar on perceptions of the university environment. *Journal of College Student Personnel, 17*(1), 66-71.

Drake, R.W. (1966). *Freshman orientation in the United States colleges and universities.* Colorado State University, Fort Collins. (ERIC Document Reproduction Service No. ED 030 923 [a]).

Drake, R.W. (1966). *Review of the literature for freshman orientation practices in the United States.* Fort Collins: Colorado State University, (ERIC Document Reproduction Service No. ED 030 920).

Emme, E. (1933). The adjustment problems of college freshmen. Council of Guidance and Personnel Associations. Recommendations. *Occupations, 21,* 46-48.

Feldman, K.A., & Newcomb, T.M. (1969). *The impact of college on students.* San Francisco: Jossey-Bass.

Fitts, C.T., & Swift, F.H. (1928). *The construction of orientation courses for freshmen, 1888-1926.* Berkeley: University of California Press.

Fitzgerald, L.E., & Evans, S.B. (1963). Orientation programs: Foundations and framework. *College and University, 38,* 270-275.

Forest, A. (1982). *Increasing student competence and persistence: The best case for general education.* Iowa City: ACT.

Forrest, D.V., & Knapp, R.H. (1966). Summer college orientation programs. *Journal of College Student Personnel, 7,* (1) 47-49.

Foxley, C.H. (1969). Orientation or dis-orientation. *Personnel and Guidance Journal, 48,* 218-221.

Gardner, D.H. (1936). *Student personnel services. Evaluation of higher education institutions.* Chicago: University of Chicago Press, p. 235.

Goodale, T., & Sandeen, A. (1971). The transfer student: A research report. *NASPA Journal, 9*(4), 248-263.

Goodrich, T.A., & Pierson, R.R. (1959). Pre-college counseling at Michigan State University. *Personnel and Guidance Journal, 37,* 595-597.

Gordon, V.N., & Grites, T.J. (1984). The freshman seminar course: Helping students succeed. *Journal of College Student Personnel, 25*(4), 315-320.

Grier, D.G. (1966). Orientation—tradition or reality? *NASPA Journal, 3,* 37-41.

Greenfeig, B.R., & Goldberg, B.J. (1984). Orienting returning adult students. In M.L. Upcraft (Ed.), *Orienting students to college* (pp. 79-92). New Directions for

Student Services, no. 25. San Francisco: Jossey-Bass.

Guber, S.K. (1970). Four approaches to freshman orientation. *Improving College and University Teaching, 18,* 57-60.

Harrison, C.H., & Varcoe, K. (1984). Orienting transfer students. In M.L. Upcraft (Ed.), *Orienting students to college* (pp. 93-106). New Directions for Student Services, no. 25. San Francisco: Jossey-Bass.

Hall. B. (1982). College warm-up: Easing the transition to college. *Journal of College Student Personnel, 23*(3), 280-281.

Herron, D. (1974). Orientation effects on student alienation. *Journal of the National Association of Women Deans, Administrators and Counselors, 37*(3), 107-110.

Higginson, L.C., Moore, L.V., & White, E.B. (1981). A new role for orientation: Getting down to academics. *NASPA Journal, 19*(1), 21-28.

Jackson, G.S., & Seegan, R.B. (1978). Ongoing orientation for freshmen. *Journal of College Student Personnel, 18*(2), 145-146.

Kamm, R.B., & Wrenn, C.G. (1947). Current developments in student-personnel programs and the needs of the veteran. *School and Society, 65,* 89-92.

Keil, E.C. (1966). College orientation: A disciplinary approach. *Liberal Education, 52,* 172-180.

Klostermann, L.R. & Merseal, J. (1978). Another view of orientation. *Journal of College Student Personnel, 19*(3), 86-87.

Knode, J.C. (1930). *Orienting the student to college with special reference to freshman week.* New York: Bureau of Publications, Teachers College, Columbia University.

Knoell, D.M., & Medsker, L.L. (1965). *From junior to senior college: A national study of the transfer student.* Washington: American Council on Education.

Knott, J.E., & Daher, D.M. (1978). A structured group program for new students. *Journal of College Student Personnel, 19*(5), 456-461.

Krall, J.K. (1981). New student welcome day program. *Journal of College and University Housing, 11*(2), 320-333.

Kramer, G.L., & Hardy, H.L. (1985). Facilitating the freshman experience. *College and University, 60*(3), 242-252.

Kramer, G.L., & Washburn, R. (1983). The perceived orientation needs of new students. *Journal of College Student Personnel, 24*(4), 311-319.

Kramer, G.L., & White, M.T. (1982). Developing a faculty mentoring program: An experiment. *NACADA Journal, 2*(2),47-58.

Lange, A.J., & Gentry, R.F. (1974). Uni-prep: An innovative program to university orientation. *NASPA Journal, 12*(2), 90-95.

Levine, A. (1980). *When dreams and heroes died.* San Francisco: Jossey-Bass.

Lowe, I. (1980/April). *Preregistration counseling: A comparative study.* Paper presented at the California College Association Conference, Monterey, CA.

McCann, J.C. (1967). Trends in orienting college students. *Journal of the National Association of Women Deans, Administrators and Counselors, 30*(2), 855-889.

Medsker, L.L. (1960). *The junior college.* New York: McGraw-Hill.

Miller, T.K., & Jones, J.D. (1981). Out-of-class activities. In A.W. Chickering & Associates (Eds.). *The modern American college.* San Francisco: Jossey-Bass.

Miller, T.K., & Prince, J. (1976). *The future of student affairs.* San Francisco: Jossey-Bass.

Moore, L.P., Pappas, E.K., & Vinton, J.C. (1979). An organizational model for orientation programs. *NASPA Journal, 17,* 40-45.

Mueller, K.H. (1961). *Student personnel work in higher education.* Boston: Houghton-Mifflin.

O'Banion, T. (1969). Experimentation in orientation of junior college students. *Journal of College Student Personnel, 10,* (1) 12-15.

Prola, M., & Stern, D. (1984). The effect of a freshman orientation program on student leadership and academic persistence. *Journal of College Student Personnel, 25*(5), 472-473.

Ramist, L. (1981). *College student attrition and retention.* College Board Report, no. 80-81. Princeton, N.J.: College Entrance Examination Board.

Riesman, D. (1961). Changing colleges and changing students. *National Catholic Education Association Bulletin, 58,* 104-115.

Ross, M. (1975). College orientation: A three-way street. *Journal of College Student Personnel, 16*(6), 468-470.

Rothman, L.K., & Leonard, D.G. (1967). Effectiveness of freshman orientation. *Journal of College Student Personnel, 10,* 12-15.

Sagaria, M.A. (1979). Freshmen orientation courses: A framework. *Journal of the National Association of Women Deans, Administrators and Counselors, 43*(1), 3-7.

Sandeen, A., & Goodale, T. (1972). Student personnel programs and the transfer students. *NASPA Journal, 9,* 179-200.

Sanford, N. (1962). Developmental status of the freshman. In N. Sanford (Ed.), *The American college.* New York: Wiley.

Santee, R.T., & Davis, B.G. (1980). The summer threshhold program: An experiment in preparatory education, *Evaluation Review, 4*(2), 215-224.

Shaffer, R.H. (1962). A new look at orientation. *College and University, 37,* 272-279.

Smith, G.C. (1984). Integrating academic advising with ongoing orientation programs. *NODA Journal, 3*(1), 9-12.

Strang, R. (1951). Orientation of new students. In C.G. Wrenn (Ed.), *Student personnel work in college* (pp. 274-292). New York: Ronald.

Tautfest, P.B. (1961). An evaluation technique for orientation programs. *Journal of College Student Personnel, 3*(32), 5-28.

Terenzini, P.T., & Pascarella, E.T. (1977). Voluntary freshman attrition and patterns of social and academic integration in a university: A test of a conceptual model. *Research in Higher Education, 6,* 25-43.

Upcraft, M.L. (Ed.). (1984). *Orienting students to college.* New Directions for Student Services, no. 25. San Francisco: Jossey-Bass.

Upcraft, M.L., Finney, J.E., & Garland, P. (1984). Orientation: A context. In M.L. Upcraft (Ed.), *Orienting students to college* (pp. 5-26). New Directions for Student Services, no. 25. San Francisco: Jossey-Bass.

Upcraft, M.L., & Farnsworth, W.M. (1984). Orientation programs and activities. In M.L. Upcraft (Ed.), *Orienting students to college* (pp. 27-39). New Directions for Student Services, no. 25. San Francisco: Jossey-Bass.

Varcoe, I.E., & Harrison, C.H. (1983). *Programs that work in transfer orientation.* University Park, PA: The Pennsylvania State University.

Wall, H.W. (1962). A counseling program for parents of college freshmen. *Personnel and Guidance Journal, 40,* 774-778.

Wharton, M.M. (Compiler). (1942). *Orientation of freshmen in colleges and universities.* Washington: National Education Association.

Whitmire, D.E. (Ed.). (1976). *Mentor handbook seminar program, university division of general studies.* Bowling Green, OH: Bowling Green State University.

Witkin, H.W. (1971). A human relations experiment in a student orientation program. *Journal of College Student Personnel, 12*(5), 372.

Wright, D.J. (1984). Orienting minority students. In M.L. Upcraft (Ed.), *Orienting students to college* (pp. 53-65). New Directions for Student Services, no. 25. San Francisco: Jossey-Bass.

CHAPTER 10

RESIDENCE HALLS

JOHN H. SCHUH

The residential milieu during college years is, for an ever-increasing number of young people, the instrument of their induction into adult social life. Too often has it merely been the extension of adolescent attitudes and forms, an extension which has led to a perpetuation of adolescent ways of thought.

(Strozier et al., p. 5)

THE PURPOSE OF this chapter is to discuss selected topics related to residence halls. Information presented includes such issues as the history and purpose of residence halls, assessment concerns associated with the residential setting, managing the residential environment, staff development, programming, the influence of residence halls on students and the future of residence halls at colleges and universities.

HISTORY

In many ways, the history of student housing in the United States reflects divergent philosophies of higher education adopted from Europe and Great Britain. Since our culture has been influenced to a great extent by ideas from Europe and Great Britain, it follows that American higher education should have been influenced as well.

During the past 350 years, the role of residence halls in American higher education has changed several times. Many of these changes were directly related to changes in the prevailing philosophical approach of the time. Even today, a consensus does not exist across higher education regarding the role residence halls should play on campus. In fact,

227

the mission of the individual campus, perhaps more than any other factor, helps determine which approach is implemented in student housing.

Historical Roots

In the Middle Ages, students who attended colleges in Europe were considerably younger (14-15 years old), often from very poor families, and lived wherever they could find a place. As time went on, students began to form their own voluntary living units which were democratic, self-governing and self-financed (Cowley, 1934). If students became dissatisfied with their living arrangements, they were free to move and find more suitable accommodations.

In England, a different approach to student housing developed. Student self determination in housing matters gave way to control by faculty members. Institutions moved from a point where they approved those who would administer the residential facilities to nominating those who administered the facilities to finally assuming total responsibility for the halls (Cowley, 1934).

The approach on the continent from approximately the fourteenth to the eighteenth centuries was similar. Toward the end of this time period, several reasons contributed to a decline in residence facilities, including lack of funding, revolution and the Reformation. Toward the end of the eighteenth century, residence facilities no longer were an important part of the collegiate scene in Europe.

The Colonial Period

Like the legal system, the language, and many other aspects of American culture, our initial model of higher education was borrowed from England (James, 1917). The founders of the earliest of the Colonial colleges had been educated in England, and their newly chartered institutions paralleled the British model. Certain factors, however, made the situation in the colonies different from the English model. The residential colleges of Oxford and Cambridge were important factors in students' education, while the early American dormitory was simply a place to eat and sleep. This difference resulted from the lack of self-contained quadrangles on American campuses, and the fact that American faculty were married whereas the English dons were unmarried and required to live within the college. In addition, students and faculty dined together in England, while in America they ate separately (Brubacher & Rudy,

1958). Moreover, colonial students were perceived as young men with souls to be saved, and therefore a profound religious influence permeated the colleges (Fenske, 1980). Because of these factors, relationships between American students and their faculty were never as close as those in England. Students' relationships with faculty were adversarial rather than tutorial. Higher education soon found itself confronting tremendous problems with student discipline (Cowley, 1934).

The Nineteenth Century

Two developments occurred in the nineteenth century that influenced the development of student housing in the United States. The first of these was the Germanic influence on our higher education system. During the nineteenth century, many faculty members of American colleges and universities pursued graduate education in Germany. The German approach to higher education was characterized by intellectual impersonalism (Appleton, Briggs, & Rhatigan, 1978) and students were considered responsible for managing their own housing, food, and social life. Financial problems plagued higher education and financial resources were not readily available to support residential construction and operations. As a result, "Dormitories built in the early nineteenth century continued in operation, but many of them had been allowed to fall into semi-decay" (Cowley, 1934, p. 712).

Toward the end of the nineteenth century a second major trend developed. Colleges and universities revived their interest in student housing. While Harvard and Yale continued their house systems during this time of disinterest and disfavor toward student housing, the rest of the country abandoned the idea of housing students. The founding of the University of Chicago dramatically contributed to the rekindling of interest in student housing (Brubacher & Rudy, 1958). William Rainey Harper, the first president of the University of Chicago, had been a faculty member at Yale and insisted that housing students be a part of the Chicago campus. As the University of Chicago became an outstanding educational institution, many other institutions modeled themselves accordingly.

The Twentieth Century

While Harper organized residence halls at Chicago, Woodrow Wilson unveiled his quadrangle system for housing students at Princeton.

Although this plan ultimately failed, Wilson was viewed as a leader in higher education and his approach influenced many of his colleagues (Brubacher & Rudy, 1958).

Another factor that led to the increase of interest in student housing was the development of women's colleges. Several private institutions were founded for women in the second half of the nineteenth century, and these institutions valued student housing. The rationale for housing focused primarily on providing close supervision of these young women. Alumnae of the women's colleges attended graduate school at the larger universities and carried with them the traditions of their residential undergraduate experiences. As larger universities began to admit women, concern for women's housing became an important agenda item for administrators. Ultimately, separate residential facilities were developed to house men and women during the first decades of the twentieth century.

Another contributing factor to the attractiveness of student housing was the development of campus life outside the classroom. Intercollegiate sports, debating societies, and student publications encouraged students to spend their out of classroom time in various extracurricular activities (Brubacher & Rudy, 1958). Campus housing became more convenient for those students who wished to participate in such activities and consequently, the demand for housing increased.

Post World War II

Campus life changed dramatically after World War II since so many young people, who might have gone to college, were involved with the war effort. After World War II, many veterans returned to complete their education and housing, especially for married students, was in short supply. Apartment style housing was constructed to accommodate married students (Schneider, 1977). This, in itself, was an oddity because previously, those who attended college as undergraduates had been single students, 18 to 22 years old. Institutions of higher education needed to exercise great flexibility in meeting the needs of these new and older students.

During the late 1960s, student housing was increasingly criticized for its restrictive rules governing student life. Institutions did not permit students to entertain guests of the opposite sex in their living quarters, and women generally had to return to their residence hall by a certain time each evening or face university disciplinary action. Students vigorously questioned these policies and, where possible, left the residence halls, or brought legal action against the institution. As a result, institutions relaxed parietal rules, often dropping requirements that students live on campus and making it possible for students to live under conditions more like their peers off campus.

Toward the middle and latter part of the 1970s, students began to return to campus residence halls because of economic conditions and the widespread indifference of students to any cause except earning a degree and finding a job (Fenske, 1980a). Inflation hindered the American economy, and residence halls became a particularly convenient and economical place for students to live. Students returned to residence halls in large numbers, and as the 1980s unfolded, a number of campuses experienced shortages in the number of available spaces for student housing.

Competing Approaches

Three approaches have characterized the development of student housing in the United States. The first, adopted from colleges in England, tried to bring students, faculty and tutors together in the residential environment. The collegiate experience was perceived as integrating learning inside and outside the classroom, and every attempt was made to provide an environment which fostered learning.

During the nineteenth century, the influence of the European continent and Germany in particular, characterized the second approach. No provision was made for student housing, and, in fact, institutions did not concern themselves with what their students did outside the classroom.

Around the turn of the twentieth century, interest was rekindled in residence halls, yielding a third approach. While attempts were made to conform to the English model with live-in faculty, the resulting residential environment emphasized the housing, feeding, and social life of students. The integration of the curriculum with residential living was never achieved. This goal may have been impossible (Brubacher & Rudy, 1958), given the differences in both the types of facilities and students who attend American colleges. It should also be remembered that the philosophy of residence halls in the U.S. is not cut from one bolt of cloth. Some universities have great concern for students' intellectual development in the residence hall, while others are more content to concern themselves with providing housing and dining services, while maintaining a successful auxiliary business enterprise. What is important is that there has been a variety of approaches to providing residential facilities on campuses throughout the United States. These approaches have their roots in Great Britain and on the Continent, and what one finds currently in American post secondary education is an eclectic approach that does not reflect either of the philosophical approaches found overseas.

PURPOSE

If you were to ask a number of student affairs administrators what they thought the purposes of residence halls were, you might receive quite a variety of answers. Among these might be to provide for a good fiscal operation, to keep physical facilities in good repair, to provide activities for students to participate in outside of class, to keep order, and perhaps to provide for student growth. This section will describe different perspectives on the purposes of student housing.

Schneider (1977) pointed out that, historically, student housing had been seen as a means of controlling student behavior. She indicated that parents were comfortable with a restricted environment because students were protected from misbehaving. As the history of higher education in the United States has shown, attempts to control student behavior were often was met with subtle student resistance and, at times, a violent backlash.

In 1961 Mueller suggested three objectives for student housing. The first of these was the physical accommodation of students. That is, a place needed to be provided where students could eat and sleep, and that place should also be convenient to classrooms and the library. Secondly, she suggested that promoting academic learning was an objective of student housing. Thirdly, she argued that residence hall staff should aid in the personal development of students. Additionally, she indicated that two minor objectives of residence halls were good public relations, especially with parents, and the supervision and control of student conduct.

In the latter part of the 1960s, Greenleaf, Forsythe, Godfrey, Hudson, and Thompson (1967) suggested eight objectives of the residence hall program. The program should (1) provide an environment which supports academic achievement; (2) assist in the orientation to college life so that students understand their purpose for being in college; (3) interpret university policies, rules and objectives to the students, and interpret student attitudes to institutional administration; and (4) help each student develop a sense of individual responsibility and discipline; (5) provide an opportunity for faculty-student contacts outside the classroom; (6) provide for the basic concerns of the individual student; (7) provide through student organizations an opportunity for students to learn to work with others and provide for leisure activities; (8) provide an atmosphere of warmth, loyalty, and high morale towards the living unit, the resident hall, and the university (pp. 10-11).

These objectives move away from earlier prescriptions related to regulating student behavior and suggest a more educational or developmental role for the residential living experience.

More recently, DeCoster and Mable (1980) proposed a five step continuum to identify the general objectives of college student housing. Based on Maslow's hierarchy of needs, this continuum included:

Level 1: Providing for a satisfactory physical environment;
Level 2: Providing adequate care and maintenance of physical facilities;
Level 3: Establishing guidelines that provide a structure for compatible and cooperative community living;
Level 4: Developing an interpersonal environment that reflects responsible citizenship and an atmosphere conducive to learning;
Level 5: Providing opportunities for growth and development.

This approach is probably the most comprenhensive statement on the purpose of residence halls and represents the basis for today's educational environment. It encompasses all aspects of student housing and underscores the interrelatedness of the physical and the programmatic environments. Students cannot be expected to be interested in learning opportunities in the residence halls unless they live in adequate physical facilities. If adequate guidelines for community living are not established, it is possible that the facilities will not be respected and may become rundown through student abuse. Each aspect makes a substantial contribution to the student's experience. None is more or less important than any other, and achieving a balance is the mark of an effective philosophical approach to student housing.

ASSESSMENT

In reviewing the various assessments that might occur in the residential situation, the two which are particularly prominent and used most frequently are needs assessment and environmental assessment. Assessment, in this context, refers to ". . . gathering data, transforming data so they can be interpreted, applying analytical techniques, and analyzing data in terms of alternative hypotheses and explanations" (Lenning, 1980, p. 234).

Needs Assessment

Students who live in residence halls bring a variety of individual needs to their living situation. Additionally, students who live in a group situation also have collective or group needs. Lenning and McAleenan (1979) pointed out that while student affairs workers are quite good at identifying and assessing individual needs, they are less proficient in assessing the needs of students in groups. They commented that "the identification and assessment of group needs tend to be subjective, overly simplistic, and as a result, often ineffective" (p. 186).

Defining need is not always easy. Kuh (1982) suggested that in many instances need is defined by the purpose for which an activity is conducted. Nonetheless, one definition which seems appropriate in this context was offered by Scriven and Roth (1978, quoted by Kuh, 1982), "Need is a factor or element without which a person cannot function satisfactorily" (p. 204).

In a residential situation, several general purposes are served by a needs assessment. Certainly, to plan the training program for staff, a needs assessment might be undertaken. How else could one determine the extent to which staff are familiar with the campus, or what specialized skills they possess for their work with students? A needs assessment also could be conducted to determine programmatic activities for students (Hunson & Yansey, 1985). Additionally, we may want to determine the value of the programs and activities sponsored by staff. To accomplish this goal, the assessment might measure how well students' needs were met.

How one conducts a needs assessment is fairly complicated. Evans (1985) outlined several ways that a needs assessment can be conducted. She suggested that a variety of instruments could be used, including objective, theory based instruments, objective empirically based instruments, theory based interviews, and general interviews. She concluded that data from surveys are as informative as those generated from interviews, and that a well-designed questionnaire with a solid theoretical base can provide a comprehensive and accurate overview of student concerns (Evans, 1985).

When thinking about undertaking a needs assessment project, the advice of Kuh (1981) seems particularly appropriate. If you have a choice of the size of your project, Kuh would suggest that you try to conduct as small a project as possible. If that means, for example, choosing between doing a needs assessment project which includes all the residents of a hall as opposed to a floor or wing, choose the floor or wing as the focus of your project.

Environmental Assessment

In reviewing the rationale for assessing the student environment, it is important to remember that paper and pencil instruments were utilized by student affairs staff to gather student perceptions of services, programs and activities available on campus. More recently interest has developed in asking students to become partners with staff in designing environments that meet the needs of students (Schuh, 1979). The ecosystem model, developed by the Western Interstate Commission for Higher Education (WICHE), is one approach to environmental assessment that encourages students, administrators and faculty to work together to design campus environments. This approach is more proactive than reactive and does not attempt to make students fit the campus environment (Huebner, 1979).

The ecosystem model has been applied in a variety of situations, including residence halls, medical schools and an entire campus. Each of the examples, according to Paul (1980), was successful in reducing discrepancies between the fit of students with the environment. At Arizona State University and Indiana University, residence life staff conducted a number of these studies and the conclusion was that the projects were successful. Environmental assessment projects conducted at Purdue University have yielded similarly successful results (Null, Hall, & Menis, 1982).

In developing the ecosystem approach to environment assessment, WICHE developed a five step model. The steps included (1) developing a planning team; (2) determining what to assess; (3) developing the assessment technique; (4) conducting the assessment and analyzing of the results of the project; and finally, (5) redesigning the environment and evaluating the process (Aulepp & Delworth, 1976). Programmatic offerings were evaluated along with physical facilities, food service, and residence hall services. Students made several helpful suggestions and it was found that the project could be completed annually without being extraordinarily time consuming.

Other approaches to assessing the student environment in residence halls have been employed at various campuses. Latta (1984) reported that a Residence Hall Environment Questionnaire (RHEQ) was developed at Michigan State University for a variety of reasons, including eliciting feedback from students on the quality of their living experience. A questionnaire with 108 items was employed and 9,595 students completed it. Latta concluded that students were pleased with their living situation and that students found their residence halls to be good places in which to live.

Waldman (1985) administered the University Residence Environment Scale (URES) to survey 244 students. His purpose was to shorten the URES and the resulting instrument included 38 items, a reduction from the original 100 items. He reported that the shortened version was quite helpful to residence hall staff who would like to gather data quickly from students at the beginning or end of a regular hall meeting.

Evans (1983) reviewed several environmental assessment approaches and concluded that much work remains to be done in this area. She suggested that the organizational structure of student groups, optimum student-environmental matches, and learning environments are all potentially fruitful areas for environmental assessment.

A Concluding Thought About Assessment

As you work with students in the residential setting, it is important to remember that there is a variety of tools available to assess the situation. Needs assessments can be used in determining the direction for programs, activities, and interventions that can be planned for and in cooperation with the resident student. An environmental assessment can be planned to determine the impact of the environment on students, and their impact on the environment. Each of these techniques will be helpful in providing direction for the staff.

ENVIRONMENTAL MANAGEMENT

Most of the existing residence halls in this country were built before the present generation of students entered the first grade. With that observation in place, it is our task to identify ways to make the physical environment of residence halls compatible with needs of our students. At times, research (Tryon, 1985) has shown that physical living arrangements actually may encourage negative student behaviors. One way of conceptualizing this problem would be to take a race car, built 15 years ago, and make it competitive in the current Indianapolis 500. It would take a tremendous amount of modifications to make the car competitive for the race. In effect, that is the problem in trying to make residential facilities, constructed years ago, attractive to current students.

Grant (1974) identified four human needs that form the basis of our dilemma in environmental management. These needs include the need for order countered by the need for stimulation, and the need for security offset by the need for freedom. How does one create an environment that preserves the conditions necessary for study (order) while at the same time providing opportunities for social interaction (stimulation)? Or, is it possible to provide a free and open environment (freedom) while simultaneously providing an atmosphere where personal safety and protection for one's belongings are assured (security)?

Grant suggested two strategies for dealing with the problems of this dilemma. One approach was to provide groupings of students who could identify with one another. He indicated that a group of approximately eight was ideal, although the range could be from two to 20. Such a small group would foster feelings of cohesiveness and increase individual productivity.

Grant's other approach was that students ought to participate in structuring their environment. Students should be able to control their own environment and provide for the degree of security, stimulation, order and freedom that would best meet their needs. Although such an approach could not meet all of a student's needs, it certainly would provide a better environment than if conditions were left to chance. The remainder of this section addresses practical issues related to environmental management, including territoriality, vandalism, special living areas and community development.

Territoriality

Territoriality, according to Grant (1974), refers to individuals being able to stake out a piece of the environment for themselves and then exercising maximum control over it. While that is a sound conceptualization of the concept, operationalizing territoriality is not particularly easy. Schroeder (1978-1979) built on several of Grant's concepts in identifying mechanisms that would mediate social behavior and the physical environment. Among his suggestions were that (1) space be personalized; (2) defensible space be identified; (3) social interaction and group stability be encouraged; and (4) individuals be provided an opportunity to regulate their privacy.

Personalizing Space

In this dimension, Schroeder referred to allowing and encouraging students to modify their physical space. Activities in the student room might include painting the walls, building lofts, paneling the walls and building furniture. In hallways, students might paint murals or graphics, could modify their lounges, build furniture for television rooms and construct other facilities which might meet studying and socializing needs. A study conducted by Werring, Winston, and McCaffrey (1981) found that a number of benefits result from students participating in painting projects. They concluded, however, that benefits accrued only to those who participated in the projects and not to everyone in the unit. This finding is not unusual given Pace's (1984) concept of quality of effort which suggests that what students get out of college will depend, to a considerable degree, on the effort they put into their experiences.

Defensible Space

A certain amount of space in any residence hall will belong to the group rather than the individual. Damage is likely to occur in these areas. Space that belongs to the entire group, such as a hallway or lounge, must be protected in ways that make it possible for residents to believe that the territory can be defended. Schroeder suggested that if residents are encouraged to paint the space, they should be able to restrict the access of nonresidents to the space and that the group be held responsible collectively for vandalism that occurs in the space. Schroeder hypothesized that these strategies will minimize problems created by those who are not part of the group.

Social Interaction

Often, lounges that are constructed on residence hall floors do not encourage interaction. Generally, they are at the ends of a hallway or in other ways are isolated from floor members. Schroeder suggested that to provide more pleasant social interaction, student rooms more centrally located within a living unit could be developed as group rooms. He pointed to work done at Auburn University where group rooms were created with great success. Additionally, he suggested that public areas, which receive minimal use, might be converted for group use. Jackson and Schroeder (1977) did this with students who sought stimulation and found the experiment to be very successful.

Privacy Regulation

Most of our residence hall rooms were built for double occupancy, although students today come from smaller families with fewer siblings (Hodgkinson, 1985). To provide more privacy for residents, perhaps more single rooms could be established, even though this would carry a certain financial risk. If that is not an option, it is possible that partitions or barriers could be constructed to provide each resident with a little more privacy.

Matching Roommates

Schroeder (1981) suggested that roommates be matched using the Myers-Briggs Type Indicator (MBTI). Briefly, the MBTI measures personality along several dimensions and by matching roommates with similar personalities, incompatibility could be reduced. Other personality tests might also be used, but the point is that by intentionally matching roommates, a more pleasant environment can be created. Much as the case with matching roommates, the MBTI or any other instrument could be used to match suitemates with the objective being greater compatibility. Where baths or other facilities are shared, greater compatibility on the part of those sharing the facilities results in a much more pleasant living situation.

Other Issues Related to Environmental Mangement

Several other issues related to managing the environment deserve comment in thisportion of the chapter. These include vandalism, special living areas and community.

Vandalism

Vandalism is a problem that is widespread in residence halls (Bowles, 1982). Strategies that deal with vandalism, however, have rarely been published even though entry level residence hall staff may spend considerable time dealing with this problem. Bowles (1982) has suggested a variety of strategies which might be employed to address vandalism. Primary strategies include (1) encouraging community development and personalization projects; (2) technical strategies which would involve indestructible materials; (3) adequate lighting and immovable furniture; (4) deterrent approaches including taking stiff action against offenders up to and including cancelling the student's housing contract; and (5) publicity, which lets students know what vandalism is costing them, both in monetary and human terms.

Special Living Areas

Lillis and Schroer (1984) reported a specialized learning environment wherein students live in a 24-hour quiet area with special support for student-initiated programming. The portability of this kind of program is difficult to assess, but it underscores the fact that special kinds of living environments can be established if there are enough students interested. These kinds of programs can include a special emphasis on the students' curriculum, such as a language or engineering house, or on the extracurricular interests of students including backpacking and hiking. These kinds of programs do provide enrichment for students and create a living situation that is a meaningful learning experience.

Community

Another concept associated with managing the residential environment which should not be overlooked is developing community. When community is well developed in a residential unit, students will share goals, responsibilities, and communications (Mable, Terry, & Duvell, 1980). As a result, they will live more harmoniously with one another and will respect and protect the residential facilities.

For a further exploration of the concept of environmental management, the reader is encouraged to consult *Making Yourself at Home* by Anchros, Schroeder, and Jackson (1978) for a detailed description of ways students can personalize their residence hall space.

STAFFING PATTERNS

While the titles of various residence hall staff positions may vary from campus to campus, functions performed remain fairly constant on most campuses. As the size of the housing department increases, additional staff will be added at the administrative level, consequently housing departments on large campuses will provide a variety of services with a large number of highly specialized staff.

The person who lives on a residence hall floor and provides direct service to students is called a resident assistant or resident advisor. At times this person is called a resident counselor, although providing advice and referral are more typical of his or her responsibilities than actually entering into counseling relationships with residents. Typically an upperclass student, the RA is responsible for working with students individually and in small groups, assessing student needs and planning programs, advising the floor government, handling certain administrative matters and enforcing university rules and regulations. There is probably no more difficult position in student affairs work than that of the RA, because literally the RA is expected to live where he or she works. RAs are always on call and deal with many problems that are quite difficult. Many senior student affairs officers began their careers as these front line members of a student affairs team.

Generally, larger residence halls will have assistant residence hall directors who are graduate students. The professional staff person in charge of the residence hall is often called a head resident, resident director or building manager. Typically, this person has a master's degree in student personnel, counseling or a related field and the position is considered entry-level in student affairs work.

Beyond the individual residence hall, a variety of administrative positions may exist to provide overall direction for the housing department. In larger housing systems, it is common to find an area director responsible for a group of residence halls. The hall directors will report directly to an area director, who frequently has several years of full time experience in addition to a master's degree. In a smaller system, the hall directors may report to an assistant director for housing or an assistant dean for residential life. This person has overall responsibility for residence life programs on campus, including such activities as coordinating the resident assistant selection and training program, advising the all-residence hall student government and judicial board, and selecting and supervising the hall directors. A person at this level usually has held several positions before moving into a situation where he or she coordinates an entire campus residence life program.

Particularly in larger institutions, other central office administrators may include an assistant director for operations, who would be concerned with the managerial aspects of student housing including room assignments, budget preparation and management, and the various business aspects of student housing such as purchasing, personnel and summer conferences. There may be an assistant director who works with physical facilities. This individual would supervise maintenance and housekeeping, work with the campus physical plant, prepare long range repair and rehabilitation plans, and serve as project administrator for major construction projects.

Food service is usually provided in one of two ways. Smaller campuses frequently will contract with a private caterer to provide food service. Other campuses, including those with a larger occupancy, tend to have a food service that is provided by the campus or by the housing department itself. Traditionally, local resources and campus facilities will be factors considered when determining whether or not the campus will provide its own food service or contract with a private vendor.

The director of housing frequently will have advanced graduate preparation and will normally report either to the Chief Financial Officer or the Chief Student Affairs Officer. There is no consistent way of handling this reporting relationship, although one dated study found that the housing director reported more often to the chief student affairs officer than to any other institutional officer (Bacon, 1966). On some campuses the housing director has been known to report to both the chief financial officer and the chief student affairs officer and in a few cases the residence life program has been established as a separate department. Indiana University and Michigan State University are examples of this later arrangement. At these institutions the residence life program is supervised by the chief student affairs officer, while the housing department reports to the chief financial officer.

STAFF DEVELOPMENT (RA ONLY)

In their book on the resident assistant, Blimling and Miltenberger (1981) listed 43 different roles that are common to the resident assistant position. Give the fact that few resident assistants (RAs) have held a similar position prior to joining the residence life staff, a training program for them is essential. In fact, it is nearly impossible for RAs to be effective without a well-designed, comprehensive training program. With that in mind, this section was designed to present a brief overview of how to develop and implement a resident assistant training program.

Staff development issues related to full-time residence hall staff will not be addressed.

Leafgren (1981) offered a particularly insightful comment on staff development when he wrote, "Like human development, staff development is a process which is continuous and cumulative. It requires time and a belief in human potential" (p. 228). Schuh (1981) suggested a four phase approach to training programs for resident assistants. These phases include (1) training in residence hall operations; (2) campus support services; (3) human relations; and (4) programming and advising. These areas can be used as a framework for planning the training program.

Residence hall operations refer to those areas which include the administrative operation and maintenance of the residence facility. Although RAs rarely have primary responsibility for fixing broken plumbing or handling custodial chores, they may find themselves in many situations when routine maintenance and facility support will not be available. For example, plumbing equipment can break at any time of the day or night or the electrical circuits may become overloaded and not function. There are other operational functions which staff must perform, such as working in the duty office, using master keys, handling meal ticket problems, assisting students who suffer injuries or sudden illnesses, and taking emergency telephone calls from families. As the training program is developed, these issues should be identified and discussed before the facility is opened to students.

Campus support services include those offices and agencies which provide assistance to the residence hall staff and students. Among them, for example, are the student health service, the counseling center, the student activities office and the recreational sports program. There are many other offices and agencies that provide support to the residence halls, and it is important that RAs understand the functions of those offices and the name of the individual to contact when assistance is needed. One way of alerting RAs to these people and offices is to have the RAs participate in a scavenger hunt on campus requiring the RAs to go to the offices and meet the staff. This technique has been used on several campuses with great success.

Training in human relations refers to the RAs' ability to interact skillfully and humanely with students. RAs provide advice and counsel to their residents and need to be able to help students in identifying their concerns or problems. Often, staff and students will work together to identify potential solutions or agencies that can provide assistance. A number of training models have been developed which are directly transferable to human relations training for RAs. Among these are the models developed by Carkhuff (1969), Ivey (1971), Kagan (1975), Danish and Hauer (1973), and Egan (1975). All of these models have strengths and weaknesses, and those planning the staff development program should be sensitive to the specific needs of the staff before selecting a particular model. At times, a combination of methods can be used in training the staff in human relations techniques.

The final area of training for RAs focuses on programming and advising. RAs often are expected to plan programs and advise student groups. To expect that RAs will know how to plan programs and advise student groups is not appropriate. Rather, RAs should be thought of as enthusiastic about programming and advising, but in need of information about how to handle their responsibilities successfully. A monograph edited by Schuh (1984) provided a great deal of information about advising student groups and is targeted at the paraprofessional group adviser. It should be a part of the residence life departmental library since it can serve as a resource for many exercises that can be used by the RA group adviser. In the program planning area, RAs ought to understand, in an elementary way, a study development theory and ought to know how to use that theory in planning programs. Forney (1986) described a workshop that introduced resident staff to student development theory. Rather than selecting programs that are traditional or of interest to staff, programs should be planned with student needs in mind. Most residence hall offices ought to have records of resources to contact for program planning, and assistance in the planning process should be available from professional staff. Additionally, each RA should be provided with a staff manual which should include program resources, along with operational and administrative information.

Although RAs face a number of new issues with each succeeding generation of students, several longitudinal studies (Schuh, Shipton, & Edman, 1986; Schuh, Shipton, & Edman, 1987) have found that the kinds of student problems that RAs encountered over 15 years did not change significantly. Most frequently, RAs encountered such issues as an academic crisis, alcohol abuse, roommate problems, and vocational issues. The point is that while such issues as wellness or AIDS capture our attention and the headlines from year to year, the training program should be designed to meet the typical concerns of the majority of the residents. This training agenda has not changed dramatically over time.

Work as an RA can be extremely demanding and stressful. Nowack and Hanson (1983) found that RAs experience considerable job-related stress in the course of their work. A subsequent study (Nowak, Gibbons, & Hanson, 1985) suggested that social support and health habits can be positive factors in the face of work and life stress. They suggested that a health lifestyle seems to be significantly associated with RA job performance and effectiveness. The implications for staff development seem obvious; mechanisms need to be developed which encourage formation of healthy habits. Among these might include special activities to build strong working teams, remembering birthdays, holidays, and other special occasions, making sure that RAs have enough time to themselves and reminding staff that their RA position should not be their highest priority. Their academic work should take precedence over their RA responsibilities, but at times, RAs scramble their priorities and become consumed by their jobs.

RESIDENCE HALL PROGRAMMING

The number and variety of programs available to the typical residence hall student are virtually limitless. On any given campus, programs can range from social to recreational, from cultural to academic. Providing enough programming in a quantitative sense rarely is a problem in a residence hall environment. Making programming meaningful to students, and linking residence hall programs to student needs is another matter. The purpose of this section is to provide a framework for residence hall programming and to identify several programs that are especially timely in today's educational environment.

There are a number of frameworks from which one might choose to plan residence hall programs. Among these are student development theories, intervention models and campus ecology models. One of the best frameworks is the dimensions of intervention for student development model developed by Morrill, Hurst, and Oetting (1980). This model identifies three specific types of programming: (1) remedial programming; (2) preventive programming; and (3) developmental programming.

Remedial programming refers to those programs which emphasize issues where something has gone wrong and the problem needs to be addressed. An example of this might be where international students have experienced subtle forms of discrimination within the residence hall because of their religious customs. Workshops might be designed for all students where the specific customs are explained. Moreover, some emphasis might be placed on the religious discrimination that, in part, was responsible for many people leaving their homelands to come to the U.S.

Preventive programming includes those programs that are implemented because student problems or issues can be predicted. Morrill, Hurst, and Oetting (1980) use the example of providing programs which help ease the transition from home to the university setting. They are designed to minimize homesickness, roommate conflicts, and academic problems.

Developmental programming sessions are those designed to foster student growth. These programs include leadership development programs, volunteer opportunities and social programs. They promote the growth and development of healthy students who desire to improve their skills and abilities.

Most educational programs can be fit into one of the three categories in the taxonomy listed above. Using this framework as a guide, program planning can be undertaken to meet the needs of students, assuming that their interests and needs have been assessed appropriately. Before describing programs which are currently of wide interest among residence hall administrators, it may be helpful to review reasons why programs fail. Hurst and Jacobson (1985) have identified seven reasons why programs fail.

At times, professional staff members plan programs around topics that are of interest to them. Staff personnel may be interested in issues related to East European cultures, so they plan programs focusing on that area, regardless of whether or not students have interests or needs in issues related to East European cultures.

Secondly, professional staff are knowledgeable in a specific area and tend to develop programs in their area of expertise. If they have undergraduate majors in physical education, they may plan programs related to recreational sports and nutrition, even though students in this hypothetical situation already are required to take courses in these areas. In effect, they repeat what students are learning in the classroom.

Thirdly, a crisis emerges on campus and programs are planned quickly to meet the crisis. In fact, what often happens is that the program focuses on the mess created by the crisis, rather than dealing with the underlying causes of the problem. We often address instances related to racist behavior rather than working on the underlying causes of racism.

Issues become popular within professional associations, and after attending a conference, staff members may plan programs on their campus because they know the programs were successful on another campus. Without understanding why the program was successful at another institution, and realizing that programs are not automatically transportable from one campus to another, they plan programs used at an engineering school dealing with using computer technology while on their own campus, with an emphasis on fine arts, computer capability is limited.

At times, programs are developed to meet political needs of the campus or simply because special interest groups have pressured us to do so. Neither is a good reason to program. Programs should be designed to meet the needs of our students. These needs should have been assessed carefully and thoughtfully.

Finally, we plan particular programs because we have always planned these programs. Student needs and interests change over time. In the late 1960s there was great interest in political issues on many of our campuses. Since then, the environment has changed to the extent that student needs and interests are quite different. We need to stay abreast of changing student needs and values and plan our programs accordingly.

Selected Programs

As was mentioned earlier, the number and range of programs that one might find in residence halls on a particular campus is large. Rather than provide an exhaustive listing of programs, an attempt will be made to focus on a few programs that represent efforts to bring faculty and students together in the residential setting to promote academic learning.

Rowe (1981) prepared a cogent discussion of living learning centers (LLC). An LLC, broadly defined is designed to "integrate the student's academic experience with his or her living environment. The goals of affective, cognitive, and physical growth and development of the resident are pursued through intentional provision of formal and/or informal . . . learning experiences" (Rowe, 1981, p. 54). Features of the LLC often include classes for credit, noncredit classes and special programming, and nontraditional experimental activities, such as an artist-in-residence or special visitors to the center. While this type of residence life program is expensive, it can provide a particularly enriched learning experience for students. Faculty can play a key role in the administration of the unit, in presenting programs, and by teaching classes within the center.

Another interesting program is the development of student-operated businesses. Valerio and Reynolds (1983) described such a program at Marquette University where students operated convenience stores in the residence halls. The stores sell snack items and prepackaged food. The purposes of the stores are to provide services for students, provide income for student government and perhaps most importantly, give students the opportunity for a "hands-on" experience with managing and operating a business. Faculty may assure a major role in the development of student operated businesses since they often serve as advisers to store management and offer courses designed to meet the needs of the students involved in marketing, managing and accounting for the stores. For a number of years, for example, a seminar for store accountants has been offered jointly by the School of Business and the Department of Residence Life at Indiana University.

Thematic housing, i.e., housing with a specific focus, has been an option available within residential housing programs for years. In earlier years these houses often had a curricular emphasis, such as providing an intensive experience for students interested in sharpening their foreign language skills. More recently, other thematic houses have been developed, including an attractive program at Illinois State University which focuses on wellness. In the Wellness House (Pope, 1987), students have available special diets, equipment and facilities designed to foster exercise, career-oriented programs, a special library and support groups. Other aspects of living in the house also emphasize good health and physical fitness, e.g., residents may not smoke while in the house. Pope (1987) indicated that the program was well received and more students applied to live in the unit than there were spaces. This kind of program could provide an excellent opportunity for faculty from physical and health education departments, for example, to work collaboratively with students in areas of common interest. While not specifically identified as part of the program, it seems clear that these faculty, as well as others, could serve as advisers to the house or program speakers or group discussion leaders in the unit.

Colwell and Lifka (1983) suggested that programs designed to provide students and faculty with an opportunity to interact at Northwestern University have yielded positive results. Their approaches include residential colleges, freshman advisor programs, faculty associates programs and individualized, ad hoc programs, such as fireside chats or informal discussions and lectures. These programs have benefits for students and faculty, including students getting to learn and appreciate faculty outside the classroom, faculty learning about the lives of students, and faculty providing useful ideas about the administration of residence programs. While Colwell and Lifka suggested starting these programs modestly, they concluded that even on a small scale, the programs were very successful. That approach is consistent with the observations of Kuh, Schuh, and Thomas (1985) who suggested that while faculty-student interaction programs add a richness to the residential experience for all participants, they are not a prescription for dramatically improving a residence hall environment. Faculty should place an emphasis on the quality of their interaction with students, not the number of students contacted.

THE INFLUENCE OF RESIDENCE HALL LIVING ON STUDENTS

Numerous studies have been conducted to determine the influence of residence hall living on students. Most, but not all, of these studies have concluded that students benefit from living in residence halls on campus.

Chickering (1974) compared commuting students with residential students and found that the residential experience accelerated the differences between the two student groups. He concluded, "Commuters and residents begin their college careers with an unequal start which strongly favors the residents. The gap between them grows. Residents have access to, find and are forced to encounter diverse experience and persons who spurt them on their way" (p. 85).

In his book on the college experience, Astin (1977) summarized information from a variety of studies which compared the experiences of commuter students with those who lived on campus. He indicated that living on campus enhances the likelihood of students to graduate and residents are more likely to aspire to graduate or professional school. Students living on campus are more satisfied with their undergraduate experience, especially in the areas of student friendships and their relationships with faculty; the reputation of their institution and their social life. Astin (1977) also concluded that residents were more likely to achieve in extracurricular areas including leadership and athletics.

Bowen (1977), however, cited a study conducted by Bradshaw who found that living on campus was not necessarily preferable to living off-campus separated from parents in apartments or rooms.

In 1985 Astin concluded that ". . . simply by virtue of eating, sleeping, and spending their waking hours on the college campus, residential students stand a better chance than do commuter students of developing a strong identification with and attachment to undergraduate life" (p. 145).

Two other studies completed recently also address the issue of the influence on students of living in residence halls. Pascarella (1985) determined that living on campus was positively associated with student development by promoting higher levels of interaction and involvement with major agents of socialization on campus. Similarly, Wilson, Anderson, and Fleming (1987) found that commuting students were more maladjusted to college than resident students.

Why does the preponderance of the evidence suggest that living on campus, be it in a residence hall, fraternity or sorority house, has such a positive influence on students? There are several reasons. As Chickering (1974) pointed out, residential students start from a favored position compared with commuters and the residential experience accelerates the differences. Such factors are family background, finances, high school academic record distinguish residential students from commuters.

Using Astin's concept of involvement as an interpretive framework, it is clear that merely by residing on campus, students have better opportunities to become involved in campus life, through leadership opportunities, recreational sports and cultural activities. These opportunities ultimately are translated into greater student growth and development.

Additionally, the environment that is created in a campus residence which provides opportunities for students to experience diversity, to be challenged by their peers, and to learn from one another contributes to student development. The challenge to residence educators is to maximize the learning opportunities available in the residential environment. That means finding ways for students to become involved with faculty, to assume leadership positions, and to participate in the myriad activities and programs available both in the residence hall and on the campus at large.

SELECTED LEGAL ISSUES

Early in a career in student affairs, one finds that the work environment is full of challenges, some of which cannot be settled anywhere other than in a court of law. Students, parents, and others will hold the staff legally responsible for their decisions and actions (Owens, 1984). As a result, a brief introduction to several legal issues will be described.

It is important to realize that individuals should not function as their own attorney. When legal advice is needed, it should be sought through appropriate channels on campus. The campus may have an office of legal counsel, or it may have an attorney on retainer. Regardless, when it is concluded that legal advice is needed, seek it!

It is important to realize the difference between working in a public institution, and working in a private or independent institution. Public institutions are more fully regulated than private ones, and those who work in public institutions are more fully constrained by the federal constitution than those who work in private institutions (Kaplin, 1985). The Fourteenth Amendment to the U.S. Constitution prescribes that the states must respect all the rights of citizens outlined in our constitution; this amendment does not apply to private citizens or institutions (Young, 1984). Consequently, private institutions have more latitude in promulgating rules and regulations, and that while due process in disciplinary situations is absolutely guaranteed in public institutions, private institutions are not held to the same standard (*Soglin* v. *Kauffmann,* 1969; Kaplin, 1985).

Fire and Safety Procedures

Perhaps the greatest danger to students living in a residence hall is fire (Schuh, 1984). Most states have laws and regulations regarding fire fighting equipment, smoke detectors, fire drills and the like. It is critical that residence life staff become conversant with these laws and regulations, and follow them explicitly. Routine inspections should be held and the staff should work closely with the staff of the physical facilities department to ensure that all equipment is functional.

Additionally, if the campus is located in a high crime area, or there is concern that students' physical safety may be threatened, resident students should be informed of ways to minimize such risks as soon as they move into the residence hall. If a series of criminal acts occur on the campus or in the residence halls and the institution fails to take steps to rectify the situation or notify students, the institution, through its administrators, could be held liable (*Duarte* v. *State,* 1979).

Physical Facilities

Usually at an inopportune time (at night or during the weekend), something will happen which will render your physical facilities inoperable or dangerous. This could be anything from an elevator breaking down to a violent act of weather resulting in making the physical facility unusable. No one can predict with absolute certainty when a snow storm, heavy rain or flood will ravage the campus. During times such as these, the resident staff will need to take steps to make sure that students are protected from injury or possibly death.

The case of *Shannon* v. *Washington University* (1978) illustrates the concept of institutional responsibility for keeping facilities in good operating condition. In this case a student slipped on a sidewalk after a storm. The court ruled on behalf of the student and several implications for management emerged from the court's decision. Firstly, an institution has a responsibility to keep facilities in good repair, no matter what time of day or night a problem occurs or how expensive it is to correct the problem. In this case, sidewalks became icy overnight after a storm. The institution, the court declared, had a responsibility to clear the walks, even though it would have been expensive to put a crew on the task at night. Secondly, the institution has to make a judgment as to what is dangerous. In the case cited above, the institution did not think that the walk was dangerous, although injuries were sustained by a person who slipped on the ice. The judgment about potential danger made by the institution should be conservative in the sense that if there is any potential for injury, the situation should be defined as dangerous and corrected. Thirdly, when the institution becomes aware of the problem, it has a duty to resolve it. When a resident staff person becomes aware of a problem, he or she should report it to the appropriate individual and it should be repaired. To protect staff and the institution, make sure that potential problems such as icy sidewalks or slippery hallways are corrected immediately. Anticipate problems that might arise such as an elevator that has been balky for the past day or two, and report any problems as soon as they are discovered.

Duty to Warn

One should accept the duty of warning a potential victim of threat. The most famous case that speaks to this point is *Tarasoff* v. *Regents of the University of California* (1976) which involved an individual threatening to do harm to a student currently away from the campus. When the student returned, she was killed. The court found that the person who received the information concerning the threat had an obligation to warn the potential victim. If this kind of information is received, even if the information may be confidential, the intended victim should be notified as well as the campus or local police department. The concept of privileged communication rarely is extended to student affairs practitioners and they are held responsible if a potential victim is not warned and becomes a victim.

Program Supervision

All kinds of programs occur in the residence halls. Most require little or no risk on the part of the participants. Some programs, however, do require a certain amount of skill or knowledge on the part of the participants or involve the consumption of alcoholic beverages. In these two instances, the risk of problems occurring increases.

For programs requiring participants to master certain skills or the use of complicated equipment, the most successful strategy for the program planner is to consult with a person on campus who has expertise in the skill area, or the use of the equipment. For example, when developing an excursion program involving mountain climbing, someone should be contacted in the physical education department to learn how to prepare participants for the activity. An expert consultant might be hired to help with the supervision of the activity as well. Activities involving trampolines, skate boards, amateur boxing or tugs-of-war need to be planned with great care since serious injuries might result (Miller & Schuh, 1981). Additionally, any activity involving water sports should be supervised by an individual with current Red Cross certification as a lifeguard.

Activities involving alcohol can result in tragedy, especially if automobiles are involved in transporting students to an event where alcohol will be consumed. The most notable case in this area is *Bradshaw* v. *Rawling* (1979) in which a sizable judgment was rendered against an institution of higher education. Although the judgment set aside subsequently by a higher court, the fact remains that institutions are at risk when students mix alcohol and automobiles. A much safer strategy is to hire public carriers to provide transportation whenever alcohol is part of an event off campus.

To minimize the risk, be knowledgable about state laws. If students are under the legal drinking age, they should not be allowed to consume alcoholic beverages. The institution should never be a part of sponsoring illegal activities. As was mentioned above, transportation should be provided through common carriers such as buses. The amount of alcohol purchased should be realistic. Planners should purchase an amount that will be commensurate with the number of participants anticipated. Food and alternative beverages should be provided. Before planning an event where alcoholic beverages will be available, the campus alcohol information center or health center should be consulted for information about program planning with alcohol.

Getting up in the morning and going to work involves some risks. The key to protecting oneself, students, and institution is to employ risk management strategies which minimize the likelihood of risks becoming real events. Never be afraid to ask for help from senior administrative staff members.

THE FUTURE

What does the future hold for residence halls? To plan for developments as we move toward the start of the twenty-first century is a challenge. The most important fact to consider is that the birth rate of traditionally college-aged students is declining (Hodgkinson, 1985). From this information alone, several changes can be expected during the coming years.

More than likely future students will request more privacy and expect to live in situations where they do not have roommates. Currently, most campus residence staff members assign two students to every room and expect that the roommates will develop into compatible partners. The roommate model was adopted at a time in history when there were more siblings in families and sharing a bedroom was the usual condition. Students of the future may not be willing to live in a situation where their privacy is limited. So, we should probably plan for more single rooms than is the case today.

If students do not have roommates, then more efforts will be required on the part of residence staff to involve students in interactive situations. Without programs and activities which encourage students to socialize and work together, isolation and alienation are possible. Given these two characteristics, the residence hall environment could become one of depression. Community building will be more difficult. Thus, strategies will have to be devised that will motivate students to leave their individual living spaces and spend time with others.

As the use of computers and cable television increases as teaching media, necessary equipment should be provided to make it possible for students to learn in their rooms. Access to computing networks, libraries, and learning resource centers will have to be a part of the well equipped student room. Cable television hookups in a student's room will be required. Therein lies a danger. As the room becomes more of a locus of learning, the possibility of isolation and depression increases. Our role will be to bring students together in meaningful ways in an effort to fight depression, isolation and boredom.

It is clear that residence halls are being expected to provide academic support facilities. Libraries, computer terminals, offices for academic advisers and classroom space will very much be a part of the future residence hall. Since more classes may be offered in the residence hall, students should be encouraged to form study groups and may be assigned to residence halls based on their prospective major or area of career interest. While some of these activities are presently being implemented, it seems clear that such will be the direction of the future.

Hand-in-hand with greater academic opportunities in the residence halls will be a strong emphasis on providing programs by which faculty and students can interact in the residential situation. As our concerns about greater isolation of students are defined, one of the ways to respond to these feelings is to design programs to facilitate faculty and students interaction in the residence hall. This may mean increasing or expanding a faculty fellow programs, more faculty/student research projects, and perhaps more faculty-in-residence or guests-in-residence positions.

Participation in student government is becoming more complicated. Student government budgets are larger and the demands placed on student government leaders by their colleagues and university administrators make service in student government less attractive. Incentives must be developed to motivate students to become involved in student government leadership positions. Perhaps a combination room assignment and office arrangement can be provided. Possibly a scholarship program could be established to assist those student government leaders who must forego part time work because of their responsibilities. The point is, student government service is becoming a burden to students, and mechanisms should be found to make this kind of service attractive.

On some campuses, the occupancy rates of residence halls and associated financial concerns will be a problem for administrators. Many residence hall systems were designed to resolve a housing shortage caused by the attendance of the baby boom generation, while today there is an over supply of capacity. Competition with housing developments off-campus is causing problems at some institutions, especially when the off-campus accommodations are newer and more luxurious. As a result, we may be on the verge of moving into rather austere financial times for many institutions. For many campuses, careful budget management will be the normal operating procedure for the foreseeable future.

It is entirely possible that students of the future will demand more services. Academic support activities have been identified earlier in this section, but we may also be moving into a closer relationship with off-campus vendors to provide services to our students. These might include convenience markets, if the students do not operate them as a government or service project, barber shops and beauty salons, and dry cleaning are a few examples. As these kinds of services are added to the auxiliary enterprises portfolio, administrators will need to be careful not to create problems for the institution in its relationships with local businesses. One approach is to operate the new service as a concession under contract to a private firm, rather than the institution operating the business by itself. A number of colleges and universities already use this approach in providing food service, bookstores, and banking services. More recreational facilities will be expected by students, including aerobics rooms, exercise areas and weight rooms. Instead of considering these as amenities or luxuries, administrators might be better served by considering them essential to the well-equipped residence hall.

Finally, the residence hall staff of the future will be faced with a variety of challenges. On the one hand they will have to carefully market their facilities because of the competition raised by off-campus housing developments for the ever-dwindling number of traditional college students. On the other hand, they also will have to be prepared to work with students who are not used to sharing living space. These students may see little value in leaving their single rooms with computer and television and thus may be less likely to participate in student activities. Special skills will be necessary for residence staff members to do their jobs effectively. The challenge, then, seems to be to identify ways that staff can stay current, that facilities remain attractive, and that students find the living experience satisfying. Residence halls that meet these challenges will be recognized as the pacesetters for the twenty-first century.

REFERENCES

Anchors, S., Schroeder, C.C., & Jackson, S. (1978). *Making yourself at home: A practical guide to restructuring and personalizing your residence environment.* Cincinnati: ACPA.

Appleton, J.R., Biggs, C.M., & Rhatigan, J.J. (1978). *Pieces of eight.* Portland, OR: NASPA.

Astin, A.W. (1977). *Four critical years.* San Francisco: Jossey-Bass.

Astin, A.W. (1985). *Achieving educational excellence.* San Francisco: Jossey-Bass.

Aulepp, L.A., & Delworth, U. (1976). *Training manual for an ecosystem model: Assessing and designing campus environments.* Boulder, CO: WICHE.

Bacon, P.A. (1966). How colleges organize housing. *College and University Business, 40*(4), 76-79.

Blimling, G.A., & Miltenberger, L.J. (1981). *The resident assistant: Working with college students in residence halls.* Dubuque, IA: Kendall/Hunt.

Bowen, H.R. (1980). *Investment in learning.* San Francisco: Jossey-Bass.

Bowles, J.K. (1982). The residence hall vandalism problem: A model for examining destructive behavior. *The Journal of College and University Student Housing, 12*(1), 15-19.

Brubacher, J.S., & Rudy, W. (1958). *Higher education in transition.* New York: Harper.

Carkhuff, R.R. (1969). *Helping and human relations.* Vols. 1 and 2. New York: Holt, Rinehart & Winston.

Chickering, A.W. (1974). *Commuting versus resident students.* San Francisco: Jossey-Bass.

Colwell, B.W., & Lifka, T.E. (1983). Faculty involvement in residential life. *The Journal of College and University Student Housing, 13*(1), 9-14.

Cowley, W.H. (1934). The history of student residential housing. *School and Society, 40*(1040), 705-712.

Cowley, W.H. (1934). The history of student residential housing. II. *School and Society, 40*(1041), 758-764.

Danish, S.J., & Hauer, A.L. (1973). *Helping skills: A basic training program.* New York: Behavioral Publications.

DeCoster, D.A., & Mable, P. (1980). Residence education: Purpose and process. In D.A. DeCoster & P. Mable (Eds.), *Personal education and community development in college residence halls* (pp. 31-55). Cincinnati: ACPA.

Egan, G. (1975). *The skilled helper: A model for systematic helping and interpersonal relating.* Monterey, CA: Brooks/Cole.

Evans, N.J. (1983). Environmental assessment: Current practices and future directions. *Journal of College Student Personnel, 24,* 293-299.

Evans, N.J. (1985). Needs assessment methodology: A comparison of results. *Journal of College Student Personnel, 26,* 107-114.

Fenske, R.H. (1980). Historical foundations. In U. Delworth & G.R. Hanson (Eds.), *Student services: A handbook for the profession* (pp. 3-24). San Francisco: Jossey-Bass.

Fenske, R.H. (1980a). Current trends. In U. Delworth & G.R. Hanson (Eds.), *Student services: A handbook for the profession* (pp. 45-72). San Francisco: Jossey-Bass.

Forney, D.S. (1986). Helping undergraduate residence staff use theory to support practice. *Journal of College Student Personnel, 27,* 468-469.

Grant, W.H. (1974). Humanizing the residence hall environment. In D.A. DeCoster & P. Mable (Eds.), *Student development and education in college residence halls* (pp. 71-75). Washington: ACPA.

Greenleaf, E.A., Forsythe, M., Godfrey, H., Hudson, B.J., & Thompson, F. (1967). *Undergraduate students as members of the residence hall staff.* Bloomington, IN: NAWDAC.

Hanson, G.R., & Yancey, B.D. (1985). Gathering information to determine program needs. In M.J. Barr & L.A. Keating (Eds.), *Developing effective student services programs* (pp. 137-157). San Francisco: Jossey-Bass.

Hodgkinson, H.L. (1985). *All one system.* Washington: Institute for Educational Leadership.

Huebner, L.A. (1979). Emergent issues of theory and practice. In L.A. Huebner (Ed.), *Redesigning campus environments* (New Directions for Student Services Sourcebook No. 8) (pp. 1-21). San Francisco: Jossey-Bass.

Hurst, J.C., & Jacobson, J.K. (1985). Theories underlying students' needs for programs. In M.J. Barr & L.A. Keating (Eds.), *Developing effective student services programs* (pp. 113-136). San Francisco: Jossey-Bass.

Ivey, A.E. (1971). *Microcounseling: Innovations in interviewer training.* Springfield, IL: Charles C Thomas.

Jackson, G.S., & Schroeder, C.C. (1977). Behavioral zoning for stimulation seekers. *The Journal of College and University Student Housing, 7*(1), 7-10.

James, E.J. (1917). College residence halls. *The Journal of Home Economics, IX*(3), 101-108.

Kagan, N. (1975). *Interpersonal process recall: A method of influencing human interaction.* East Lansing, MI: Michigan State University Educational Publication Services.

Kaplin, W.A. (1985). *The law of higher education* (2nd ed.). San Francisco: Jossey-Bass.

Kuh, G.D. (1981). Guiding questions for needs assessments in student affairs. *Journal of the National Association for Women Deans, Administrators and Counselors, 45*(1), 32-38.

Kuh, G.D. (1982). Purpose and principles for needs assessment in student affairs. *Journal of College Student Personnel, 23,* 202-209.

Kuh, G.D., Schuh, J.H., & Thomas, R.O. (1985). Suggestions for encouraging faculty-student interaction in a residence hall. *NASPA Journal, 22*(3), 29-37.

Latta, W.J. (1984). The residence hall environment questionnaire. *Journal of College Student Personnel, 25,* 370-373.

Leafgren, F. (1980). Student development through staff development. In D.A. DeCoster & P. Mable (Eds.), *Personal education and community development in college residence halls* (pp. 218-228). Cincinnati: ACPA.

Lenning, O.T., & McAleenan, A.C. (1979). Needs assessment in student affairs. In G.D. Kuh (Ed.), *Evaluation in student affairs* (pp. 185-205). Cincinnati: ACPA.

Lenning, O.T. (1980). Assessment and evaluation. In U. Delworth & G.R. Hanson (Eds.), *Student services: A handbook for the profession* (pp. 232-266). San Francisco: Jossey-Bass.

Lillis, C.J., & Schroer, T. (1984). An alternative residence environment for participatory learning. *Journal of College Student Personnel, 25,* 469-470.

Mable, P., Terry, M.S., & Duvall, W.H. (1980). Student development through community development. In D.A. DeCoster & P. Mable (Eds.), *Personal education and community development in college residence halls* (pp. 103-113). Cincinnati: ACPA.

Miller, T.E., & Schuh, J.H. (1981). Managing the liability risks of residence hall administrators. *Journal of College Student Personnel, 23,* 136-139.

Morrill, W.H., & Hurst, J.C. (1981). Preface. In W.H. Morrill & J.C. Hurst (Eds.), *Dimensions of intervention for student development* (pp. IX-X). New York: Wiley.

Morrill, W.H., Hurston, J.C., & Oetting, E.R. (1981). A conceptual model of intervention strategies. In W.H. Morrill & J.C. Hurst (Eds.), *Dimensions of intervention for student development* (pp. 85-95). New York: Wiley.

Mueller, K.H. (1961). *Student personnel work in higher education.* Boston: Houghton-Mifflin.

Novack, K.M., & Hanson, A.L. (1983). The relationship between stress, job performance and burnout in college student resident assistants. *Journal of College Student Personnel, 23,* 545-550.

Novack, K.M., Gibbons, J.M., & Hanson, A.L. (1985). Factors affecting burnout and job performance of resident assistants. *Journal of College Student Personnel, 26,* 137-142.

Null, R., Hall, P., & Mines, P. (1982). Environmental assessment of Purdue residence halls. *The Journal of College and University Student Housing, 12*(2), 20-27.

Owens, H.F. (1984). Preface. In H.F. Owens (Ed.), *Risk management and the student affairs professional* (n.p.). NASPA Monograph no. 2, N.P.: NASPA.

Pace, C.R. (1984). *Measuring the quality of college student experiences.* Los Angeles: Higher Education Research Institute—UCLA.

Pascarella, E.T. (1985). The influence of on-campus living versus commuting to college on intellectual and interpersonal self-concept. *Journal of College Student Personnel, 26,* 292-299.

Paul, S.C. (1980). Understanding student-environment interaction. In W.H. Morrill & J.D. Hurst (Eds.), *Dimensions of interaction for student development* (pp. 58-82). New York: Wiley.

Pillinger, B.B. (1984). Early residential life: Vassar College in the nineteenth century. *The Journal of College and University Student Housing, 14*(1), 7-9.

Pope, R.L. (1987). Wellness life-style: A residence hall housing option. *Journal of College Student Personnel, 28,* 82-84.

Rowe, L.P. (1981). Environmental structuring: Residence halls as living learning centers. In G.S. Blimling & J.H. Schuh (Eds.), *Increasing the educational role of residence halls* (pp. 51-64). New directions for student services sourcebook No. 13. San Francisco: Jossey-Bass.

Schneider, L.D. (1977). Housing. In W.T. Packwood (Ed.), *College student personnel services* (pp. 125-145). Springfield, IL: Charles C Thomas.

Schroeder, C.C. (1978-1979). Territoriality: Conceptual and methodological issues for residence educators. *The Journal of College and University Student Housing, 8*(2), 9-15.

Schroeder, C.C. (1981). Student development through environmental management. In G.S. Blimling & J.H. Schuh (Eds.), *Increasing the educational role of residence halls* (pp. 35-49). New directions for student services sourcebook No. 13. San Francisco: Jossey-Bass.

Schuh, J.H. (1979). Assessment and redesign in residence halls. In L.A. Huebner (Ed.), *Redesigning campus environments* (pp. 23-36). New directions for student services sourcebook No. 8. San Francisco: Jossey-Bass.

Schuh, J.H. (1981). Staff training. In G.S. Blimling & J.H. Schuh (Eds.), *Increasing the educational role of residence halls* (pp. 81-93). New directions for student services sourcebook No. 13. San Francisco: Jossey-Bass.

Schuh, J.H. (1984). The residential campus—high risk territory! In H.F. Owens (Ed.), *Risk management and the student affairs professional* (pp. 57-82). NASPA Monograph No. 2. N.P.: NASPA.

Schuh, J.H. (Ed.) (1984). *A handbook for student group advisers.* Bloomington, IN: ACPA.

Schuh, J.H., Shipton, W.C., & Edman, N. (1986). Counseling problems encountered by resident assistants: An update. *Journal of College Student Personnel, 27,* 26-33.

Schuh, J.H., Shipton, W.C., & Edman, N. (1984). *Counseling problems encountered by resident assistants: A 15-year study.* Manuscript submitted for publication.

Schuh, J.H. (In press). Community development. In G.S. Blimling (Ed.), *Structured group experiences and case studies for working with resident assistants.* Dubuque: Kendall/Hunt.

Tryon, G.S. (1985). An exploratory study of the relationship between residence hall design and student alcohol consumption. *Journal of College Student Personnel, 26,* 372-373.

Valerio, V.R., & Reynolds, K. (1983). A business-oriented student program: Residence hall stores. *The Journal of College and University Student Housing, 13*(1), 15-18.

Waldman, D.A. (1985). Development of a modified university residence environment scale. *Journal of College Student Personnel, 26,* 70-72.

Werring, C.J., Winston, R.B., & McCaffrey, R.J. (1981). How paint projects affect residents' perceptions of their living environment. *The Journal of College and University Student Housing, 11*(2), 3-7.

Wilson, S.J., Anderson, S.A., & Fleming, W.M. (1987). Commuter and resident students' personal and family adjustment. *Journal of College Student Personnel, 28,* 229-233.

Young, D.P. (1984). The student/institutional relationship: A legal update. In H.F. Owens (Ed.), *Risk management and the student affairs professional* (pp. 15-31). NASPA Monograph No. 2. N.P.: NASPA.

LEGAL CASES

Bradshaw v. *Rawlings,* 612 F.2d 135 (3rd Cir., 1979).

Duarte v. *State,* 151 Cal. Reptr. 727 (Ap. Ct., Fourth District, Division 1, 1979).

Shannon v. *Washington University,* 575 S. W. 2d 235 (Mo. Ct. Ap., St. Louis District, Div. 3, 1978).

Soglin v. *Kauffmann,* 418 F.2d 163 (7th Cir., 1969).

Tarasoff v. *Regents of the University of California,* 551 P. 2d 334 (Cal. Sup. Ct., 1976).

CHAPTER 11

STUDENT ACTIVITIES

GERALD L. SADDLEMIRE

HISTORY

THE STRUCTURED events in which students participate outside of class are generally labeled student activities. Occasionally these activities are called extracurricular or cocurricular activities. Since everyone on campus can be affected by various aspects of the activity structure and program, the popular term campus activities may also be appropriate. The chief student affairs officer is responsible for bringing together the varying interests of student organizations, student government, union activity boards, and special interest groups ranging from Peace Coalition to the Society for Anachronistic Warfare or the Japanese Club. On a small campus the chief student affairs officer may give direct supervision to most of these activities. On a larger campus the office of student activities or the union activity organization will have the delegated responsibility for such supervision.

College faculty and administrators have learned that where there are groups of students there will be a variety of ways to supplement and complement their class activities. A look at the history of student activities indicates that students will find ways to be active out of class. The challenge for faculty and administrators is to determine how to structure these activities so that they have the highest possible potential for contributing to the total development of the student. To put it simply, since students will create activity, appropriate structured intervention can help this activity become a positive contributor to the education experience.

Student activity programs allow the student to participate in volunteerism, plays, films, music, politics, lectures, concerts, outdoor recreation, and intramurals. Students can determine, through their contribution to the student activity fee, the degree to which they wish to support each of the sponsoring organizations.

Mueller (1961) indicated that a student activities program should provide: (1) a favorable continuation of the socialization process of the individual; (2) opportunities for experiences in good group interaction and relationships; and (3) the development of leaders for leadership on the campus and in later life.

The current high level of acceptance and support for organized student activities is a relatively recent feature in higher education. The early threads of activities outside the classroom are described by Morison (1935) in England, Scotland, and the Netherlands during the American colonial period. Young men were left largely to their own devices which often meant brawls and rebellions directed primarily at the faculty members of the institution.

> In the eighteenth century, German students formed clubs called Landsmannschaften (students from the same province). Activites included fencing, drinking, and initiating freshmen into the clubs. The same period in England saw a more extensive program of activities than was the case in Germany. Card parties, plays, riding, fox hunting, and horse races were all popular. Political clubs were formed to keep students abreast of the politics and party strife of the period. Literary clubs, social debating societies, philosophy clubs, social clubs, and athletic clubs entered the campus scene at this time. In many instances, members of literary, debating, and philosophy clubs discussed academically related material. (Lewis, 1981,p. 18).

Student life and the activities of students in the colonial colleges were dominated by religious activity, a strict moralistic discipline, and a classical curriculum. It is hardly surprising to find that riots and rebellions were common among the students who reacted negatively to the strict regimentation and discipline. Since students were grouped for the first time by four distinct levels, freshman, sophomore, junior, senior, the early planned activities made use of this structure. Early forms of hazing can be credited to the upperclassmen who took it upon themselves to assure that new freshmen showed proper respect for the upperclassmen.

From the mid-eighteenth century to the mid-nineteenth century, literary clubs and debating societies were the common form of organized student activities. Students had found that the classical curriculum did not provide a means of discussing the political and social issues of the time and established these groups as a supplement to the curriculum.

The instructional methods of lecture and limited recitation did not allow for discussions that permitted students to interact with each other or the instructor. One measure of status of these organizations was the extent of their library collections which often competed successfully with the holdings of the college library. Faculty were sympathetic to these activities and recognized their importance as supportive of the curriculum and not competitive. This marked an improved faculty-student relationship as compared to the colonial period when the live-in faculty tutor was often alienated from his students.

The literary societies developed such strong loyalty among their members that they formed judicial bodies that disciplined students whose behavior violated organizational, dormitory, or community rules. Those members found guilty were subjected to "fines, public reprimands, ostracism and expulsion from the society for such crimes as profanity, lying, playing cards, intoxication and acting in a disorderly manner so as to bring disgrace on fellow members, inattention to studies, neglect of duties as members, and cheating in any form of student contest" (Leonard, p. 62). These actions illustrate efforts on the part of students to control themselves and represented a rudimentary type of student government.

Other student societies were more interested in restricted membership and secret meetings at places inaccessible to college authorities. Some of these evolved into the first Greek letter social fraternities in the 1820s and 1830s. When colleges were unable or unwilling to build adequate housing, the fraternities responded by constructing club houses to provide meals and housing for their members. Later in the nineteenth century the appeal of the Greek letter societies was enhanced when more faculty spurned any close student interaction out of class and devoted their complete attention to research and scholarly activities in the same Germanic tradition present where many prepared for their academic careers. This faculty attitude in the post Civil War period contributed to expansion of activities by students with little attention from college authorities. The term extracurricular was particularly appropriate during the 1870s and 1880s when faculty preferred to consider the student as an adult whose out of class life was of no concern to others.

College presidents in the late nineteenth century found that the diversity and growth of the student population brought about a similar diversity in student activities that now included Greek letter societies, cultural programs, athletics, lectures, student government, and class activities. The presidents responded by assigning responsibility for some aspects of student behavior to selected faculty who then were given the title dean of men or dean of women. This was a move away from the authoritarian or simple neglect style of supervision to a more student oriented approach by faculty who worked with students in structuring out of class activities.

In the years immediately preceding World War I student run clubs, various forms of student government and intercollegiate athletics became more common.

> The nineteenth century saw significant changes and innovations in the fields of higher education and student activities. The classical curriculum evolved into practical and vocational teaching. Education for the elite evolved into education for all. A trickle of student activities evolved into a tide of organized clubs, athletics, and activities. Strict religious training evolved into a concern for moral development and social awareness. The student activities were beginning to adopt the form by which it would be known in the future. (Lewis, 1981, p. 56).

The twentieth century brought a continuation of the efforts to bring the extracurriculum into a more harmonious, noncompetitive relationship with the curriculum. Hand (1938) describes the goal of the early student activity program as follows:

> Through cooperative work in a group pursuing a common interest, students achieve the emotional security which a knowledge of being socially acceptable and of belonging invariably engenders. Through working diligently and happily with others at self-imposed tasks in pursuit of a common purpose, students grow out of themselves and acquire self-confidence, personal poise, and charm, and the ability to get on pleasantly and effectively with others. (p. 117)

These lofty goals were consistent with the professional viewpoint espoused by the growing number of student personnel staff members that played an increasingly important role in the campus scene after World War I. Student personnel workers helped convince the academic sector that learning was not limited to the classroom. As a result, student government, religious groups, drama, choral competitions, forensics, departmental clubs, intramurals, and intercollegiate teams flourished.

As the diversity and number of student activities grew, higher education institutions also increased the use of specialists making a career of advising student activities and union management work. The student affairs staffs now included such titles as director of student activities, director of counseling, as well as the original title of dean of women, dean of men.

Any discussion of student activities must also include attention to the growth of the college union. The word "union" in America initially was used in the nineteenth century by the debating societies. Later the term became associated with a physical facility for campus activities programming. The first building that was planned as a common meeting place for faculty and students was erected in 1901 at the University of Pennsylvania. The growth of the union building as a center for recreation and culture was rather slow until post World War II. Prior to this time unions were generally found at large universities but since 1946 unions have rapidly spread to two-year colleges and small four-year institutions as well (College Unions—50 Facts, 1986).

The post World War II growth period meant expansion of trained personnel to continue the move to integrate the curriculum and the extracurriculum. Student affairs staff found it necessary to help student groups plan a wide variety of social, recreational, and political activities for a student body that had a growing population of women, veterans, minorities, and adult learners. Coffee houses, films, artists-in-residence, rock stars, folk singers, craft centers, outdoor centers, and spring break travel came into vogue during this period.

As with most professional fields, the student union and student activity staffs have found national professional associations to be an invaluable vehicle for sharing ideas, concerns, and programs for inservice staff development. The Association of College Unions-International was founded in 1914 by student and staff representatives of seven midwest institutions. In 1986 there were more than 700 colleges and universities that held membership in this organization.

The National Association of Campus Activities was formed in 1960 to help book various lecturers and major speakers for campus appearances. Both organizations sponsor a variety of publications, workshops, and regional and national conferences that are directed to the inservice needs of student activity and union staffs.

ADMINISTRATION

The organizational arrangement for student activities is closely related to the size of the student body and the institutional mission. Student activities on a small campus are generally administered by one or more members of the central student affairs staff such as the assistant dean of students or the director of student activities reporting to the chief student affairs officer. If the campus has a union building, another position as director of the union is required. Typical titles for two person staffs are director of student activities and union and associate director of student activities and union. Since some aspects of the union include income producing facilities, the person serving as the building director must have a close working relationship with the business office. On smaller campuses staff members who commonly report to the chief student affairs officer must be generalists performing a wide range of responsibilities.

On large campuses, the breadth of staff members' functional responsibilities are more defined because of the larger numbers of students served and the program complexity. Typical titles of staff who are part of the student activities team include orientation director, organization and program advisor, leadership development coordinator, financial and budgeting officer, and Greek life advisor.

When there is a large union facility, the union director has additional staff responsible for such areas as conferences, programs, operations, special events, and business. Since most unions are open seven days a week, some staff must provide technical assistance in the interest of safe practice and equipment operation during the entire period that the building is open.

Greek life may be affiliated with either the student activity office or the residence life office if on campus housing is provided. On a smaller campus the assistant or associate dean of students may also serve as the Greek life director.

PROGRAMS

The breadth of activities that occur on the campus or are sponsored off campus suggests a comprehensive label. While student activities is the traditional term, the term, campus activities, more accurately describes the array of events that occur outside the classroom. In many circumstances campus-community activities would be an even more accurate term to use. The Board of Directors of the National Association of Campus Activities acknowledged in 1983 the breadth in the activities field when they approved the change in the title of their journal from *Student Activities Programming* to *Campus Activities Programming*. An examination of the diverse events being held in College Unions shows how the broad interests and needs of the campus and community are served through conferences, community education, retail stores, lectures, etc.

The direct involvement of students in campus activities encourages them to use their energy and creativity in ways that benefit themselves and the quality of life for all segments of the campus—fellow students, faculty, administration. Scholars who report their research on higher education indicate that the involvement of students is widely acknowledged as a way to improve retention, a high priority agenda item at every college and university (Astin, 1982; Boyer, 1986). The nature of the structured activities will be governed by the student body composition, the mission of the institution and the type of relationship that exists among students, faculty, and student affairs staff.

The professional activities staff is expected to be able to contribute to the growth and development of students by helping them analyze programming possibilities that range from cultural and entertaining to social justice and legal concerns. Such programming calls for an understanding of student development and, in particular, the effect of interaction between students and their environment on behavior.

LEADERSHIP

Leadership and its relationship to institutional effectiveness is one of the most discussed topics under study by both students and staff. New leaders move into existing positions annually, thus, orientation for these people must be scheduled annually. Arrangements must be made for current and new staff members to discuss well designed meetings, become familiar with an organization procedure manual and adopt a needs assessment instrument (Woolbright & Delahunty, 1980).

Leadership training should extend for much of the year because of the potential usefulness of inservice learning. Staff members must understand the sequential leadership development that moves from the technical phase of helping individuals understand how to fit and work within the organization through the team building phase and ultimately, to a leadership phase that assures that decisions are made by the entire group based on the goals of the organization. Leadership properly employed requires one to know the organization, to have effective communication skills, to possess a valid set of values and attitudes, to be tolerant and flexible, to invest the required amount of time, and to have a positive self concept.

Rick Miller (1987) in discussing the ingredients needed to help students become leaders points out that the recipe for leadership can work for all types of persons from the "strong, silent type" to the "quiet, outgoing type." He describes the leader as an achiever who gets things done consistently and well by using surrounding talents and resources to attain a worthwhile goal. Leaders have learned what it takes to get the job done while working with other people. Leadership training is based on the conviction that leaders are made, not born.

An interest in finding out what is happening on campuses to encourage the development of young leaders prompted Gregory and Britt (1987) to conduct a survey assessing the leadership training efforts of higher education institutions. Responses from 469 institutions were analyzed and the following general guidelines for effective programs were identified: (1) proper selection of participants is critical to program success, (2) good programs have a sound philosophical basis, (3) effectiveness of a program depends on its goals, (4) interdisciplinary programs hold more promise, (5) the more comprehensive the program, the better, (6) effective programs pay explicit attention to leadership, (7) effective programs tend to be longer term, (8) programs that award "credit" earn more respect and credibility, (9) the more successful courses and programs use a variety of training methods, (10) effective leadership education programs use evaluation plans. This survey is a useful summary of current practice, but it has the limitation of not including scientific studies evaluating program effectiveness.

Student leaders can experience frustration and bewilderment when confronted with the politics of the campus environment. Politics need not be a dirty word, in fact, it is in many ways, the art of the possible. Only recently has the political dimension of higher education been systematically included in conceptual frameworks and models (Baldridge, et al., 1978; Bennis and Nanus, 1985). The new models of leadership point out the necessity for including the political dimension.

Rest and Cosgrove (1987) describe the following specific political strategies that can be learned by students to help them become effective leaders: (1) identify interest groups on campus and their status and stands, (2) identify appropriate communication strategies, (3) seek the power resources student leaders can use to have influence, (4) understand the coalitions and how student leaders can build them, (5) develop realistic priorities, (6) use skills for holding open meetings on controversial topics, (7) be aware of the organization's legacy. Students who understand the political elements of their leadership roles can expect to use these same skills in the community after they graduate.

MULTICULTURAL ENVIRONMENT

Recently campus union and student activity staffs, along with a few faculty and administrators have recognized the educational advantages of initiating programs that expose the majority of students to different cultural groups on campus. Encouraged by the civil rights movement of the 1960s, the recognition of the need for cultural diversity has taken the form of such events as Hispanic Culture Week, Black History Month, and International Student Festival. The planning and participation of minority and international students has been a source of pride for the sponsoring groups but has also been a disappointment becase of the fact that traditional white, middle class students seldom indicate much interest in any attempt to interpret diverse cultural backgrounds (Ivey, 1982).

Chavez and Carolson (1985) provide a blueprint for a multicultural approach in programming with the first step pointing to the recognition of the value of cultural diversity to both individuals and the society. Through an awareness of their own cultural heritage and a willingness to share these cultures with others, students may grow in their knowledge about themselves. The exposure to various cultures enhances tolerance and understanding. In addition to helping the students establish a budget, the staff can encourage use of art, music, dance, theater, fashion shows, literature, films and speakers in order to challenge the audiences to learn more about different cultures.

Multicultural programming is an excellent vehicle for collaboration with the faculty, both those who represent a different cultural heritage and those who teach multicultural courses (Quevedo-Garcia, 1983).

The Association of College Unions-International (ACU-I) has only to look to its own statement, "Role of the College Union," to know that it must embrace multicultural programming to respond effectively to the needs of a new generation of college students (Stewart & Hartt, 1985). The ACU-I capitalized on its international nature by locating a regional conference at the Oxford University Union in England in 1986.

In order to accomplish multicultural programming objectives, leadership training must develop a sensitivity for and/or awareness of these objectives. Jefferson (1986) details both a theoretical model and a functional training design that provides educational exercises to help student leaders move through various stages of multicultural development.

By reviewing the literature on international programming, Stewart and Hartt (1987) uncovered "several themes relating to the international students and their experience on the American college campus: the differences between the international students and traditional American students, the concepts of adaptation and alienation and the components of the multicultural personality." After examining the student development literature, Stewart and Hartt concluded that many notions expressed by Sanford, Perry, and Astin apply to the cross-cultural setting. It is apparent that student activity and union staffs are called upon to promote the development of all students, but not in mutually exclusive clusters. The multicultural viewpoint celebrates diversity and works to integrate elements of that diversity into the group and individual lives of students.

VOLUNTEERS

The success of the American social system depends to a large degree on the existence of millions of people who serve in volunteer organizations. About a half million students work on college and university campuses. The involvement of students in these organizations assures a flow of volunteers prepared for effective participation in later life in a wide variety of community organizations. Students participate as members of groups that range from Greek letter organizations to the campus affiliates of religious groups. Students generally are interested in contributing meaningfully and directly into the lives of individuals who are poor, handicapped, or disadvantaged. Humanitarian activities extend from helping with child care to providing programs for the elderly in nursing homes.

The degree of effectiveness of these volunteer organizations rests largely on the quality of the internal communication process. (Boatman, 1987) concludes from a study of organizational communication as it applies to the campus that

> successful student organizations have systems in place to make information available to members, a structure to allow information to flow smoothly throughout the organization, and processes that involve members in the communication activities of the organization. (p. 31)

Boatman points out that the uniqueness of volunteer organizations affects their communication and general operation. Many students make an ad hoc commitment to particular causes so there is a tendency for a rapidly changing membership. The leadership must use diplomacy rather than a system of rewards and punishment, and be aware of the need for a constant recruitment and orientation program. Volunteer organizations may have short ranged, poorly defined goals and purposes that are difficult to evaluate.

The satisfaction for students which depends partly on the social interaction within the organization must be strong enough to hold the loyalty of the student despite the competition from other activities outside the organization. The need to assure a sound financial base can intrude on the time and energy that can be used to achieve the organization's goals.

By using four key variables, information availability, organizational and communication structure, member involvement and friendship or social relationships, Boatman forms a communication process model that is useful to members, leaders and advisers of volunteer groups. This model addresses such questions as:

> Information: How much information do you receive either about new
>   developments or mistakes and failures within the organization?
> Structure: Who makes the decisions in this organization?
> Involvement: Who feels responsible for achieving the organization's
>   goals?
> Friendship or social relations: Do you trust others in the organization
>   and do leaders and advisers trust you and other members? (p. 33-34)

STUDENT DEVELOPMENT—
A THEORETICAL BASE

Student activity and union programming staffs find that student development theories have very practical applications in the many settings where informal education is occurring. Practitioners accept the use of theory as a guideline for designing cocurricular activities so that reinforcement and enhancement of the learning process is intentional and directed. The theories of Arthur Chickering, William Perry, and Douglas Heath can be applied to cocurricular education when programming for student groups as well as when interacting with individual students as consultant and advisor (Boatman, 1985). Boatman offers examples of group programs and individual interventions for each of Chickering's seven vectors, examples of programs that relate to each of Heath's five dimensions in his model of maturing, and examples of how students can be given experiences that may help them move through the positions in

Perry's explanation of how students develop intellectually during the college years.

The need for involvement of students, faculty and staff in order to initiate an institution wide program of student development is described by Borski, Moore, Serotin, and Taylor (1985). These writers document the frustrations and barriers that exist and the need both for support from the top administration and for generating products and results that are tangible evidence of positive movement.

Reber (1983) notes that "the opportunities for systematically applying human development theories to educational practices are endless." The supervision and training of student employees requires the teaching of skills that help the employee to grow in each of Chickering's seven vectors of competence. Allen (1985) has systematically identified life skills that employees use in their daily tasks and describes educational sessions to help develop these skills.

In order to be effective educators, it is incumbent on the student affairs and union programming staffs to include an understanding of student development theory with learning theory, group dynamics, student demography, educational philosophy, institutional governance, supervision, and organizational development (Marine, 1985; Kirkland, 1987).

ADULT LEARNERS

The adult learner has moved to center stage in the higher education scene. Student activities and union staffs in four year colleges are becoming aware of a population segment that has enjoyed majority status on most two year colleges since the early 1970s. Lifelong learning as a means of job advancement and personal enrichment is bringing persons of all ages to most campuses in unprecedented numbers. The search for the proper response to the adult learner, whether full time or part time, has the full attention of the entire higher education community. Everyone must adapt and change. Student affairs staffs are no exception. In fact, since student affairs staffs focus on the total educational environment of the student, these educators should be in the vanguard of designing programs in an environment that shows a sensitivity to the unique circumstances that surround the adult learner.

The two year college and urban universities have had the most experience in dealing successfully with this new type of student. Publications from the National Clearing House for Commuter Programs housed at the University of Maryland are the first successful attempts to provide a vehicle for professionals who want to share their insights and help others become aware of the unique circumstances of the nontraditional student. The terms "nontraditional," "commuter," and "adult learner" all may apply to the student population represented on campus who are 25 years of age and older, who commute, and who are either part-time or full time students.

Every part of the campus must examine its process and product to see what changes are required to meet the needs of the adult learner. The student activities and union programmer is in an excellent position to help the campus modify its environment appropriately. The student handbook and organizational directories should include material on renting, escort services, child care centers, and support groups both on campus and in the adjoining community. Luncheon forums and brown bag lunches fit the schedules of those who are likely to be returning home in the late afternoon. Program publicity must go beyond the residence halls to the classrooms, parking lots, commuter mail boxes and home mailboxes.

Adult learners are intensely anxious about competing academically and fitting in at a strange environment. They can be frustrated by requirements, unaware of independent or experiential learning options, concerned about the necessary commitment of time and money, preoccupied with unanticipated emergencies at home (Carlson & Basler, 1986; Boyer, 1985). Penning and Keller (1982) describe an approach to program planning for a campus of 10,000 with an average age of 26, 65 percent attending classes in the evening, 70 percent married, 85 percent employed. Care is taken to keep the cost low, to involve adult learners on advisory boards, to publicize in publications, classrooms, and by direct mailing, to provide professional staff at noon and in the evenings, to evaluate each event and to learn from user response.

Professional preparation programs for student activities and union programming staffs are recognizing the need to include course work that addresses the latest research on adult life stages, both male and female. Conferences and workshops are planned with increasing frequency for those staffs who need in service education as a way of improving their role as advocates for the students who no longer fit the traditional mold. The well being and retention of the adult learner is closely tied to the successful efforts of the professional student affairs staff to help the institution make necessary changes to fit new needs.

STUDENT GOVERNMENT ASSOCIATIONS

The current status of student government on campuses varies from being virtually non-existent to highly visible representative associations that take responsibility for such items as involving students directly with the board of trustees and funding services essential to the quality of life on campus. In the late 1970s several student governments (Fleischman, 1982) ceased to exist after national political and social issues of interest to students seemed resolved and a sense of purpose lessened. However, student groups with special interests or with well identified constituencies continued to flourish and became the basis for a new coalition of organizations.

Many students do desire to participate in an organizational life that meets the need of the student body. Fleischman, after surveying professionals who advise successful student government associations, reported four tactics that have worked on some campuses: (1) reorganize an outmoded structure to accommodate new interests and new students; (2) evaluate use of funds and the way administrators use student government for communication; (3) define expectations and role of adviser; (4) promote large-scale involvement of students.

Boyd (1985), in analyzing student government, points out that the more diverse student body and the emphasis on career orientation and the pragmatic causes have pushed the broad-based, ideological student organizations into the background and are often replaced by the single purpose interest group.

This movement, in turn, requires the student government to analyze its own composition to see how well it matches the profile of the student body. Boyd suggests that for the staff member most closely affiliated with student government to increase student leaders' awareness, plus train and motivate "them to be responsive to and responsible for all segments of the campus population is an ambitious task." (p. 51)

The role of the adviser is identified by Chiles and Pruitt (1985) as critical on campuses where student associations are an embarrassment to themselves and the institution they allegedly serve. Program boards, fraternities and sororities and honors service organizations have all "recovered" and advanced since the rebellious 60's. Many college administrators are wary of strong student associations, so are content "to let sleeping dogs lie." Professional advisement for student associations is not a high priority, and little attention is given in the literature of higher education to the historical and current role of student associations.

The improvement of student association productivity according to Chiles and Pruitt (who speak from the context of the large university) will follow by using such suggestions as: (1) use of qualified, full time student association adviser, (2) engage in a self study of the student association, and (3) seek the authority to operate as a viable partner in the institutional governance process by meeting with key administrators (Chair of Faculty Senate, Institution President, Board of Trustees).

A study conducted by Cuyjet (1985) surveyed the role played by student government on 407 campuses where responses were obtained from both student government presidents and advisers. The majority of both groups see student government as the official representation of the student body to the administration and faculty. Both students and advisers agreed that student government has minimal influence on the major decision making councils of the college/university.

Regardless of the student government format or visibility on a particular campus, it is a viable way to bring student opinions and concerns into the policy making offices and committees on the campus. Earl McGrath (1970) concludes that students should be encouraged to play a significant role in determining the purposes and practices of higher education. He points out "hardly any institution remains untouched by the activities of students aimed at gaining a voice in major policy-making decisions . . . Where students have been fully involved in academic government, they have typically discharged their responsibilities with effectiveness and with dignity" (p. 105).

FRATERNITIES AND SORORITIES

On campuses where Greek organizations are located, the student affairs division assigns supervisory staff usually from the campus activities, union programming office or sometimes the residence life office. The Greek organizations with national affiliation are also subject to policies and procedures that are prescribed by the national office.

The stereotypical view of Greeks comes from the large, well established Greek system that features large structures with pillars that house 50 or more students and are located near each other in an area referred to as Greek Row. Weekend, and even mid-week parties, are well attended by affluent traditional aged students who also find time to be heavily involved in community service, intramurals, and student organization leadership (Heida, 1986).

A broader look at the Greek system shows a wide variety of housing styles that range from the large single off campus dwelling to individual college-owned units on campus, to small houses in deteriorating neighborhoods, to meeting rooms in residence hall lounges. Accurate, up to date research that examines the Greek systems is a scarce commodity. Schwartz and Bryan (1983) in the introduction and overview of their book *The Eighties: Challenges for Fraternities and Sororities* note the lack of substantive information and research on fraternity and sorority life. Their book is intended to encourage others to produce that much needed information in future publications. Kuh, Bean, Bradley, and Coomes (1986) in their review of research based contributions to the student affairs journals since 1977 conclude that studies in Greek life have become increasingly rare to the point that this aspect of campus life is virtually ignored in the current literature.

R. Shaffer (1983), in reviewing the available research in Greek life, reinforces the danger of stereotyping the Greek system. "Just as there are enormous differences among colleges and universities, so are there enormous differences within the Greek system not only from campus to campus but also from chapter to chapter on any one campus. A review of research pertaining to fraternities and sororities tells the reader just one thing — local factors and conditions are the most significant in determining the quality of fraternal experience." (p. 6)

Research on academic achievement indicates in one situation that Greek membership contributes to higher scholastic achievement while in another situation the opposite conclusion can be made. Greek affairs leaders need to learn about the particular institutional and organizational dynamics on each campus in order to understand how the local environment contributes to the variability of scholarship of chapters of the same national organization having the same, or at least similar, pledge training and scholarship programs.

Toward the end of the activism period, Packwood, Casse, Lyerly, and Maklehurst (1972) found that Greeks felt that the individualistic philosophy arising out of the 1960s had lowered the attention to tradition and group solidarity, but increased the interest in more flexible rules, individualized programming and stronger interpersonal relationships. Although no research is available, the identified continuing trend toward a more diverse student body make such gross generalizations about social attitudes and behavior unsupported.

"One generalization that can be drawn from the literature is that Greeks provide leadership on the campus" (Shaffer, p. 15). However, it is not clear whether this is the result of attracting members who already possess traits, interests, and qualities that encourage participation in campus activities or whether leadership development in the Greek system is the major contributing factor. Greek letter affiliates have been reported to come from families of higher socioeconomic levels and have enjoyed considerable participation in social and extracurricular activities in high school.

When discussing issues facing Greek life that compel greater emphasis upon evaluation, Shaffer and Kuh (1983) point to the contributions to the performance of the advisers from such groups as the Association of Fraternity Advisors (AFA), the National Panhellenic Council (NPHC) and the National Interfraternity Conference (NIC). Many campuses have professionally prepared staff members responsible for campus Greek organizations to assure consistency and desirable outcomes from the Greek organizations.

While describing a comprehensive evaluation plan within the Greek system, Shaffer and Kuh list a series of generic questions that must be addressed to "keep Greek affairs staff sensitive and help the system's capacity to remain current with the changes in the larger campus environment. (1) What is it that we, as a Greek system, are trying to do? (2) How else have we considered doing it? (3) What are we doing differently this year as individual chapter houses and as a Greek system? If nothing is new or innovative, why not? (4) Can a case be made for changing Greek affairs policies? (5) If we are going to change policies and procedures, who will be affected in what ways? (6) How are we going to determine the quality of Greek life on this campus?" (p. 46)

Sutherland (1983) identifies one of the most significant current needs of the Greek system is a clearly defined relationship between the Greek organization and the institution where they are located. Greek organizations must have a strong cooperative relationship with the institution in order to achieve their goal of providing educational and leadership opportunities for small groups of students. The local adviser and the field consultants need to work together toward a quality educational environment.

In summarizing the expectations, challenges, predictions, and recommendations of the 1980s, W. Bryan and R. Schwartz (1983) conclude that

> Over the years Greek organizations have survived institution opposition and/or indifference, economic depressions, wars, state laws banning membership, faculty bans, and student movements. Their

survival is due to their potential for contributing to the total development of their members. These organizations would be well advised to reflect on their early beginnings. The Greek organization can provide a learning environment by establishing learning centers for seminars and in-depth discussions of topics not covered in the classroom. It can be a community of students living and working together. This community can involve faculty and their adviser actively in the operation of the chapter; alumni living in the university community can participate through house corporations and other means. Faculty can participate positively by serving as advisers, helping to enrich programs so that chapter life is productive and beneficial. (p. 162).

STANDARDS AND ETHICS

Standards and guidelines for use by the student activity and union programming staff have been prepared by professionals from related student affairs associations that have responded to the need for criteria to guide professional practice. This initial set of professional standards and guidelines published by the Council for Advancement of Standards (CAS) contains elements of form, substance and philosophy for the co-curricular life and educational experiences of college students.

The goals of both the college union and student activities show how they can complement the academic offerings. The Union is described as a "laboratory" for learning and practicing leadership, programming, management, social responsibility and interpersonal skills. The student activity standards state that the primary functions of full time professional staff members include advising student groups, planning, implementation and assessment of programs and activities, and coordinating the overall student activity program.

In order to achieve the student activities and union mission as well as the institutional mission, the staff should possess the following qualities. It should be noted that these qualities may be achieved by combining the talents of the entire staff.

Desirable qualities of professional union staff members are: "Knowledge of and ability to use management principles, including the effective management of volunteers; Skills in assessment, planning, training and evaluation; Interpersonal skills; Technical skills; Understanding of union philosophy; Commitment to institutional mission; Understanding of, and the ability to apply, student development theory." (CAS, p. 21)

Desirable qualities of professional student activity staff members are:

"Ability to relate to and work well with superiors; Ability to relate to and work well with peers, subordinates, and students; A keen interest in professional and personal development; Ability to be creative and innovative in the delivery of services; Ability to train and assist students in their development; Undergraduate leadership experience; Understanding of group dynamics and the ability to work effectively with groups; Ability to interpret student concerns and interests to the campus community." (CAS, p. 91-92)

The CAS Standards call for all persons involved in the various functional areas of student services to maintain the highest standards of ethical behavior. The ACU-I responded by developing a Code of Ethics that was adopted by the Executive Committee in July 1985 (Plakidas, 1985). The code calls for (a) appropriate professional behavior including honesty and integrity in job performance, (b) need to examine the part played by values in decision making and problem solving, (c) guidelines for anticipating and resolving ethical problems.

The NACA adopted a *Statement of Professional Ethics* in 1986 that has important philosophical uses in the student affairs field. Boatman (1986) notes that this statement "serves as a tool to teach potential members of the profession about the ideals and ethical values of the profession; provides guidelines to consider when making practical decisions as a professional, serves as the basis for defining 'competent behavior' by members of the profession, serves as a basis for evaluating individual performance, serves as a protection of the integrity of the profession, and is a public statement of what members of a profession stand for." (NACA, p. 23).

The CAS *Standards and Guidelines for Student Activities* states that, "The Code of Ethics should address at least the issues of: accuracy of information, conflict of interest, fiscal accountability, fair and equitable administration of institutional policies, effective disclosure of and respect for relevant civil and criminal law, and student involvement in related institutional decisions. Professional staff members should teach and adhere to established ethical guidelines for contractual agreements and relevant standards for the use and operation of facilities." (p. 93)

The high volume of staff-student interaction creates many opportunities for the staff members to model the standards and ethical codes that have been adopted by the professional associations (NACA and ACU-I). The moral climate of the campus depends, in part, on the way students are encouraged to follow the suggestions and the example set by the staffs who work so closely with them.

TRENDS

The student activities and union programming staff, along with the rest of the institution, are faced with financial constraints. Students are reluctant to impose fees upon themselves without careful justification and documentation. The budget preparation process will need to include student participation in order to earn student approval.

Union management staffs are watching the trends that show students moving away from interest in bowling, billiards, crafts, big name concerts, and outdoor recreation to determine whether space reserved for these activities should be reallocated to make space available for automatic tellers, computer access centers, copy machines, and retail stores. Since some of these activities are revenue producing, the effect on the financial well being of the union is apparent.

In view of the increased influence of the single purpose student groups, student activity staffs are in a unique position to serve as an integrating factor for the single purpose organizations that can become cosponsors of events such as international week. Such planning and programming could bring unique and sometimes disparate groups together and perform an important educational function.

Campus union and student activity staffs are also finding it necessary to learn about the theories of development of the new constituencies on campus, the female majority, adult learners, minorities.

Herman-Betzen and Carlson (1986) emphasize the need for the union to be an integral part of the academic enterprise so that financial resources will follow the educational thrust of the institution. Another vision they suggest is the need to adopt the concepts that are discussed by Thomas J. Peters and Robert H. Waterman, Jr. whereby the union management shows concern not only for the customers but also for the employees, and encourages innovation. Evidence of new and innovative responses that are within the context of the union mission are an insurance of viability in the future.

Nancy Davis (1985), as Editor of the *ACU-I Bulletin,* listed topics that the professional staff members should consider when preparing manuscripts. These topics include both continuing and emerging concerns that are becoming trends: employee motivation, liability, student leadership training, microcomputer application, union concept and philosophy, supervising student employees, building use policies, strategic planning, professional development programs, implementing a marketing plan, organizational dynamics, ethics and standards, alcohol beverage policy, creative management, evaluation, remodeling, teleconferencing in higher education.

ACU-I Executive Director, Richard Blackburn (1987), in observing trends from professional meetings and campus visitations reports that alcohol is the overriding problem as the 21 drinking age legislation requires careful monitoring of campus alcohol service, checking IDs, finding alternatives for dwindling pub income. An emerging response is the increasing use of the nonalcoholic alternative, sometimes referred to as Dry Dock. Campus Activities directors are becoming increasingly wary of the use of corporate support for events by companies providing tobacco, firearms, or alcohol so that limits are sometimes imposed on the extent of subsidy allowed.

Renovation rather than new construction is the current method used to provide facilities and meet new utilization requirements. Computers are being introduced as a way of managing energy use. Labor saving equipment is considered a good investment, particularly in areas where there is a shortage of workers employable at the minimum wage.

The continuance of campus activities and union programming seems assured, but the precise function and operational format is less predictable. The lack of predictability because of the constant change in the student clientele, in the role of higher education, and in the surrounding community requires that the professional staff remain on the cutting edge of the types of programming that contribute significantly to the quality of life for those on the campus.

REFERENCES

Allen, K. (1985, April). Student development: Applying theory to student employers. *ACU-I Bulletin, 53*(2), 17-22.

Baldridge, J.V., Curtis, D.V., Ecker, G., & Riley, G.L. (1978). *Policy making and effective leadership.* San Francisco: Jossey-Bass.

Bennis, W., & Nanus, B. (1985). *Leaders: The strategies for taking charge.* New York: Harper & Row.

Blackburn, R. (1985, February). Director's concerns reflect issues facing unions. *ACU-I Bulletin, 53*(1), 4-6.

Blackburn, R. (1987, March). Trend shifts evident on college campuses. *ACU-I Bulletin, 55*(2), 4-8.

Boatman, S. (1982, October). Group development, *Programming, 15*(4), 40-43.

Boatman, S. (1985, April). Student development: Practical applications for campus activities. *ACU-I Bulletin, 53*(2), 12-16.

Boatman, S. (1987, May). A model for communication in volunteer organizations. *Programming, 20*(1), 30-35.

Boyd, R. (1985, September). Analyzing student government: Strategies for representing special interest groups. *Programming, 18*(3), 47-51.

Boyer, J. (1985, August). Serving the new majority. *ACU-I Bulletin, 53*(4), 4-6.

Brattain, W.E. (1981). *The administration of college unions and campus activities.* Bloomington, Indiana, T.I.S. Publications.

Bryan, W., & Schwartz, R. (1983). *The eighties: Challenges for fraternities and sororities,* 170 pp. ACPA Media. Carbondale, IL: Southern Illinois Press.

Bryan, W., & Schwartz, R. (1983). *The 80's: Expectations, challenges, and recommendations,* 150-163. In Bryan, W. and Schwartz, R., *The eighties: Challenges for fraternities and sororities.*

Carlson, J.M., & Basler, M.L. (1986, December). The quiet revolution: Student activities and the nontraditional student. *Programming, 19*(6), 52-56.

CAS Standards and Guidelines for Student Services/Development Programs. (1986). 111 pp.

Chavez, E., & Carlson, J. (1985, October). Building a multicultural environment. *ACU-I Bulletin, 53*(5), 4-6.

Chiles, R., & Pruitt, D. (1985, May). Student associations: Viable partners in institutional governance? *Programming, 18,* 21-24.

Code of Ethics — Association of University Unions-International. (1985).

Council for the Advancement of Standards for Student Services/Development Programs. (1986).

Cuyjet, M. (1985, May). Student government: The nature of the beast. *Programming, 18,* 25-31.

Davis, N. (1985, August). Editor's message. *ACU-I Bulletin, 53*(4), 3.

Fleishman, B. (1982, March). The changing faces of student government. *Programming, 14*(8), 39-44.

Heida, Debbie. (1986, Summer). Greek systems on predominantly commuter campuses. *NASPA Journal, 24*(1), 48-50.

Herman-Betzen, M., & Carlson, J. (1986). Visions for the college union. *ACU-I Bulletin, 54*(1), 4-7.

Hodgkinson, H.L. (1985). *All one system: Demographics of education — kindergarten through graduate school.* Washington, D.C.: Institute for Educational Leadership.

Ivey, J. (1982, October). Taking stock of the foreign student exchange. *Programming, 15*(4), 33-36.

Kirkland, R. (1987, September). Moving from philosophy to practical: Student development theories can help in the transition. *ACU-I Bulletin, 55*(5), 23-27.

Kuh, G., Bean, J., Bradley, R., & Coomes, M. (1986, July). Contributions of student affairs journals to the literature on college students. *Journal of College Student Personnel, 27*(4), 292-304.

Leonard, E. (1956). *Origins of personnel services in American higher education.* Minneapolis: University of Minnesota Press.

Lewis, H.M. (1981). *Student activities past, present, future.* Thesis no. 3824, Bowling Green State University (Ohio).

Marine, J. (1985, February). The college union's role in student development. *ACU-I Bulletin, 53*(1), 22-23.

Miller, R. (1987, Summer). The elixir of leadership. *Programming, 20*(2), pp. 29-31.

Morison, S.E. (1935). *The founding of Harvard College.* Cambridge: Harvard University Press.

Mueller, K. (1961). *Student personnel work in higher education*. Boston, Houghton Mifflin.

National Association of Campus Activities (1986, October). Statement of Professional Ethics, *Programming, 19*(4), 23-24.

National Clearinghouse for Commuter Programs. University of Maryland.

Quevedo-Garcia, E.L. (1983, April). Meeting the challenge of ethnic minority programming. *Programming, 15*(9), 48-51.

Packwood, W.T., Casse, R.M., Lyerly, B.J., & Maklehurst, J. (1972). Greek individualism and activism: A new identity. *Journal of College Student Personnel, 13,* 224-228.

Pennington, W.D., & Keller, M.H. (1982, October). Program primer for "Road Scholars." *Programming, 15*(4), 28-32.

Peters, T.J., & Waterman, R.H. Jr. (1982). *In search of excellence*. New York: Harper & Row.

Plakides, S. (1985, October). Association adopts code of ethics. *ACU-I Bulletin, 53*(5), 13-14.

Reber, C. (1983, March). Implementation of student development theories. *Programming, 15*(8), 42-45.

Shaffer, R. (1983). *Review of research in Greek affairs*. Chapter 1, pp. 6-29. In Bryan, W. and Schwartz, R. *The eighties: Challenges for fraternities and sororities*.

Shaffer, R., & Kuh, G. (1983). *Evaluation and decision making*, 31-48. In Bryan, W. and Schwartz, R. *The eighties: Challenges for fraternities and sororities*.

Sutherland, S. (1983). *Issues for the Eighties,* 73-93. In Bryan, W. and Schwartz, R. *The eighties: Challenges for fraternities and sororities*.

Stewart, G., & Hartt, J. (1985, November). Multiculturalism: A prescription for the college union, *ACU-I Bulletin, 53*(6), 4-7.

Stewart, G., & Hartt, J. (1985, January). Multiculturalism: A community among differences, *ACU-I Bulletin, 53*(1), 4-8.

Stroup, H. (1964). *Toward a philosophy of organized student activities*. Minneapolis: University of Minnesota Press.

CHAPTER 12

CAREER PATHS IN STUDENT AFFAIRS

AUDREY L. RENTZ AND GERALD L. SADDLEMIRE

THE NEW PROFESSIONAL

THE ANXIETY LEVEL of the full-time graduate student goes up in direct proportion to the nearness of the graduation date. The two primary reasons are the memory of their experience of the tight job market when they completed their undergraduate degree and secondly the realization that advertisements of college student personnel entry level positions generally peak about six to eight weeks before the beginning of the next academic year. Most candidates however, find that persistence, patience, and job hunting skills are rewarded since 95 percent of the graduate students secure employment in full time positions (Evans & Bossert, 1984; Saddlemire, 1988).

Job seeking skills needed by graduates are taught in many of the graduate preparation programs and are also included as part of the convention placement services of the national student affairs professional associations. The importance of the placement process is underscored by the endorsement by the American College Personnel Association of *The Guidebook for the Successful Job Search in Student Development*. Backhuber (1986) presents a step-by-step approach to a successful job search process with illustrations and charts to use as an individual plans their search. Areas of self-assessment, preparing the necessary paperwork, inquiring about potential opportunities, preparing for interviews, participating in placement services and deciding on contracts offered are explained.

The process of finding full-time work as a professional begins several months before the completion of the graduate degree. Stamatakos (1983) describes the steps to be taken in planning strategies for convention placement, making on-site visits and accepting the new position. Even the well designed, apparently successful job search only opens the door to a career in student affairs. Once a person is fully immersed in the new position, changes can cause a reassessment of the working environment. A change in supervisor, an administrative realignment and/or differences between the institution's mission statement and actual practice may make a change at the end of the first year desirable. Previously learned job search skills will be used again. Although early discomfort may dissipate during the year, a change after one year can be justified and does not prevent a person from continuing on the career ladder.

Stamatakos (1983) discusses the need for both beginning and experienced practitioners to manifest professionalism in their work. He points out the need for staff members to maintain preeminent moral and ethical standards of conduct. Staff members must be familiar with both the ethical statement of the professional associations and with the professional standards adopted for practitioners and preparation programs. While all three national associations have adopted ethical statements, the ACPA Statement is the most detailed guideline for individual behavior. The various associations for specialty areas within student affairs all have ethical statements that serve as additional resources. Winston and McCaffery (1983) have provided a comprehensive schemata for viewing professional ethics within student affairs from both a theoretical and historical perspective. Their work includes a paradigm for ethical decision-making, vignettes showing applications of the ethical decision-making process and recommendations for enhancing ethical practice.

Mable and Miller (1983) describe the process used by the Council for the Advancement of Standards for Student Services/Development Programs since its inception in 1979. The publication of these CAS Standards marks a major triumph for a large number of professionals who were convinced of the need for institutions to insure the integrity, self-evaluation, and achievement of objectives in student affairs.

The great majority of young professionals find their first job to be a satisfying setting in which they can apply competencies already acquired and can develop new ones. Both new staff members and their supervisors are well aware of the importance of the initial position in starting a successful career in student affairs. Stamatakos (1978) offered a number of suggestions to keep young professionals moving successfully through the first critical months of a new position. His suggestions that follow have been endorsed and distributed by other graduate faculty who prepare new professionals for careers in the student affairs field.

Assignments: Determine your supervisor's expectations at the earliest opportunity. Keep her/him informed of the progress on unfinished tasks. Use the discussions of unfinished tasks to clarify the reporting style expected by the supervisor.

Environment: Expect to live with ambiguity and contradiction within the student affairs team. Learn about the local customs, the history of current issues and why some situations do not seem to be properly influenced by the student personnel point of view or by intervention strategies that operationalize student development. Look for ways to make positive contributions to staff meetings.

Faculty: Seek ways to cultivate faculty relationships. Read the faculty charter, minutes of the faculty senate and attend open meetings of governance groups. Many faculty are interested in data that describe student characteristics, values, and attitudes. Student affairs staffs and the institutional research staffs can collaborate to make data about students available to the wider faculty audience. New professionals often find that by participating in institutional research they can serve as a bridge between student affairs and the institutional research office.

Professional Development: Maintain a plan for self development that is shared with the supervisor. New professionals find that they need to be committed to lifelong learning as a necessary way to keep up with new developments in both student affairs and in higher education in general. A development plan will include short term and long term goals and the competencies necessary to achieve them.

The work habits and personal qualities of the young professional will soon become important determinants for future moves up the career ladder. Demonstrating such characteristics as optimism, maturity, and loyalty, both to supervisor and to those who are supervised, helps to increase the new professional's value as a staff team member.

Mentoring: Maintaining a relationship with a mentor may require moving away from a faculty mentor in the graduate preparation program to a mentoring relationship with colleagues at work and/or in professional associations. The opportunity to be involved with experienced professionals in association work can be a valuable learning experience whether at the state, regional, or national level. It is in this context that one can become a loving critic of the profession.

Administration: The unpredictability of events in the student affairs environment, regardless of the organizational structure that may exist, can be a source of concern to the new professional. It is possible that input from students and junior staff may be disregarded and purely political considerations may serve as the basis for a decision that affects student affairs policies and programs (Hull, Hunter, & Kuh, 1983; Kuh, 1984). Since the way things are decided is not always clear, rational, and consistent, the level of frustration of the staff will rise accordingly. Kuh (1984) described sanity maintenance behaviors that help student affairs staffs take advantage of seemingly unexplainable situations.

1. Look at alternatives to the traditional bureaucratic model to understand the influences and input that affect policies, procedures, or staff performance.
2. Learn to tolerate the diverse values and approaches to student development that may arise from student activities, residence life, and financial aids.
3. Know the organizational chart, but don't let it stifle initiative. The associate dean responsible for staff development will welcome an activity initiated by someone else.
4. If a change in policy, procedure, or practice seems sensible, find out if political or traditional barriers have prevented this change.
5. Determine the "shock" effects of change to decide if change will create new problems for staff wedded to the "old way."
6. Keep the job in perspective with the other areas of your life such as family relationships, community involvement, faith in a deity.
7. When the unpredictable or uncontrollable interferes with the routine, look for the humor in the situation. A sense of humor helps maintain a positive view of the situation. (pp. 56-59)

Kuh's suggestions can help new professionals live with the ambiguities by learning to respond to what "is" rather than what "should be."

New professionals who are going to small colleges (under 5,000) may have some particular problems in adjusting to that setting. Richmond (1986) notes that moving from the preparation program setting in the large university to the small college can put a person in unfamiliar turf where much time is spent tending to individual problems and building personal relationships. It is also unlikely that there will be a number of new professionals employed in any one year, making it difficult to find kindred souls. However, Richmond's tips for professional success and survival are applicable in any setting.

> Cultivate faculty relationships, make changes for the better, but do so carefully, get the lay of the land, get to know your supervisor, move quickly to establish support systems, take care of yourself, become active in professional associations, maintain your sense of humor. (p. 36)

Persons entering the student affairs field have an obligation to understand the concept of professionalism and manifest it in their work through constant renewal and expansion of skills and understanding (Carpenter, 1983; Miller, Winston, & Mendenhall, 1983; Mueller, 1961; Stamatakos, 1983).

The career path followed by the student affairs professional will have four developmental stages: (1) formative, (2) application, (3) additive, and (4) generative (Carpenter, 1983). The new professional has completed the developmental tasks necessary to obtain a position in student affairs (formative) and is beginning to apply the skills and competencies involved with student affairs practice (application). Additional developmental tasks at this stage are:

1. Learning to take responsibility for professional decisions.
2. Attaining the respect of the campus community.
3. Making a firm commitment to student affairs as a profession.
4. Applying established ethical standards in direct contact work with students.
5. Contributing to newsletters that report on current practices in specific student services.
6. Taking part in inservice education, workshops, and other methods of gaining knowledge and skills to aid performance in one's current position.

                                        Miller, Winston, and Mendenhall, p. 156

New professionals should keep a developmental awareness of the tasks and activities they attempt as they move up the ladder to positions of greater responsibility in practice and with professional associations.

The professional associations have combined their efforts through the Council for the Advancement of Standards for Student Services/ Development Programs (CAS) to give professionals a document that gives the new professional the benefit of the best thinking in the field about the specific functions that are to be performed. Mable and Miller (1983) discuss the rationale for professional standards and how they are to be used as an instrument for assuring integrity of post secondary institutions. Familiarity with general standards and those for the various functions is essential for the young professional.

MENTORING

Literature describing the career development of male managers and executives in the corporate sector first revealed the significance of the mentor-protege relationship (Kanter & Stein, 1979; Knox, 1978; Levinson, 1978; Roche, 1979). The relationship between a younger professional or protege and a mentor has been characterized as one of the most developmentally important relationships a person can experience during early adult years (Levinson, 1978). Several authors have described mentors in a variety of ways. They have been viewed as individuals: interested in passing on their wisdom and experience to others (Dalton, Thompson, & Price, 1977); who teach technical aspects of the career as well as the information about the social and political factors affecting career development (Hill, 1976; Levinson et al., 1976; MacGregor, 1960); and who serve as sponsors, facilitators of dreams and providers of moral support (Levinson, 1978). Traditionally mentors are more experienced, 10-15 years older, more powerful, more creatively productive, and are usually considered prestigious colleagues who have access to policy making groups within an organization (Burton, 1977; Pierson, 1982; Schmidt & Wolfe, 1980). Mentors have also been characterized as "more than a supervisor or fellow employee . . . a teacher who is also a friend . . . who provides discipline, guidance and advice . . ." (Halatin, 1981, p. 36). Discussing the role of mentors within academe, Moore (1982) suggests that many mentors "operate, not to teach directly, but to awaken, test, or exercise the protege's talents" (Moore, 1982, p. 26).

The relationship between a mentor and protege has been compared to that of a bonding between lovers. Levinson (1978) viewed the interrelationship as "a serious, mutual, non-sexual, loving relationship with an older man or woman" (p. 334). Consequently it is a relationship that exists only when the mentor and protege are willing, compatible and the "chemistry is right." Similarly it is a relationship not to be entered into without sufficient thought and without a willingness to commit considerable personal and professional time. Literature discussing cross-gender mentoring indicates that these types of relationships are fewer in number. Same gender mentoring, while historically rooted in male groups, has received considerable attention in the literature recently associated with the professional development of women. As the concept of mentoring was adopted from the business community and applied to higher education, the early literature addressed issues of concern in the career development of teaching faculty (Moore, 1972; Moore & Salimbene, 1981). Subsequently the focus changed again to the advancement of corporate women executives (Hennig & Jardim, 1977). The significance of mentors in the lives of student affairs professionals is well known. In a study of student affairs professionals in 1984, two-thirds of the respondents reported having participated in a relationship with one or more mentors. Same gender relationships were reported by 68 percent of the staff respondents (Kelly, 1984). Specifically, a young professional's socialization within the profession can be assisted by the role a mentor may play in helping the individual become involved in professional associations, research, publication, and networking.

Several authors have proposed models to describe the mentor-protege relationship. Most models include four stages: (1) initiation, (2) development, (3) termination, and (4) becoming a mentor (Levinson, 1978; Missirian, 1982).

Three major functions of mentors have been identified. These are: "(1) role model: 'If you can, I can,' (2) consultant/advisor: 'I've traveled this route before,' and (3) sponsor: 'I'd be happy to recommend.'" (Schmidt & Wolfe, 1980, pp. 46-48). Although imitation is sometimes perceived as part of the role modeling process, the younger professional generally does not seek to emulate every characteristic of the mentor. Frequently a partial role modeling process occurs wherein the protege selects desired traits from several mentors (Schmidt & Wolfe, 1980). Another form of the modelling relationship, termed stage modeling, occurs when the younger professional desires information about future periods of personal and professional advancement (Bucher & Steeling, 1977).

Although Stage One of the relationship is typically the responsibility of the mentor, there are two factors which may increase the likelihood of a mentor-protege relationship: (1) familiarity with the concept of mentoring and (2) the successful completion of a highly visible task involving some degree of risk (Kelly, 1984). After deciding that a mentor is desired, the younger professional should observe potential mentors within the current environment and attempt to select someone who possesses desired traits or who is assuming a position the protege views as a career goal. The next task of the protege-to-be is to bring his/her talents and skills to the attention of a potential mentor. This is often accomplished through shared committee assignments or special projects. The relationship may be formalized after a "testing period" during which the newcomer's abilities and achievements have been evaluated. Frequently, the protege is unaware of this review process underway.

Once the relationship has been formally initiated, proteges may benefit in several ways. Within the mentor-protege relationship (MPR), the younger professional typically learns by trial and error, identification with the mentor and observation (Levinson, 1976; 1978; Polanyi 1958). The mentor can provide information about existing informal organizational communication patterns, suggest assignments the protege should seek to develop additional skills and offer advice in handling new situations encountered by the protege. As the relationship progresses and the mentor continues to be satisfied and remains committed to the protege, the mentor may recommend the younger professional for particular assignments or responsibilities more directly under the supervision of the mentor or that will permit the two of them to work collaboratively. As the relationship continues there is a "deepening emotional commitment and maintenance of the relationship" (Missirian, 1982, p. 66). More overt behaviors to promote, protect, and publicize the protege may follow. Specifically within student affairs, the mentor may guide and assist the involvement of the protege in professional associations through committee assignments and nominations for leadership positions. Opportunities to participate in research projects or manuscript preparation are frequently offered.

Typically, mentors usually are members of one of the following groups: (1) faculty members in graduate preparation programs; (2) past supervisors in professional positions; (3) chief student affairs officers; or (4) individuals in leadership positions in professional associations. Some New Professionals have had mentors during their undergraduate years and many broaden their base of support, advice, and counsel during their graduate degree programs. The duration of the mentor-protege relationship will vary depending on the goals and desires of both parties. Relationships may continue for many years becoming one of the more significant friendships during an individual's life. Eventually, the time may come when one or both of the parties wishes to terminate the relationship. This may happen when the mentor senses that he/she can no longer benefit the protege or when the protege decides that additional advice, support and encouragement may no longer be necessary. Termination can be a traumatic experience for either or both individuals. Letting go "is often the most difficult task of all for the mentor" (Daloz, 1983). As in other emotional bondings, Levinson (1978) suggests that the relationship may end amicably or as a result of increasing tension and bitterness. Such an observation is not offered to dissuade young professionals from seeking mentors but to alert individuals to the intensity of the bond that often develops.

A REVIEW OF CAREER PATH RESEARCH

Student affairs literature contained few references to research efforts describing career mobility patterns among its professional members before 1970. The decade of the 1970s seemed to herald the beginning of an era of interest in collecting information about job availability, hiring practices, position qualifications and career moves. Several representative studies are presented to illustrate the variety of career development and advancement issues that have received attention during the past 15 years. One of the first surveys attemped to describe characteristics and career paths of top level administrators within student affairs. Sherburne (1970) analyzed levels of administrative responsibility and gathered information describing career moves of the chief student affairs officer (CSAO). Three levels were identified: (1) executive (CSAO and staff directing the student personnel program); (2) managerial (direction of welfare, control, activities, and teaching functions); and (3) entry-level (Sherburne, 1970). His conclusion that most senior administrators, with the exception of female executive level staff, moved to their current positions from previous employment outside their present institution lent support to the hypothesis that mobility was in fact related to advancement. Differences in the career patterns of male and female CSAO's were noted. Greater mobility was found among male administrators despite equal or superior qualifications of women.

In a subsequent landmark study by Grant and Foy (1972), characteristics of CSAO's were identified and the authors concluded that these individuals were indeed "people in transition" (p. 112). While insignificant differences were discovered in the marital status of the administrators, more female CSAO's were single (98%) than their male counterparts (24%). An interesting observation was made concerning a traditional conflict confronted by the CSAO. Of all CSAO respondents, 33 percent indicated greater loyalty to their institution, while 27 percent expressed greater allegiance to their profession.

Ferrari (1972), in an analysis of manpower needs within student affairs, concluded that 43 percent of all new staff members hired during 1970-1972 by NASPA member institutions came directly from graduate preparation programs or a prior position within the field. The prevailing trend of hiring non-student affairs prepared or experienced people was changing.

Issues related to women and minority staff members received increasing attention during this same time period. Myers and Sandeen (1973) completed a study of coeducational and non-Black NASPA member institutions. Of the 11,705 employed professionals responding, 39 percent were female and 14 percent were minority staff members. The highest numbers of women and minority staff members were concentrated on four-year plus campuses, i.e., universities with large enrollments. An analysis of women's career paths revealed that nationally women were overrepresented in entry-level positions (69%) and underrepresented within top-level CSAO positions (7%).

Several observations about graduate preparation programs and the placement of their graduates during 1973-74 were made by Packwood (1976). Northeastern and mid-western institutions were the source of most college student personnel graduates and residence halls was the specialty area in which most graduates (25%) secured employment. Other functional areas listed in decreasing frequency were student activities, placement and career planning, admissions, minority programs, and financial aid. Positions at four-year institutions attracted more than two-thirds of all graduates hired. Job advertisements originated from institutions in the South (56%), the Midwest (45%) and the Northeast (41%); while graduates were hired in the Midwest (32%), the Northeast (28%), and the South (26%). The percentage of graduates who secured positions outside of student affairs was 15 percent.

Interest in the career development of women and minority staff members and employment practices continued to characterize the literature of the late 1970s and early 1980s. The Women's Movement and the effects of the Civil Rights and Student Activist Movements, as well as an economic recession and an emphasis on retrenchment influenced research efforts of those interested in career mobility and advancement. Escott (1976) studied the individuals who made career moves and the methods used to secure new employment by concentrating on the placement activities at the 1974 ACPA, NASPA, and NAWDAC Convention. He determined that available positions were listed by public and private institutions in almost equal numbers. Among entry-level positions, employers' most frequent sources of candidates were "Conference Placement Services" (51%) and "Referrals from Colleagues" (25%). For all new positions listed, these two sources accounted for 68 percent of all individuals hired.

Candidates and employers were also the subjects for a study by Armstrong, Campbell, and Ostroth (1978). The area of Housing, still a primary source of employment positions, accounted for 39 percent of all vacancies listed in the 1978 NASPA Placement Supplement. At the same time, 48 percent of all graduates sought positions in Housing. Student affairs candidates taking positions outside the field continued to be a small group (8%).

The marital status of women remained a topic of interest. Arnold concluded that "(i)t should come as no surprise that a larger percentage of mid-career women than men in our profession are unmarried" (Arnold, 1982, p. 4).

As retrenchment and the competition for jobs increased, attention shifted to the study of those individuals leaving the field. Of the M.A. and Ph.D. graduates surveyed during the summer of 1980 from two Eastern universities, 39 percent left student affairs to secure employment outside academe (Burns, 1980). Of those graduates who earned their degrees before 1975, 49 percent remained in the field while 51 percent did not. Gender differences revealed that women withdrew from the field in significantly larger numbers than men at both educational levels. Of all who remained, 46 percent had earned their degrees within the past five years, while 38 percent of those who exited the field graduated within the past five years.

A comparison of traits associated with leavers and persisters was reported. Service, dedication, independence, and work were not as highly valued by those who left the field when compared to those who stayed. Leavers valued expertise, knowledge, and advancement more than those who persisted. Interestingly an almost equal number of those who left returned to graduate school (48%) as those who felt they were insufficiently challenged in their student affairs positions (51%). "Up or out" was the most common expectation of those who remained in the field (Burns, 1980).

Considerable attention continued to be directed toward the career development of the CSAO (Evans & Kuh, 1983; Harder, 1983; Kuh, Evans, & Duke, 1983). Comparisons of data collected in 1969 with those of 1980 revealed that: (1) more CSAO's held the doctorate in 1980, (2) more had been in their jobs for longer periods of time than those in 1969, and (3) the 1980 CSAO's anticipated that their next career move would be to a vice-presidency in academic administration rather than to teaching as stated in 1969 (Grosth, 1980).

The changing pattern in the use of the titles Dean of Students and Vice-President for Student Affairs was described by Paul and Hoover (1980) and Rickard (1985). Their major conclusion was that the former title was being used less frequently among current CSAO's than it had been in the past. Additionally, two percent of all CSAO respondents indicated the use of dual titles in their positions, combining student affairs responsibilities with such duties as enrollment management, marketing, and student life (Rickard, 1985).

An assessment of the career patterns of women CSAO respondents disclosed that although only 11 percent of the CSAO's were women, this total represented twice the figure identified in 1977 (Paul & Hoover, 1980). Of these women, 82 percent used the VPSA title in contrast to only 76 percent of all male CSAO's studied.

Also of significant relevance here are the changes that have occurred in the characteristics of student affairs professionals and those enrolled in graduate preparation programs. During 1977-1979 enrollments in many preparation programs at the masters' level shifted from a majority male population to a predominately female group (Holmes, 1982). The percentage of female CSAO's ranged from seven percent to 20 percent in the mid-1960s and rose to only 26 percent by 1982 (Rickard, 1982). Minority CSAO's represented two percent of all top-level administrators in the mid-1960s and were 13 percent of the population in 1982 (Rickard, 1985). Rickard (1982) reminds us that "two-year institutions grew twice as fast as four year, and private institutions nearly tripled the growth in the public sector" as reported in 1980-1981 by the National Center for Education Statistics (Rickard, 1982, p. 37). Women continue to be overrepresented in entry-level positions and underrepresented at top levels of administration.

In a follow-up study of alumni who had completed their master's degree work at Bowling Green State University, it was learned that 67 percent of those graduating in the five year span between 1977 and 1982 were still employed in higher education. In a subsequent study of the period 1982-1986, 81 percent of the graduates in the five year span between 1982 and 1986 remained in higher education positions (Saddlemire, 1987).

Earlier studies of Bowling Green State University alumni show that of those individuals who leave higher education for employment in another field approximately four percent return to higher education within a two year period.

Master's degree graduates of college student personnel programs find an open job market for entry level positions in the various student affairs functions. In the 1980s, the employment areas that provided the greatest opportunity for the 250 Bowling Green State University graduates were residence life, student activities/student union and career planning/placement. Other functions that have shown a steady demand for the entry level professionals to fill vacancies are: (1) admissions, (2) academic advising, (3) alumni/development, (4) cooperative education, (5) counseling, (6) financial aid, (7) off campus student central office, (8) international student programs, (9) orientation, and (10) minority student programs.

The career paths of 37 graduate students who held assistantships in student activities at Bowling Green State University from 1977 to 1983 are described to illustrate the variety of specialty areas and levels of positions to which a young professional in student affairs might aspire. Twenty-six of the graduates have remained in the field. Their administrative titles include: Associate Dean of Community Education, Director of Student Activities, Associate Dean of Students, Assistant Director of Admissions, Director of Career Services, and Director of Admissions. In addition, three have completed their doctorate. Four-fifths (81%) of the more recent graduates from 1982-1986 have remained in higher education. Their titles include Student Activities Coordinator, Admissions Counselor, Career Counselor, Orientation Director, Assistant Director of Activities and Orientation. Just over one-half of the 25 graduates who remained in student affairs have continued in student activities positions. (Saddlemire, 1983, 1986).

The geographic areas that show promise for growth in higher education are the states that are not the victim of regional economic problems such as a price collapse in oil or farm products. In 1988 the relative economic prosperity of the New England and middle Atlantic states provides a positive climate for requesting money from the legislature. A high level of employment assists the students to consider private higher education as an option when selecting colleges although public education continues to increase the percentage of enrolled students.

DOCTORAL PROGRAMS

Doctoral programs are not subject to the same CAS preparation program standards as master's degree programs. Each university's graduate faculty has designed a degree according to the university's mission and particular strengths. The characteristics of the university department that grants the degree are a major influence on the curriculum. Departments of Higher Education, Counselor Education, Counseling and Human Development Services, Administration and Leadership are examples of departments that offer a doctorate attractive to those pursuing a career in student affairs.

In addition to the completed master's degree, the doctorate usually requires an additional 60 hours, including a dissertation that demands thorough investigation of a specific topic.

Universities that offer both a Doctor of Philosophy and a Doctor of

Education degree will describe the Ph.D. as having a greater research/ scientific emphasis, while the Ed.D. will be more oriented to the needs of the practitioners in higher education. The fact that the degree requirements are determined by the graduate faculty of the university makes it imperative that the literature describing the Ph.D. and the Ed.D. be reviewed carefully before making a decision early in the program. It is usually possible to switch from one degree program to the other. In either case, the dissertation will be a major requirement. It is also useful to find out which faculty members are available as dissertation advisers and what their professional interests are. These faculty members are a likely source for a mentoring relationship (Saddlemire, 1987).

The Directory of Graduate Preparation Programs in College Student Personnel (1987) lists 17 institutions with doctoral programs in higher education that have a student affairs emphasis and also meet the ACPA Commission XII standards at the master's level—one faculty member involved 100 percent in the program, at least one student personnel practicum opportunity, and at least two content courses in college student personnel. The Directory contains doctoral program information about admission requirements, program content, number of graduates, assistantships available and the number of persons enrolled. The Directory lists an additional 17 institutions that offer a degree in higher education without a student affairs emphasis.

The following course offerings are representative of those offered at the doctoral level:

Environmental Design and Problem Solving Through Campus Ecology (The Ohio State University)
Research in Higher Education (Michigan State University)
Evaluation Models and Techniques (Indiana University)
Higher Education in the United States (Southern Illinois University)
American College Student (Florida State University)
Advanced Student Development Theory (University of Maryland)
Practicum in Student Services Administration (Oregon State University)

By earning a doctorate, the student affairs professional has a credential that is often listed as a necessary qualification for either upper level administration or a teaching position at the graduate level. Since student affairs is an applied behavioral science/management field, admission to the doctoral program generally requires successful experience as a practitioner.

GRADUATE FACULTY POSITIONS

The 116 graduate preparation programs described in the 1987 ACPA Directory list from one to six full time graduate faculty members in college student personnel/development appointments. The increasing emphasis on theories of human development from adolescence through adulthood requires faculty who can teach courses in socio-cultural foundations, psychosocial, cognitive, person-environment, humanistic and behavioral perspectives. Since the context of student affairs is higher education, offerings must be available in the history, philosophy, legal aspects, and administrative structures of higher education. Management, supervision, resource allocation, planning and policy analysis have recently been given more attention in the curriculum.

Those preparation programs with a counseling emphasis require coursework in the helping relationship, group counseling, life style and career development, and individual appraisal. Regardless of the emphasis, all programs require courses in research and evaluation and opportunities for supervised experiential learning.

Student affairs professionals who are interested in graduate faculty positions need to be prepared to teach the courses described previously. The smaller programs will require faculty who possess a broader generalist background to teach the variety of courses necessary. Within larger departments, faculty may be assigned to teach specific courses that reflect their particular experiential and academic interests. Position vacancies commonly call for evidence of ability to conduct research and to guide graduate students in their theses and dissertations. Graduate faculty members are expected to contribute to the quality of the academic program through research, teaching, and service.

REFERENCES

American College Personnel Association. (1987). *Directory of graduate programs in college student personnel.* Commission XII, Professional Education of Student Personnel Workers in Higher Education. Carbondale, IL: Southern Illinois University Press.

Arnold, K. (1982). Career development for the experienced student affairs professional. *NASPA Journal, 20*(2), 3-8.

Armstrong, M.R., Campbell, T.J., & Ostroth, D. (1978). The employment situation in college and university student personnel. *NASPA Journal, 16*(1), 51-58.

Backhuber, T. (1986). *A guidebook for the successful job search in student development.* American College Personnel Association.

Bucher, R., & Steeling, J.G. (1977). *Becoming professional.* Beverly Hills: Library of Social Research, Sage.

Burton, A. (1977). The mentoring dynamic in the therapeutic transformation. *The American Journal of Psychoanalysis, 37,* 115-122.

Burns, M.A. (1982). Who leaves the student affairs field. *NASPA Journal, 20*(2), 9-12.

Carpenter, D.S. (1983). The student affairs profession: A developmental perspective. In T.K. Miller, R.B. Winston, Jr., & W.R. Mendenhall (Eds.), *Administration and leadership in student affairs* (pp. 147-166). Muncie, IN: Accelerated Development.

Carpenter, D.S., Guido-DiBrito, F., & Kelly, J.P. (1987). Transferability of student affairs skills and competencies: Light at the end of the bottleneck. *NASPA Journal, 24*(3), 9-14.

Daloz, L.A. (1983). Mentors: Teachers who make a difference. *Change, 15,* 244-27.

Escott, S.B. (1976). Anatomy of a placement cotillion. *NASPA Journal, 14*(1), 40-52.

Evans, N.J., & Kuh, G.D. (1983). Getting to the top: A profile of female chief student affairs officers. *NAWDAC Journal, 46,* 18-22.

Ferrari, M.J. (1972). National study of student personnel manpower planning— 1972. *NASPA Journal, 10*(2), 91-100.

Grant, W.H., & Foy, J.E. (1972). Career patterns of student personnel administrators. *Journal of College Student Personnel, 10*(2), 106-113.

Halatin, T.J. (1981). Why be a mentor? *Supervisory Management, 26*(2), 36-39.

Harder, M.B. (1983). Career patterns of chief student personnel administrators. *Journal of College Student Personnel, 24,* 443-448.

Harragan, B.L. (1977). *Games mother never taught you: Corporate gamesmanship for women.* New York: Rawson.

Hennig, M., & Jardim, A. (1977). *The managerial woman.* New York: Anchor/Doubleday.

Holmes, D.R. (1982). Exploring career patterns in student affairs: Problems of conception and methodology. *NASPA Journal, 20*(2), 27-35.

Hull, D.F., Hunter, D.E., & Kuh, G.D. (1983). Alternative perspectives on student affairs organizations. In G.D. Kuh (Ed.), *Understanding student affairs organizations* (pp. 27-38). New directions for student services, no. 23.

Kanter, R.M., & Stein, B.A. (1979). *Life in organizations.* New York: Basic Books.

Kelly, K.E. (1984). Initiating a relationship with a mentor. *NASPA Journal, 21*(3), 49-54.

Kinnick, B.C., & Bollheimer, R.L. (1984). College presidents' perceptions of student affairs issues and development needs of chief student affairs officers. *NASPA Journal, 22*(2), 2-9.

Knox, A. (1978). *Adult development and learning.* San Francisco: Jossey-Bass.

Kuh, G.D. (1984). Suggestions for remaining sane in institutions that don't work the way they're supposed to. *NASPA Journal, 21*(3), 55-61.

Kuh, G.D., Evans, N.J., & Duke, A. (1983). Career paths and responsibilities of chief student affairs officers. *NASPA Journal, 21*(1), 39-47.

Levinson, D.J. (1978). *The seasons of a man's life.* New York: Knopf.

Levinson, D.J., Darrow, C., Klein, E., Levinson, M., & McKee, B. (1976). Periods in the adult development of men: Ages 18-45. *The Counseling Psychologist, 6,* 21-25.

Mable, P., & Miller, T.K. (1983). Standards for professional practice. In T.K. Miller, R.B. Winston, Jr. & W.R. Mendenhall (Eds.), *Administration and leadership in student affairs* (pp. 193-212). Muncie, IN: Accelerated Development.

Mendenhall, W.R., Miller, T.K., Winston, R.B. Jr. (1983). Roles and functions of student affairs professionals. In T.K. Miller, R.B. Winston, Jr., & W.R. Mendenhall (Eds.), *Administration and leadership in student affairs* (pp. 503-533). Muncie, IN: Accelerated Development.

Missirian, A.K. (1982). *The corporate connection.* Englewood Cliffs, NJ: Prentice-Hall.

Moore, K.M. (1982/Winter). The role of mentors in developing leaders for academe. *Educational Record,* 23-28.

Moore, K.M., & Salimbene, A.M. (1981). The dynamics of the mentor-protege relationships in developing women as academic leaders. *Journal of Educational Equity and Leadership, 2*(1), 51-64.

Moore, L.A., & Burns, M.A. (1983). Recruiting the entry-level professional and the middle manager in student affairs. *The Journal of College and University Student Housing, 13*(1), 19-23.

Myers, E.M., & Sandeen, A. (1973). Survey of minority and women student affairs staff members employed in NASPA institutions. *NASPA Journal, 11*(1), 2-14.

Packwood, W. (1976). College student personnel graduate placement. *Journal of College Student Personnel, 17*(1), 22-27.

Paul, W.L., & Hoover, R.E. (1980). Chief student personnel administrators: A decade of change. *NASPA Journal, 18*(1), 33-39.

Pierson, J. (1982). *Moving women up.* Silver Spring, MD: National Association of Social Workers.

Richmond, D.R. (1986). The young professional at the small college: Tips for professional success and personal survival. *NASPA Journal, 24*(2), 32-37.

Rickard, S.T. (1982). Turnover at the top: A study of the chief student affairs officer. *NASPA Journal, 20*(2), 36-41.

Rickard, S.T. (1985). Career pathways of chief student affairs officers: Making room at the top for females and minorities. *NASPA Journal, 22*(4), 52-60.

Rickard, S.T. (1985). Titles of chief student affairs officers: Institutional autonomy or professional standardization? *NASPA Journal, 23*(2), 44-49.

Roche, G.R. (1979/January). Much ado about mentors. *Harvard Business Review,* 14-28.

Saddlemire, G.L. (1987). Alumni Career Paths, unpublished report, Bowling Green State University (Ohio).

Saddlemire, G.L. (1988). Young Professionals Mobility. Paper presented at American College Personnel Association Conference, Miami, Florida, March 21, 1988.

Schmidt, J.A., & Wolfe, J.S. (1980). The mentor partnership: Discovery of professionalism. *NASPA Journal, 17*(3), 45-51.

Sherburne, P.R. (1970). Rates and patterns of professional mobility in student personnel work. *Journal of College Student Personnel, 8*(2), 119-123.

Stamatakos, L.C. (1983). Maximizing opportunities for success. In T.K. Miller, R.B. Winston, Jr., & W.R. Mendenhall (Eds.), *Administration and leadership in student affairs* (pp. 477-502). Muncie: IN: Accelerated Development.

AUTHOR INDEX

303

SUBJECT INDEX

315